Congregate
Housing for
Older People

Congregate Housing for Older People

A Solution for the 1980s

Edited by

Robert D. Chellis
James F. Seagle, Jr.
Barbara Mackey Seagle

LexingtonBooks
D.C. Heath and Company
Lexington, Massachusetts
Toronto

Library of Congress Cataloging in Publication Data
Main entry under title:

Congregate housing for older people.

  Includes index.
  1. Aged–Housing. 2. Congregate housing. I. Chellis, Robert D. II.
Seagle, James F. III. Seagle, Barbara.
HD7287.9.C63   363.5'9   81–47983
ISBN 0–669–05210–8   AACR2

Published simultaneously in Canada

Printed in the United States of America

International Standard Book Number: 0–669–05210–8

Library of Congress Catalog Card Number: 81–47983

Contents

Chapter 9   **The Congregate-Housing Model: Integrating
                Facilities and Services**
                Thomas O. Byerts   127

Chapter 10   **Elements of Geriatric Design: The Personal
                Environment**
                Joseph A. Koncelik   139

Part IV   *Services and Management*   159

Chapter 11   **Service Options in Congregate Housing**
                Elaine M. Brody   161

Chapter 12   **A Management Overview**
                Diana L. McIver   177

Chapter 13   **Health-Care Needs of Elderly in Congregate
                Housing**
                Richard W. Besdine and *Sylvia Sherwood*   189

Part V   *The Future*   207

Chapter 14   **Daring to Explore and Apply: A Research
                Agenda for Congregate Housing**
                Sandra C. Howell   209

                Index   217

                About the Contributors   225

                About the Editors   227

Preface: A Needed Alternative

Robert D. Chellis and
James F. Seagle, Jr.

Society's response to the perceived needs of older people has too often been to establish institutional services, which may or may not meet their real needs. Independence and, consequently, the quality of life are often diminished. Public policy influencing housing designed specifically for impaired elderly has assumed a heavy service orientation, and designs have been based on the nursing-home model without consideration of its appropriateness. (The nursing home, in its turn, has been far too heavily modeled on hospital prototypes.) Many elders do, indeed, need supportive services, but there is a wide variation in individual needs and in type and degree of service required. Typically, initial residents of new housing need relatively few services, but they will need progressively more over the years, as the original group ages.

Congregate housing can be the flexible alternative to the current extremes of custodial care versus complete self-sufficiency. Congregate housing can provide for changing needs and varied populations in ways that reduce isolation and stress while encouraging independence.

The philosophical base for congregate housing should be the assumption that even the very frail elderly should remain an integral part of the community and not be shunted aside as a faction or subset best served in isolation. They should remain as individuals within many small groupings, and as a part of the community at large. Any effort to plan or provide services or facilities must assert the normality of aging and the integrated place elders should have in society. Close bonds and identification among all members of a community may actually increase the opportunities for health and happiness in that community.

It is demonstrable, without venturing too far into social theory, that all people need to feel some control over their lives and environment. Older people find opportunities to exercise control diminishing rapidly as, in a grim progression, they lose roles as workers, parents, or spouses, and find that income and physical abilities are also diminishing. We should not presume to know what is best for them, but rather, listen carefully to their requests and demands. All older people should be encouraged to remain active—physically, intellectually, politically, sexually, and in every other way—and as independent of outside support as possible.

Societies have been plagued by misapprehensions of their aged populations. To be old in our society is to be considered increasingly helpless, childlike, sick, or mentally deteriorated. Efforts to deal with the often-overstated needs of this group have resulted in self-fulfilled prophecies and a system that leaves few choices. The system fosters dependence. Incentives are for providers to care for sick people, not to help people to stay well. Among the elderly themselves, that may account for as much functional disability as any of the pathologies accompanying aging.

Older people hold the same biases and values as does the rest of society. The notion that they will rapidly physically decline is, in some respects, reality for them. They are confronted by service-providers who are paid to serve functionally disabled elders, but not necessarily to rehabilitate them. Both in institutions and in the community, this interface weighs against a healthy outcome. Older people, providers, and the community at large must be apprised of the facts, starting with providers. A more positive view and true understanding of the aging process must be made available. New concepts are absorbed more easily by new sponsors or by managers moving into new fields than by those involved with entrenched existing services.

Most communities now have a fairly broad range of services and facilities for older residents, but they are not always the most appropriate ones. To be effective and efficient they should be planned and managed under a philosophy that recognizes the dangers inherent in the overprovision of care. The only healthy dependency is one that the older individual chooses for himself. Even tender loving care may, in overdoses, stifle or smother the recipient's efforts at self-sufficiency.

Congregate housing is a practical way to achieve a balance between dependence and independence. A broad definition of congregate housing must include reference to private living space, with the types and intensities of shared services varying in response to specific resident and community needs, staff limitations, and financial considerations. Our contributors have examined a broad range of issues relating to the nature of congregate housing and its design, implementation, and maintenance. We expect the reader to be impressed with the flexibility within the definition of congregate housing as to sponsorship, size, services, staffing, social programs, and so on.

It is our hope that this volume will help readers to understand and appreciate the adaptability of congregate housing and that this will result in material improvement in the living alternatives available to older people. It has been rewarding and a pleasure to work with all concerned in the preparation of this book.

Acknowledgments

Robert D. Chellis and
James F. Seagle, Jr.

Charles H. Farnsworth, the concerned Boston gentleman whose will, drawn in 1930, recognized the need for sheltered housing, left a bequest that has great potential for helping frail, elderly people in Massachusetts and across the country. Under the enlightened stewardship of the State Street Bank and Trust Company of Boston, and trust officers George G. Robbins, senior vice-president, and Deborah Robbins, senior trust officer, much has already been accomplished. Within three years they have sponsored a major national symposium, which provided the chapters for this book, encouraged this publication, and, as a tangible milestone, are sponsoring the construction of a model seventy-five-unit 202/8 building, documenting each step of the development process for the possible future benefit of others.

In a field where so much is needed—sponsors, innovative ideas, money, good management, and so on—the Farnsworth Trust has made its mark early, and even more can be expected in the future.

Other specific acknowledgments include our thanks to Patricia Eliot for her cheerful and effective help in organizing the Farnsworth Symposium and to Claire Wasserboehr for her invaluable assistance with typing, spelling, matters of consistency, and deadlines, no matter how unreasonable.

1

Enriching Environments for Older People

Marie McGuire Thompson

There probably is no field of social action more replete with conferences or publications than the field of gerontology today. There are conferences and publications on the health benefits of exercises, accepting death with poise, the sex drive and satisfaction of older people, long-term care and short-term care, and so forth.

This extensive body of information, composed of both myth and fact, concerning the elderly can be confusing to legislators, agencies, planners and architects attempting to formulate programs and design facilities; yet we can anticipate no decrease in gerontological problem solving.

In a 1980 press conference Secretary Patricia Harris of the Department of Heath, Education and Welfare (HEW), in an answer to a question on the cost of the "greying of America," stated:

> The aging phenomenon will have a significant impact on HEW's activities. By 2030, 18 percent of the population—55 million, will be 65 or older. Today, only 1 man in 5 and 1 woman in 12 are in the work-force at age 64 or older. Thirty years ago half of all men 65 or older remained in the workforce. By 2030, the ratio of active workers to retired citizens will change from the present 6 to 1 to only 3 to 1. One of the most obvious results of these demographic changes will be increased costs for programs serving older people. By 2010, the cost of Social Security, SSI, Medicare and Medicaid, Disability Insurance, and Black Lung programs is expected to triple to $350 billion. It will jump to $635 billion by 2025 . . . the vast majority of these payments will go to older people. (HEW 1980)

If we add to these startling figures the increase in Medicaid cost over the past decade, from $1.8 billion to $11 billion (with 40 percent for nursing-home care), the economic picture is indeed grim. If we further note that 40 percent of these payments are for nursing care and then consider that 25 to 50 percent of older persons in nursing homes do not need that level of care, the need for housing alternatives within communities, new sources of interest and financial support, and improvement of the product becomes dramatically clear. Beyond cost elements, there is the social concern that assigning older persons to a medical atmosphere prematurely or unnecessarily constitutes cruel and unusual punishment that may herald dependence and death. Should we expect older citizens to accept neglect and yet live, despite a restricted environment and their consequent diminished interest in it?

In the development of nonmedical environments, Currie (1977) notes that the many factors influencing facility design include statistics, demographic projections, economic profiles, indexes of varying disabilities by age group, life-style preferences, migration trends, dependence versus independence, familial networks, social and psychological needs, health-care services, ethnic traditions, transportation, communications, and security. These and other elements are essential to shaping the environments required to serve that diverse population of active and passive, able and handicapped, younger-old, older-old, alert and confused, who collectively make up the broad category called the elderly. We must recognize that the housing needs of the elderly are diverse and complex. We should not expect that one service or setting will be adequate for ever-changing and increasing needs. We also must recognize, however, that the large percentage of persons sixty-five and over continues to function in society with minimal dependence upon special settings or programs. Nevertheless, by analyzing one segment of the built environment we can lay the foundation for a workable congregate-housing alternative.

This book is published at a time when resources are inadequate to both present and clearly foreseen demands. Housing for the elderly is often given second place to the shelter needs of families. The *Journal of Housing* (February 1980) reports that "city officials [of Los Angeles] announced the intention of freezing the number of elderly housing developments until commitments for a sufficient number of family units have been obtained. Developers providing housing will have priority." Such curtailment has been more or less underway since 1968 when the Department of Housing and Urban Development (HUD) announced a similar policy of approving public housing for the elderly only if applications included an appropriate number of family units—this despite long waiting lists, large numbers of elderly poor in sub-standard housing, and more middle-income elderly seeking housing with services. Add to this the late start in recognizing the impact of the growing aged population and the strong trend toward planning for and changing living arrangements in retirement years. The Los Angeles illustration provides one more example that cities now and in the future will become more and more active in housing-policy development and construction due to the effects of revenue sharing, block grants, historic preservation, and the neighborhood-revitalization responsibilities placed upon municipalities to generate and prioritize local housing solutions.

It should also be recognized that no matter how many billions of public dollars are invested, or how much housing is produced by the government, the regulatory duties of governments inevitably hamper the flexibility and creativity of housing programs, limit choice and variety, cause expensive delays, and often ignore the use of competent research findings as a basis for policy formulation. Government activity must be reinforced by other leadership elements. Especially important is the involvement of private initiative, directed to the common good, with freedom to apply the planning, theory, practice, techniques, and expertise developed in the competitive arena of business. The conference sponssorship of organizations such as Farnsworth Trust, therefore, is most significant, as it may encourage others to become involved in this urgent area of need and thus help to achieve the more ideal, more workable, and more varied environmental solutions beyond the potential of the strictly regulated we seek. There is no legal barrier to combining funds from different sources either to achieve more enriching environments beyond the limits of regulatory-agency approval or to guarantee the service element in the housing which also will increase the chances of capital funding by government. Such guarantees are rare today; rather, there tends to be a determination to remain uninvolved. Whatever the reasons for combining resources, undoubtedly it is the way of the future if we are to achieve any acceptable level of improved housing-opportunities for aging people in our communities.

Involvement of varied private groups will reflect, in part, the historic American tradition of volunteerism, the acceptance of responsibility for the well-being of one's neighbor that marked the early years of this country's growth. In *Democracy in America,* Alexis de Toqueville recorded 150 years ago his surprise at the individual and collective effectiveness of the average citizen in promoting good works.

> If a man gets the idea of any social improvement whatsoever, a school, a hospital, a road, he does not think of turning to the authorities. He announces his plan, offers to carry it out, calls for the strength of other individuals to aid his efforts and ... fights against each obstacle.... In the total, the general result of all these strivings amounts to much more than any administration could undertake" (Schleifer 1980)

The involvement of the private sector reaffirms this principle of personal and corporate responsibility for meeting the needs of neighbors. While it is true that governmental programs have, in many instances, replaced nongovernmental activity, it is quite clear now that unless private interest is regenerated, either through individual action or in combination with government, we will see a decrease in the development of well located and designed housing with services appropriate to all stages of the aging process.

The development of national policies and housing legislation bears a brief review. Past events still cast their shadows. We continue to select unhappy or isolated locations, accident-prone designs, activity programs that may inhibit rather than promote sociability, and a host of questionable inherited concepts. We continue to assume that if we operate a service agency, all older people will seek us out; if we build a fine building, everyone will want it by choice; if we provide nutritious meals, even in dark basement settings, we are quite sure any who are hungry or isolated will come; if we provide one bus with a limited schedule, our transportation effort is adequate, and so on. We seem peculiarly unruffled by the fact that these services may be scattered in a dozen or so places among many agencies with dissimiliar requirements and controls. We have in the past found no systematic means of adequately linking community-service programs with people's needs, including the needs of those who only require help with daily living chores. When housing for independent living is provided, no provision is made to meet the realities of the aging process, the time when full independence will become impossible. We provide reserves to maintain the building as it ages, but none to maintain the residents as they age. While we cannot hope to always match the housing-and-services needs of all people all the time, we could, in our housing policies, at least recognize the inevitability of the decrements of aging and provide space to accommodate basic supportive services when that need comes about. We must accept responsibility as conscientious housing operators to plan so that we make possible the longest span of community living, regardless of whether public or private funds are used. The small additional construction-cost to equip spaces for conversion to the accommodation of basic services is more economical than is adaptation when the structural system is locked in.

Every national housing act since 1961 has contained programs that either include specially designed housing for the elderly or maintain or expand existing programs; yet, only 3 to 4 percent of the older population can live in these special facilities. The vast majority still live in their own homes, in old-age homes, in lifetime-care, campus-type arrangements, or in substandard and unlicensed boarding homes, in old hotels in crime-prone neighborhoods, or, sometimes unhappily, with children or friends.

It is time that policymarkers and housing developers recognize that the aging process for most is gradual and that there is an inherent responsibility to assure continued residence, if at all possible, when residents already in their seventies are admitted. We generally do not change overnight from being well to being sick and yet our past housing programs present an either-or situation: one is either completely well and able and can do quite well in housing for independent living, or one is ill and needs care in a medical facility. Between these two extremes there is a large group, estimated to be from 4 to 6 million, who, over time, as the aging process gradually takes its toll, will need assistance with the daily chores of living, even though medical supervision or care is not needed. They should be able to remain in residential environments and should be provided the sustaining services.

This concept was recognized first by President Kennedy when, in 1963, he recommended to Congress a program of group living with services. No action was taken until 1970 when Congress passed the first congregate-housing act. However, because the national nutrition act was pending at that time, Congress provided for the cost of dining rooms and kitchens with all necessary equipment, but did not provide for the purchase, preparation, and serving of meals. Therefore, very little congregate housing resulted.

It was not until the Congregate Housing Services Act of 1978, that the key element, the service subsidy, finally appeared. This subsidy made available 10 million dollars to help defray that portion of the service cost which could not be paid for by limited-income residents of congregate housing who needed them. Developments in only thirty-eight locations could be approved under three-year service-subsidy contracts.

Let us look more closely at what is involved in this seemingly simple concept of housing with services, its gap-filling potential in the housing continuum, its objectives and goals and, of course, its limitations.

Referring to congregate housing as "assisted residential living," the International Center for Social Gerontology offers the following definition:

> Assisted independent residential living is a planned group living environment that offers the elderly who are functionally impaired or socially deprived, but otherwise not ill, the residential accommodations and supporting services they need to maintain or to an independent, semi-independent or semi-dependent life style and prevent premature or unnecessary institutionalization as they grow older. (Lawton et al, 1980)

The basic issue is no place better stated than in Powell Lawton's (1980) article in a recent issue of the *Gerontologist*. Dr. Lawton describes two contrasting models of the housing environment and what each is designed to accomplish. He identifies them as either constant or accommodating environments. According to Lawton, the constant model attempts to preserve, as much as possible, the original character of the living environment. While the individuals living in the constant environment would change, the service needs of the group would remain virtually the same over time.

An accommodating environment, on the other hand, would tolerate the extended residence of tenants despite declining health and functional capacity, and would allow far less stringent admission requirements as the resident population becomes more aged. If allowed to continue to its logical extreme, an accommodating environment would, therefore, evolve slowly into a long-term care facility.

Dr. Lawton suggests that sponsors and administrators develop a clear perspective at the outset of the original planning and design phases of the housing project, on the long-term goal they wish to achieve in the housing project. This should be considered both for the initial rent-up period, and for the period twenty to thirty years in the future.

Presuming a level of relative independence of tenants, those sponsors adhering to a basically constant model, which is and has been the most usual concept, will be faced with the task of finding alternative living arrangements for tenants whose declining health and functional capacity may eventually exceed the capabilites of the housing environment. Sponsors wishing to adopt an accommodating position, must have long-range plans with regard to the extended-service package that will eventually have to be provided to the increasing number of tenants whose functional independence will decline with advancing age.

One method by which to insure a stable population has been suggested by Fowles (1978), who offers an acturial approach to the problem. Using age and mortality data for the year 1976, Fowles develops a statistical model for the selection of tenants that would stabilize the tenant population and obviate the progressive aging of such groups.

A stable population is defined by Fowles as a "population 60+ years of age of constant size with a stable age distribution over time." The model uses the number of deaths that occur with a five-year period as being equal to the number of persons in the sixty to sixty-four age tenant group. A stable population can thus be maintained if the tenant selection process is made by replacing all deaths of all ages with the addition of new members from the sixty-to-sixty-four year-old age category.

For example, table 1-1 contains the distribution of members of five different stable populations by age. It can be seen that a stable population of 125 persons, for example, could anticipate a death rate of approximately thirty individuals over a five-year period. In order to maintain the age distribution of the original population, that is maintain a stable population, thirty new members must be added during the same five-year period. However, each new member must be selected from the sixty-to-sixty-four-year-old age cagegory.

Table 1-1
Age Distribution of a Stable Population
60+ Years Old, by Size of Population

Age	Size of Population				
	25	50	125	250	500
60+, total	25	50	125	250	500
60-69	12	23	57	115	231
60-64	6	12	30	60	121
65-69	6	11	27	55	110
70-79	8	17	42	84	167
70-74	4	9	23	47	93
75-79	4	8	19	37	74
80-89	4	8	21	41	83
80-84	2	5	13	25	51
85-89	2	3	8	16	32
90+	1	2	5	10	19

Note: Based on estimated mortality rates for 1976.

This approach can be used by a planner wishing to create such a stable population in the initial rent-up of a new congregate-housing community, or it can be applied to an existing housing community by simply filling all vacancies with new members from the youngest age group. Fowles notes, however, that in the latter case it might take anywhere from five to twenty-five years before the age composition of the population becomes stable. He further cautions that any attempt to create a stable population would undoubtedly encounter different mortality rates than were used in his sample, due to geographical and temporal variations in mortality as well as to differing sex and racial composition. However, the effect on the distribution would be minimal, particularly for populations as small as the examples indicated in table 1-1.

Although determination of the building's use over time is of basic concern, a variety of other policy issues also must be considered. A major question to be addressed as we plan to operate congregate housing concerns the determination of the applicant's functional ability and the appropriateness of this type of housing over a reasonable period of time. If the federal subsidy is used, the law requires a professional assessment committee (PAC) composed of not fewer than three people from the health, social service, or mental health fields, and the housing manager. This committee has two major responsibilities: to interview all applicants to determine functional ability and to prescribe what services are needed by individual applicants or residents. The committee undoubtedly will be aware that over-serving could lead to dependency and therefore will recommend only those services required to maintain individual independence in congregate housing. The PAC also will be called upon by the manager when there is resident resistance to termination of residency even though removal to a higher level of care has become essential.

Of course, if a federal subsidy is not used, the PAC requirements would not apply; nevertheless, a professional measure of functional ability should be established. The alternative would be a manager capable, by experience and training, of determining functional ability and of prescribing the service plan required. Outside professional judgment is recommended to both relieve and bolster the manager's judgment. There are a number of evaluation instruments that measure an applicant's ability to perform the activities of daily living and these can be useful. In any case, the tenant-selection process in congregate housing ascends to the professional level and is no longer a routine clerical duty with age and income the only factors.

We have spoken of maintaining the residential ambience of the development by admittting only a limited percentage of persons who have need for one or more of the supportive services. This bears repeating, since it has economic implications for the private investor. The attractiveness of the development will be diminished if the majority of the tenants are visibly impaired or obviously near the end of their independent life-span. This would create a quasi-institutional atmosphere that would discourage the hale and hardy from moving in or remaining in residence.

When considering the specific service programs to be offered, a number of questions must be addressed. What type of meal service is preferable, cafeteria or served meals, catered or in-house preparation? Due to lack of experience in this field, and often the absence of an adequate kitchen, it appears that many of the new HUD congregate-housing sponsors plan to use caterers based on the HEW Title III experience. Overlooked is the monotony, the limited response to individual tastes or appropriate ethnic or religious factors, and the lack of variety often attributed to mass-produced meals. I would rest my recommendations for in-house meal preparation by asking whether we would want airplane-type meals, even those that might be served in first class, served every day.

What type of housekeeping schedule should be offered: daily, weekly, or monthly? At what cost? Could interested tenants be trained and paid through the CETA program to become housekeepers? Should heavy laundry be included in this service package? Should the housekeeper also provide personal services as needed? If not, what resource should be called upon to provide these services: residents, outside volunteers, paid escorts and helpers?

What kind of health services, if any, should be provided in-house? What arrangements are essential to handle health crises?

How does one best develop a workable, sliding-scale, service-cost plan, part of which will be paid by the resident and part of which will be defrayed by subsidy? What is an equitable amount of disposable income for tenant use for essential needs not included in the service plan?

There are a host of design questions that obviously have to be considered. For example, what are the design differences, if any, in congregate housing? How can the design conserve energy, reduce frustration, and encourage social contact to help keep the elderly person mentally active, physically fit, and socially fulfilled?

The staffing of a congregate-housing facility also poses a variety of questions. What should be the background and training of the manager of a development where some of the residents are semidependent? Also, what is the role of the manager in relation to service programs provided by community agencies? How can a quality service be assured under a system of split responsibility? Will the manager know that an underlying managerial concept respects the right of the elderly to be masters in their own homes?

What is the role of the agencies on aging required under the federal statute to review and comment on the adequacy of the services component in congregate housing?

For staff convenience of economy, will the congregate housing tenants requiring services be identified by set-aside locations within the development, thereby being made to feel different and perhaps inferior? Should we build congregate housing for all impaired people and disregard the greater social benefits inherent in a mixed population?

Should meal and leisure services be available not only to the residents but also to elderly people in the neighborhood, or is this an invasion of the privacy of the residents, particularly at the family dinner hour?

A listing of these many questions tells us clearly that, while the congregate housing concept is easily grasped, its operation poses many questions that are quite beyond the experience of most housing developers.

James Sykes from Wisconsin, in testimony before the U.S. Senate Special Committee on Aging, stated firmly that the pattern of services fround in a statewide survey of public housing falls far short of the need if, indeed, any basic services were provided. While the need for services increased with age, the availability of services at housing sites did not increase. Numerous surveys reveal the same picture. It is as if an automobile were built without a gas tank.

The state of Maryland has had a program of housing with services called sheltered housing under state legislation for over five years. It was enacted primarily to reduce the cost of unneeded nursing-home care. Based on Maryland's experience, the cost-effectiveness of sheltered housing compared with that of institutional care leaves no doubt as to its economic and social validity. Dr. Matthew Tayback, Director of the Maryland Office on Aging, has stated before a U.S. Senate Subcommittee hearing (1978) that "what was proposed in the then pending congregate housing bill (S 2691) is feasible and there is no question about it, that it is cost effective. It is an arithmetic that is of benefit to the American public."

Most conferences on elderly housing deal with the urban scene. Thus, we find rehabilitation loans, no-interest elder-loans, home-equity conversions, neighborhood reinvestment plans, historic preservation and its impact on the elderly population, common in older urban neighborhoods, Section 312 loans, special security programs and a host of other activities directed to the well-being of the urban elderly. It is a fact, however, that the rural elderly, who by and large have less income and even graver housing needs, are only now beginning to receive the level of attention warranted. Of course, there are exceptions. One is the exemplary Colonial Club Senior Center in Sun Prairie, Wisconsin, which is surrounded by a variety of housing types developed by Jim Sykes with the help of a generous and concerned corporation.

Increased interest by the Farmers Home Administration (FmHA) of the Department of Agriculture is evidenced by their three-year demonstration of congregate housing in the ten regions of the United States. Capital funding is provided under the Section 515 rural-rental program, which was previously mostly used for families. The services are the responsibility of the Administration on Aging through funding and working with its state and area agencies on aging. There is growing interest among the national and state FmHa offices in the housing needs of rural-elderly and rural-handicapped as well.

On the government agenda for housing are on-site services for all elderly congregate housing, revised HUD/FmHA minimum property standards incorporating local conditions and cost-reducing measures, and development of blueprints to assist both small and self-help builders. The objective is to shift emphasis so that departments and agencies will manage their programs in ways that recognize local priorities and facilitate local decision making in rural America with federal investment complementing state-local development plans and priorities.

Federal leverage is expected to attract private investment in rural economic and community development. High priority will be given to disadvantaged persons, including the elderly.

With the leadership of the Farmers Home Administration and the increasing interest of states, we can expect in the immediate future to reach more rural and small-town elderly people with appropriate housing and services or with services in their own homes. It has been the experience in some European countries that, if housing is built in the village or commune closest to the farm areas, it will in time, if not immediately, attract the elderly farm-people as their needs for services grow. Growth of rural interest, however, must be accompanied by technical assistance, particularly if congregate housing is planned.

In conclusion, it appears to me that this publication may initiate a creative process freed from the constraints of both past and present, daring to apply some foresight about the future. Above all, it is important to demonstrate that we are not a nation that operates solely through public institutions, but one which, through private concern, dares to explore the unknown, dares to provide the animation, vibrancy, and freedom that too often is discouraged by governmental regulations. Just as public-private forces need to combine to add strength to a democracy and variation to our fabric of life in the housing field, so, too, do health and social forces need to combine as an important component of shelter programs in the later years. Let us hope that the more mundane aspects of housing development will not overshadow the ultimate goal: to offer hope where there is despair, and joy where there is sadness caused by the physical, mental or personal losses in the later years. We must take care, however, that our intense concern does not create the feeling that older persons are another species, even though the eighty-year-old may not want to listen overlong to the eighteen-year-old, and vice versa. To design and build for older people one must know older people, accept older people, and enjoy older people. Such knowledge is basic whether we design and build new housing, convert older housing, renovate, winterize, share a home, or pitch a tent. Our primary objective must be to relate the physical structure and the services to human values, most particularly to the changing needs of older citizens.

References

U.S. Department of Health, Education and Welfare. 1980. *Human Development News,* January.

Currie, L.; Ast, G.; Cohen, S.; Gordon, E.; and Macsai, J. 1977. *Designing Environments for the Aging: Policies and Strategies.* Chicago: University of Illinois.

Lawton, M.P.; Greenbaum, M.; and Liebowitz, B. 1980. The Lifespan of Housing Environments for the Aging. *The Gerontologist* 20, no. 1:56–64.

Fowles, D.G. 1978. A Model for Creating a Stable Population in Congregate Housing Residences. In *Assisted Independent Living in Residential Congregate Housing for Older People,* ed. W.T. Donahue, P.H. Pepe and P. Murray. Washington, D.C.: International Center for Social Gerontology.

Schleifer, J. 1980. *The Making of Tocqueville's Democracy in America.* Chapel Hill: University of North Carolina Press, p. 123.

U.S. Senate. 1978. Hearing before the Subcommittee on Housing and Urban Affairs of the Committee on Banking, Housing and Urban Affairs. Washington, D.C.: U.S. Government Printing Office.

Part I:
Psychosocial Factors
of Need

The need to feel in control of one's environment does not diminish with age. The exercise of survival skills is as important to well-being as is physical exercise. Elders need to be presented with opportunities for mastery and challenged to make choices. The choice of where to live and with whom is extremely important. At the heart of a fairly strict self-selection process is the ongoing need to continue old routines. Given proper support, however, elders will continue to adapt to group norms and they can be accepting of a wide variety of functional abilities among neighbors.

2

Impact of the Psychosocial Environment of the Elderly on Behavioral and Health Outcomes

Ellen J. Langer and
Jerry Avorn

Epictetus once said that it is not events themselves that cause stress, but rather the views one takes of those events. That is, our own subjective reality, rather than an objective reality, largely determines the way the world impinges on us. The full age-related implication of this idea has only recently been felt in the scientific community. In the past decade, researchers have been devoting extensive study to the importance of perceived control over events in one's life. One focus of our own research has been the importance of this variable in appreciating the problems of the elderly. Much research in this area suggests that the belief that one can affect outcomes relevant to one's own life is of paramount importance to psychological and perhaps even physical health. Interestingly, this has been shown to be true regardless of whether or not such belief in fact reflects the reality of control.

There are several subtle ways in which physical and interpersonal environments lead us to believe that we have no control over our actions and our experiences. The consequences of such perceived loss of control may be devastating. In this chapter, we will describe the negative consequences of believing one has lost control over one's environment, some of the factors that lead to such a belief in institutionalized elderly adults, and possible ways of ameliorating the situation.

In 1942, the great Harvard physiologist W.B. Cannon helped make the scientific community aware of the strange phenomenon of voodoo deaths. People who, for one reason or another, are led to expect they will die, do in fact die, often despite previously good health. Autopsies often reveal no apparent medical cause. Bettelheim's (1960) descriptions of some concentration-camp victims reveal similar findings. While some victims starve to death, others die without apparent physical cause. This phenomenon has been documented in numerous other reports, particularly in the literature of sudden cardiac death (Lown et al. 1977).

Laboratory investigation confirmed the validity of these observations and suggested some clues to its physiological basis. Richter (1957) found that if he held a wild rat in his hand until it stopped struggling and then placed it in a tank of water, the rat drowned within a half hour. He repeated this with several rats and in each case found the same result. He compared this finding to another group of wild rats that swam around for approximately sixty hours when placed directly into the tank. Why did the former group drown so quickly? It was as if the rats had simply given up.

The effects of giving up are real and the consequences may be extreme. Additional evidence of the phenomenon comes from epidemiological studies that reveal a markedly increased rate of death among surviving spouses in the year following bereavement (Parkes 1964). Patients judged prospectively to have a sense of helplessness or hopelessness have been found by Schmale (1969) to have a much higher likelihood of subsequently being diagnosed as having cancer. Dr. Ellen J. Langer has attempted experimental interventions to test this hypothesis in the institutionalized elderly. Nursing-home residents were randomly assigned to two groups. The control group was told that the home's staff was there to care for them and to make decisions for them regarding their day-to-day lives—in their best interest, of course. Residents in the experimental group, by contrast, were encouraged to make their own decisions as much as possible concerning meal times, recreational activities, and so forth. The latter group was found to show significant improvement in psychological well-being and activity (Langer and Rodin 1976). A follow-up study eighteen months later suggested that the residents in the experimental group also seemed to have a lower rate of mortality when compared with controls (Rodin and Langer 1977).

The physiological mechanisms through which such learned helplessness can be transformed into physical illness are not totally clear, but some intriguing evidence exists. Some investigators invoke the notion of a parasympathetic death—death resulting from overactivity of the parasympathetic nervous system. This could be mediated, for example, through excessive stimulation by the brain of the vagus nerve, which innervates the heart as well as many other vital organs. Vagal impulses slow the heart rate; extraordinary activity of the vagus nerve can result in cardiac standstill and, consequently, death.

Recent cardiovascular research has focused on another mechanism, perhaps more important. This is the sympathetic nervous system, the apparatus responsible for the fight-or-flight emergency response that quickens the heart, constricts the blood vessels, releases adrenalin, and creates the hyperaroused state we have all experienced at times of extreme stress. Evidence from dogs and humans has shown that psychological stress that initiates this emergency response makes it likelier that the heart will become over-stimulated and go into ventricular fibrillation—a disordered and ineffective twitching of the heart muscle that pumps no blood and is therefore incompatible with life (Lown et al. 1977). Excessive activity of the sympathetic or parasympathetic nervous systems has been suggested as the means through which psychological stress can be transformed into physical illness or even death.

Of course, in daily life the physiological effects of the psychosocial environment are considerably subtler, but even when death does not result, successful living is clearly undercut by a threatening milieu, and unnecessary debilitation can result. The loss of perceived control is stressful at first; if it persists, the individual becomes passive and dependent, feels incompetent, and may display symptoms characteristic of reactive depression.

The early psychological experiments in this field focused on the effect of negative outcomes in producing these feelings of helplessness. People typically were put in situations where they were going to experience some aversive event over which they had no control. To make the appropriate comparisons, other people in these studies were made to experience the same aversive consequence, but were led to believe that they were doing so by choice. Thus, the same negative outcome was experienced by the two groups and all that differed between them was their belief about their control over the outcome. One group believed they could control the outcome, the other believed they could not. In virtually all of the studies of this type, although neither group exercised control, the group that believed that control was possible experienced less stress. In other studies, subjects were given prior experience with uncontrollable negative outcomes in which their attempts to terminate the negative consequences were repeatedly met with failure. No matter what they did, they were unsuccessful. After this experience, they were then placed in a second situation where control was possible. The prior experience with uncontrollability led people not to exercise control in this second situation even when control was possible. They have learned that responding is futile and hence they have given up and become passive. However, they were giving up in situation in which giving up was clearly maladaptive. Comparison groups not given the prior experience with uncontrollable outcomes readily exercised control in the second situation. It would seem that much passivity and giving up in general is a result of prior experience with loss of control (Seligman 1975).

The relevance of control to the environment of the elderly becomes much clearer when we consider other factors that may lead residents of nursing homes to give up because they believe themselves to be helpless. First, there may be a discrepancy between what nursing-home residents are permitted to do and what they think they are permitted to do. Residents may indeed be able to exercise control over some aspects of their lives; however, if the subjective experience of that reality is such that the individual believes no control is available, then the negative physical and psychological consequences resulting from this belief will exist regardless of the reality. Further, Baltes and Barton (1979) have shown that the reality of nursing-home life may, in fact, not be so benign. In a study of staff and resident behavior, they found that independence-affirming behaviors on the part of residents were generally met with negative reinforcement by staff, while dependence-affirming resident activity was rewarded.

The power of the environment to induce helplessness and giving up is made even more apparent when one considers the following observation: belief in one's own incompetence may evolve even if the individual is not given direct experience with uncontrollable outcomes. Incompetence may be inferred from very subtle environmental and interpersonal cues, quite independent of a direct-failure experience. It is these subtle factors that insidiously communicate loss of control that will be considered in the remainder of this chapter.

What interpersonal aspects of nursing-home environments tell the elderly resident that he or she is incompetent and unable to control his or her environment? First is the very decision to institutionalize—usually made by families or health care professionals, and not by the elderly themselves. Ironically, the need to place a parent is often a result of the inability of society to provide adequate noninstitutional support for partially disabled elderly (Avorn 1982); yet such societal inadequacy is perceived as inadequacy of the elder to perform in that society. Even before the elderly adult takes up residence in the nursing home, staff may unwittingly communicate their belief in his or her helplessness. They do this by speaking almost exclusively to the children who are placing their parent in the home, rather than to the elderly adult who is actually moving to a new home.

Simply bearing the label "nursing-home resident" may be debilitating if the resident accepted, in younger days, a set of negative, preconceived ideas about why one goes to a nursing home. We found in our own research (Langer and Benevento 1978) that when people were assigned labels that connoted inferiority, they performed poorly on tasks that they not only could perform but in fact did perform quite well before they wore the label. Labels may also be a problem from the perspective of the staff's behavior. In other research (Langer and Abelson 1974) we asked professional psychotherapists to evaluate a person whom we called either a "patient" or a "job applicant." Both groups saw a videotape of the same person; nevertheless, their evaluation differed considerably depending on the label. The person labeled "patient" was generally seen as sick and in need of help, while the same person labeled "job applicant" was seen as well-adjusted. (Professionals who were specifically trained to observe behavior and not use labels saw the person as well-adjusted no matter what we called him, but most people do not receive this kind of training.) A great deal of social psychological research tells us that people behave differently with people for whom they have different expectations and that the latter group in turn comes to behave in a way that confirms those expectations (see Rosenthal 1971, Kelley 1967, Snyder 1978). The label instigates this process (Rodin and Langer 1980).

If those caring for the elderly expect them to be generally incompetent because they are nursing-home residents, they will unwittingly behave as if they are incompetent, and the residents, in turn, may come to believe that they are incompetent and act accordingly. In this kind of a system, all expectations may receive confirmation so no one knows that it could have been otherwise. This point of view has been documented as well in *Stigma* by Erving Goffman (1963) and in medical research. In the latter case, patients who were told that they had high blood pressure immediately began to experience more illness-related absenteeism, though their physiological condition had not changed from previous months or years—they had simply been labeled as sick (Haynes 1978).

Another interpersonal factor that may subtly lead to an erroneous belief in incompetence is one that denies what would seem to be the guiding principle of most institutions: tender loving care. Because the elderly as a group are seen as frail and vulnerable, the tendency of society in general is to treat them with special care—always being ready to "help the little old lady across the street." In this case what is true in the general population would seem to be even more prevalent in nursing homes. Here the people are pictured as more frail than average and the staff are hired primarily to help them; yet simply helping people may make them incompetent (Langer and Avorn 1982). Although well-meant, such attention may communicate belief in the inability and inadequacy of the recipient. If the person faces no difficulty, if there are no challenges, large or small, feelings of mastery are precluded and consequences as involution, depression, and morbidity are real possibilities. Helping the resident get dressed to to go breakfast (either out of concern for the resident or to save time for the staff) may only result in feelings of incompetence and dependence for the resident and ultimately take more of the staff's time, since the individual will soon come to assume the need for such help.

A fourth interpersonal factor worth considering is the effect of uniforms. Uniforms constantly remind residents that they need to be taken care of, that they are not members of the higher-status group, and that they can never hope to join the ranks of these potential role models. Since uniforms make it easy to recognize who is doing what in the institution, they also make salient to the resident what they themselves or others in their same position are not doing. Watching someone else do things that one used to do oneself, but is no longer doing, may lead to the sense that one has become incapable of performing those activities. This can occur even when the only reason the person is not engaging in the behavior is an institutional decision based on other matters and not at all an assessment of the individual's competence. The expectation of incompetence on the part of the individual, facilitated by similar expectations held by the staff, is often so pervasive that there may be no other explanations offered for why an individual is or is not doing something. When there is a ready explanation for an event, one rarely searches for other possible causes. The lack of systematic and recurrent functional-assessment of institutionalized elderly in most settings makes it more likely that such a "lowest common denominator" approach will be used instead of a more person-specific, accurate measurement of what each individual can (or could) do.

The physical aspects of most nursing homes also nurture this belief of no control. One simply cannot feel much control over that which is unfamiliar; however, we can exercise control by making the unfamiliar familiar if the environment suggests that this is possible. In fact, it is the very process of making the unfamiliar familiar that gives rise to the perception of control and the feeling of mastery. Residents come from homes that they have lived in all their lives, that had kitchen facilities they could use, rooms with furniture and belongings that were familiar, doors that could be open or locked closed, decorations that were unique and aesthetically appealing, and so on. Obstacles were dealt with as

the environment was mastered, and new obstacles were forever revealing themselves. Mastering the environment led to general feelings of mastery; however, if
the individual is faced with an already-mastered environment, mastering will not
take place and the positive and life-sustaining consequences of perceived control
will be lost.

Attempts by professionals, family, or the residents themselves to explain
disorientation in the elderly may not take these issues into consideration. This
is not surprising. One typically tries to explain behavior based on what there is
to be seen, rather than on what is missing; yet the disorientation could be a function of the lack of salient, easily discriminated cues. The negative effects of this
misattribution would be likely to multiply and may rob the individual of the
motivation to find more subtle cues to help make the discrimination (Avorn
1981a). Why bother looking if you do not think you are capable of finding?

Perhaps the biggest problem for the elderly resident is that the environment
is either too easy or too difficult to negotiate. Those aspects perceived as too
difficult will be ignored entirely. Those aspects that are too easy are just as
problematic. Having doors that are always opened for you, food that is always
served to you, ramps for entering or leaving instead of a few steps, almost preclude feelings of control. How can one feel a sense of mastery if there is nothing
to master?

In a series of studies testing the illusion of control (Langer 1975), this kind
of physical involvement with the environment was found to be important to
people even when the situation they were trying to control was, in fact, uncontrollable. For example, in one study, subjects were face to face with an elec-
trical apparatus with three paths displayed on it. They were told that a buzzer
would sound if the correct path were traveled with a stylus. Subjects in the
high-involvement group traversed their chosen path themselves while those in the
low-involvement group chose the path for someone else to travel. In fact, only
chance determined whether the buzzer rang; yet, even in a situation as con-
strained as this, where the outcome was, in fact, random, involvement mattered.
Subjects who were more actively involved felt more confident and perceived
greater control over the outcome. Similar effects of feeling involved with the
environment have been found in other settings (Langer and Roth 1975). How
many times has each of us pushed buttons on elevators that were already lit to
exercise control and because doing nothing is so difficult? Thus, obstacles that
are mildly to moderately difficult to overcome (but not dangerous) should not
be quickly removed from the environment of the elderly; instead they should be
dealt with by the residents.

Another factor that is worth examining when considering the environment of
the elderly is routinization. Detailed analysis of the ways in which routinization
is a problem have been dealt with elsewhere (see Langer 1978a, 1978b; Langer
1979). We will present here only the results of those analyses. If an environment is almost perfectly predictable, the hallmark of routinization, then there

is nothing for the individual to think about. However, the individual must be in a mindful state to perceive control over the environment; thus, routine does not promote perception of control. We all perform many tasks (particularly the so-called activities of daily living) mindlessly; that is, in doing them we do not think carefully about what we are doing or how we are doing it. This is possible because many of these activities have been overlearned through decades of practice; we have become so adept that we can do these things without thinking. Ironically, however, it is just such overlearned tasks that are the most likely to make us feel incompetent. The reason for this paradox is straightforward: because we perform the tasks almost automatically, we have lost conscious awareness of many of the intermediary steps necessary for their completion. This explains the familiar sensation of having to perform an entire overlearned task (such as tying shoes) from the beginning in order to get it right.

Normally, when our competence is called into question, we can satisfy ourselves that we are in fact competent by mentally retracting the steps required to do such a task. For an overlearned task that is normally done mindlessly, this ability may be lost. For an elderly person in an institutionalized setting, it becomes very easy to imagine that one is not competent to perform many tasks: many self-care needs are performed by others, and it is no longer possible even to remember how one used to perform such tasks for oneself, because they were overlearned many years earlier.

Implications for the Design of Environments for the Elderly

The above experimental data and clinical observations can have immediate and far-reaching applications to the care of the elderly. These include: changes in existing institutions, alterations in policy to discourage institutionalization, the development of healthier alternatives, and the identification of potential obstacles inhibiting such developments. We will conclude by discussing each of these in turn.

Changes in the Nursing-Home Environment

The evidence we have presented argues strongly in favor of a number of specific changes in the design of nursing homes. Some are quite readily accomplished, requiring virtually no changes in the present management and reimbursement structure of long-term care; others would require more far-reaching developments. Among the more do-able changes would be architectural diversification of the nursing home, so that rooms and wings of a facility would look quite distinct from one another. It is striking how rarely variations in paint color are used in nursing homes to accomplish this end. While there may be a certain small economy in using the same institutional color throughout a facility, the cost in terms of confusion, loss of mobility, and psychological debility of residents is far greater. Permission for residents to bring in their own furniture and memorabilia would also go a long way toward reducing the institutionalization syndrome that is such a predictable aspect of life in an anonymous environment. A sense of control would further be heightened if residents who are at no risk of harming themselves were allowed keys to their rooms. Where possible, the medical model of a hospital setting with four-bedded or two-bedded rooms should be abandoned; it is not a living arrangement that is ever chosen voluntarily. Being forced to share a room means, besides the endurance of loss of privacy, further exposure to the problems of partner-changing and the need to tolerate the idiosyncrasies (often irritating) of another—a constant reminder of lack of control of the environment.

It is striking how carefully nursing-home environments have been made to conform to life-safety-code provisions to guard against fire hazard. While tragic, nursing-home fires are rare and certainly do not seem to us to present the greatest threat to the health and well-being of institutionalized elderly. What is needed is a mind-safety-code enforcement, a series of environmental and behavioral standards to guard against the much more debilitating psychological hazards that form the nursing-home environment. A general guideline would require impressive and documented evidence to justify a change in the life-space or a diminution of personal control, the elements that make the institution look very different from the real world. We believe that many restrictions of nursing-home life would then be found unsupportable.

Public-Policy Considerations

Our present reimbursement system for long-term care obviously is heavily biased in favor of the institutionalization of frail elders. No matter how enlightened the institution, certain built-in bureaucratic considerations make institutional life inherently more destructive of control and of independence. There will be a limit to the extent to which nursing homes can be humanized. The needs of mentally and physically handicapped residents and the pervasive needs of staff members will constantly work toward creating a milieu that is not in the best interests of the nonhandicapped resident. The full solution to this problem awaits an enlightened public policy that will adequately fund noninstitutional services for impaired elderly as generously as it has funded nursing homes in the past. Implicit in such a reorientation is a strict limitation of the medical model for long-term care adapted so enthusiastically over the past two decades in this country. This approach, in which the recipient of care is viewed as inherently ill and incompetent, may be appropriate in the operating room or in an intensive-care unit (though probably not completely in the latter), but it is certainly not a fit way to view people who may have only slight problems with mobility or sensation, and are otherwise quite able to care for themselves.

In recent years, a number of alternatives to institutional care for the elderly have received increased attention in the United States: home care, respite care, and congregate-living facilities. A number of studies have suggested that significant numbers of the institutionalized-elderly population could be dealt with in less-restrictive, but reimbursable, alternative-care programs. It is not yet clear whether such alternative forms of care, if available, will in fact be more cost-effective than institutional care. For many nonfrail elderly misplaced in nursing homes because of inadequate housing opportunities or because of poor judgment by a referring agency, noninstitutional alternatives will save money. We are concerned here with, however, a larger issue: the saving of psychological well-being and ability for self-care that are clearly better enhanced in noninstitutional settings. From the bulk of psychological and geriatric evidence, we can now conclude with some certainty that there is good reason to favor options such as congregate housing over conventional nursing-home care.

Obstacles to Be Overcome

The mere preponderance of evidence, however, has never been enough to assure the acceptance of an idea. Powerful institutional and economic interests will continue to favor the nursing-home model of care for the frail elderly. There is tremendous inertia in the present system, a result of both the reluctance of people (particularly health-care professionals) to change, and, more important, the enormous economic motivation of the nursing-home industry to maintain its current hegemony over the long-term care scene. Attempts to construct a more psychologically (and medically) health environment for the elderly will be met, but rarely head on with considerable resistance. Of course, no discussions will take place in the language of capital investment or profit. As always, "the welfare of the patients" will be voiced as the main rationale for policy decisions that might in fact work against their interests. It will be particularly important to be certain that the proprietary (that is, profit-making) nature of the present long-term industry not to transferred to a burgeoning new alternative care industry. We make this argument on clinical, rather than on economic grounds (although persuasive arguments can be based on the latter as well). If our focus is to be upon the preservation of individual competence and sense-of-self in the elderly in whatever setting, we have an inherent contradiction between this goal and the development of a for-profit sector to serve the elderly. Concerns of business will necessarily require standardization, routinization, streamlining, and efficiency, often at the expense of idiosyncrasies, individuality, personal attention, diversity, and all of those "minor" aspects of human life which distinguish it from that of an ant colony. It will always be cheaper and "more efficient" to house elderly people four to a room instead of individually; to have staff feed them rapidly instead of letting them try it for themselves in a more time-consuming and "inefficient" manner, to design facilities, whether nursing homes or congregate-living arrangements, with the sameness and drabness that mark public-housing projects instead of the variety in private homes; to hire the cheapest available labor for the most intimate contact with residents, with predictable results.

It is evident now that the direction of public policy in the mid-1960s to excessively reimburse institutional care and nearly ignore home-based alternatives has led to a long-term care crisis in which costs have escalated out of control (Avorn 1981*b*). The quality of life for the elderly thus cared for has fallen into a state (at least in terms of psychological well-being) not in their best interest. In this decade, as we look ahead to patterns of long-term care that are more consistent with the variety and individuality of human life, we must base our public policies on clinical and experimental evidence that will further those goals, and not once again construct policy around misguided reliance on inappropriate commercial or medical paradigms that do not fit the people we hope to serve.

References and Additional Resources

Avorn, J. 1982. "Beyond the Bedside: The Social Context of Geriatric Practice." In *Health and Illness in Old Age,* ed. J. Rowe and P. Besdine. Boston: Little, Brown & Co.

Avorn, J. 1981*a*. "Studying Cognitive Performance in the Elderly: The Need for a Biopsychosocial Approach." In *Aging and Cognitive Processes,* ed. F. Craik and S. Trehub. New York: Plenum Press.

Avorn, J. 1981*b*. Nursing Home Infections: The Context. *New England Journal of Medicine* 305:759–760.

Avorn, J. and Langer, E. 1981. Helping, Helplessness, and the "Incompetent" Nursing Home Patient: An Empirical Study. *Clinical Research* 29:633A.

Baltes, M.M., and Barton, E.M. 1979. Behavioral Analysis of Aging: A Review of the Operant Model and Research. *International Journal of Behavior and Development.* 2:297–320.

Bettelheim, B. 1943. Individual and Mass Behavior in Extreme Situations. *Journal of Abnormal Social Psychology* 38:417–452.

Cannon, W.B. 1942. Voodoo Death. *American Anthropologist* 44:169–181.

Chanowitz, B., and Langer, E. 1980. "Knowing More (or Less) Than You Can Show: Understanding Control through the Mindlessness/Mindful Distinction. In *Human Helplessness,* ed. M.E.P. Seligman & J. Garber New York: Academic Press.

Goffman, E. 1963. *Stigma: Notes on the Management of Spoiled Identity.* Englewood Cliffs, N.J.: Prentice-Hall, Inc.

Haynes, R.B., and Sackett, D.L. 1978. Increased Absenteeism from Work after Detection and Labeling of Hypertensive Patients. *New England Journal of Medicine* 299:741-744.

Kelley, H. 1967. Attribution Theory in Social Psychology. In *Nebraska Symposium on Motivation,* ed. D. Levine. p. 192-240.

Langer, E. 1975. The Illusion of Control. *Journal of Personality and Social Psychology,* 32:311-328.

Langer, E. 1978. "Rethinking the Role of Thought in Social Interaction. In *New Directions in Attribution Research,* ed. J. Harvey, W. Ickes, and R. Kidd, Hillsdale, N.J.: Lawrence Erlbaum and Associates, Inc.

Langer, E. and Benevento, A. 1978*b*. Self-Induced Dependence. *Journal of Personality and Social Psychology,* 36:886-893.

Langer, E., and Abelson, R. 1974. A Patient by Any Other Name: Clinician Group Differences in Labelling Bias. *Journal of Consulting and Clinical Psychology,* 42:4-9.

Langer, E., and Imber, L. 1979. When Practice Makes Imperfect: Debilitating Effects of Overlearning. *Journal of Personality and Social Psychology,* 37:2014-2025.

Langer, E., and Rodin, J. 1976. The Effects of Enhanced Personal Responsibility for the Aged: A Field Experiment in an Institutional Setting. *Journal of Personality and Social Psychology,* 34:191-198.

Langer, E., and Roth, J. 1973. Heads I Win, Tails It's Chance: The Illusion of Control as a Function of the Sequence of Outcomes in a Purely Chance Task. *Journal of Personality and Social Psychology,* 32:951-955.

Lown, B.; Verrier, R.; Rabinowitz, S. 1977. Neural and Psychologic Mechanisms and the Problem of Sudden Cardiac Death. *American Journal of Cardiology,* 39:890-901.

Parkes, C. 1964. Effects of Bereavement on Physical and Mental Health. *British Medical Journal* 2:274-279.

Richter, C.P. 1957. On the Phenomenon of Sudden Death in Animals and Man. *Journal of Psychosomatic Medicine* 19:191-198.

Rodin, J., and Langer, E. 1980. Aging Labels: The Decline of Control and the Fall of Self-esteem. *Journal of Social Issues* 36:12-29.

Rodin, J., and Langer, E. 1977. Long-Term Effects of a Control-Relevant Intervention among the Institutionalized Aged. *Journal of Personality and Social Psychology,* 35:895-902.

Rosenthal, R. 1971. Pygmalion Reaffirmed. In *Pygmalion Reconsidered,* ed. J. Elashoff and R. Snow Worthington, Ohio: C.A. Jones, p. 139-155.

Schmale, A.H. 1969. Somatic Expressions and Consequences of Conversion Reaction. *N.Y. State Journal of Medicine* 69:1878.

Seligman, M.E.F. 1975. *Helplessness.* San Francisco: W.H. Freeman & Co.

Snyder, M., and Swann, W. 1978. Behavioral Confirmation in Social Interaction. *Journal of Experimental Social Psychology* 14:148-162.

3

Grouping Elders of Different Abilities

Lorraine G. Hiatt

Social scientists have amply documented the tendency for people to form groups that, like the clusters of a kaleidoscope, create patterns more evident to the observer than to those intimately affected. People, particularly mobile, older people, may be uniquely influenced by factors that direct them into new associations with their peers—factors such as housing, services, technology or finances—which have little to do with traditional reasons for forming friendships or families.

Grouping will be used here to refer to situational factors that result in either the overt or subtle manipulation of the social encounters of older people who reside in a congregate-housing facility or engage in a senior-center program. These situational factors may derive from formal administrative policy or be manipulated through location, design, or setting arrangement. Grouping may also result as an unintentional by-product of other decisions.

The purpose here is to examine residentially created groupings of older people and the implications for design, and, conversely, of the effects of design on group formation. Case studies will demonstrate some long-term effects of planning and design decisions. The objective is to suggest options for older people, planners, managers, and policymakers, and for those involved in congregate-housing design.

Awareness of the external pressures on group formation in retirement settings may result in facilities and programs sufficiently flexible to meet the needs of people to form groups, formal and informal, large and small, and joined by choice or through coincidence.

This will not be a reiteration of the extensive literature on the pros and cons of developing retirement communities restricted to older people (see Davis 1973; Lawton 1976; Snyder 1972; Thompson 1978; Urban Systems Research 1976; U.S. Department of Housing and Urban Development 1979); nor is the intent to persuade sponsors that the grouping process is wholly within anyone's control.

The issues raised and examples presented were culled from several distinctly funded research programs I was involved in across the United States from 1972-1981 (Snyder, Ostrander and Koncelik 1973; Snyder 1972; Snyder and Bowersox 1976; Berkowitz, et al. 1979; and Snyder and Ostrander, 1974) and from individual consultation on planning and design—approximately fifty-five projects.

Initial Findings from Site Visits

On-site visits to residences and programs for older people suggest:

1. *Grouping is occurring.* Very few apartment and long-term care settings have an equal probability assignment of older people to any apartment or residential unit in a building or section of that building even though the entire structure may be covered by a single license or certified as a single level of care. Even senior centers, rehabilitation centers and recreation programs typically have formal and informal procedures which encourage the entry of some people while discouraging the participation of others. The mechanisms for creating groups may include admission procedures and inadvertent qualifications such as that a person must be mobile, able to drive, or have access to transportation in order to participate.

2. *Selection procedures may be paradoxically overt and subtle.* In some instances, staff and the older people themselves can articulate the requirements for residence or participation. In other instances, the factors controlling admissions may be a function of historic charter, marketability, personal preference, or sponsor ideology. In still others, membership may be unwittingly restricted, as when the policies and procedures are borrowed from some other agency and implemented without considering the appropriateness for this particular set of services.

3. *Design, location, and equipment influence program entrants and participation.* Building design may work independently of management procedures in some residences and reinforce programs of internal subgrouping in others. For example, creating areas with larger apartments or rooms, setting aside a portion of the building for wheelchair-accessible apartments, or otherwise distinguishing an area according to equipment, space and furnishings may all become influential social forces. Management of some organizations work diligently to overcome unintentional design-imposed groupings.

4. *Many decisions that affect group formation are made long before a building or service formally opens.* Planning decisions made to secure funding, reduce construction costs or to market and publicize the building may impose upon the services and influence the individuals and groups served later on. Sometimes, the ramifications of such policy decisions are not anticipated. For example, the decision to create a dining room and require entrants to take a meal, may become a major source of conflict in the operation and success of a program after a facility opens.

5. *The question of balancing the types of people served is important.* One of the most perplexing questions faced by those planning and evaluating environments for older people pertains to population mix or balance. What admissions or discharge policies result in what mix of people? Should a concerted effort be made to group people in one building or portion of a building because they share similar physical, mental or economic characteristics?

Too many planners neglect to consider the changing needs of older people in whatever initial plans they make regarding the mix of clients. Older people do not represent a stable set of needs over the life-course of a building. There may be periods when they become similar (Lawton, Greenbaum and Lebowitz 1980) but this may be a function of initial entrance requirements.

There is evidence that setting the initial age of entry at seventy, rather than the more common sixty-two or sixty-five, or over may yield some longer tenure or stability to the population. It appears that many of the high-risk health crises, such as heart disease and stroke, may occur during the sixties (depending upon the ethnic composition of the population). Much congregate housing has appeared to provide services in excess of the needs of clients, particularly during the first four to six years of operation. This may result from focusing the marketing on a relatively younger, less frail population with a strong bias toward self-care. The motives of relatively younger-old people to move may involve the economic hedge against inflation resulting from lower-than-market-value rentals. Those who live to seventy and would apply for apartment residences may be survivors who accept their aging and are interested in the support services necessary to sustain energy and good health.

6. *Grouping is a problem.* The major difficulties resulting from restricted entry-requirements and externally imposed systems for setting a population mix seem to arise because the stability of a group cannot be maintained or predicted. However, the chief proponents of strict admissions policies and firm systems for relocation may not be corporations or managers, but rather older people themselves.

The following material will illustrate the previous points:

Evidence of Grouping

In practice, few older people or administrators label their current questions about lifestyle in existing buildings or community programs as issues of grouping. More frequently, their concerns are stated as:

> This building was designed for one type of user. The "independent" ones. Now these folks have become dependent and our applicants seem to be more needy as well. We haven't got the right kind of programs and facilities to meet these needs, but the community pressure to accept increasingly "helpless" people is strong. Then, once they're in, trying to get them out is our greatest headache. (Congregate housing manager)

> I'm not happy. I can't find my own kind any more. Fewer people to talk to. We used to go out—a group of us. But, there's less interest now. (Tenant of five years)

> They seem to be letting in a new kind of person. I don't like that. This place was supposed to be for independent people. Now just look at that

[a woman with a walker, having great difficulty going through a front door] . . . or them [a group of people sitting and watching the woman have difficulty]. We have some here who just shouldn't be. They may burn us all down or make us look bad. (Tenant of six years)

I don't go out of my room much; they have all types here. It's best not to trouble with anyone, you never can tell how they are in the head, don't you know. (Resident of three years)

"What are *they* doing *here*?" (Resident of apartment upon seeing residents from an adjacent nursing home arrive for a picnic)

Older people and staff are not the only people with opinions:

Mother's feeling she has to do so much to keep up here. She's exhausted. Maybe it's time for her to move. (Adult daughter)

Bases for Grouping

Admittedly, the most extensive administrative and design-imposed grouping of older people occurs in skilled and intermediate nursing-homes and in retirement campuses. In the first example, staffing and health are often given as explanations for clustering people of similar abilities. In multi-level-care geriatric centers, the facilities are available to reinforce complicated schemes of both administrative and resident-initiated clustering.

Administrative criteria for admissions, which become criteria for grouping and are imposed on top of existing regulations, have included:

1. Age (either minimum or maximum);
2. Mental clarity, alertness;
3. Capacity for self-care ("Must be able to prepare own meals" or "Must need to take one meal a day from us");
4. Mobility ("Must walk in the front door under his or her own power"; or use of a wheelchair or independence with a mobility aid);
5. Diet (need for salt-free, sugar-free foods);
6. Admission status (new versus being evaluated versus longer-term resident);
7. Financial status;
8. Personal habits (smoking, drinking, and so forth);
9. Assistance required in relation to location of offices, services or equipment;
10. Deafness, blindness.

Architectural means of establishing groups include: (1) Natural features of building change: sections, floors, wings; (2) Apartment or room configuration and size; (3) Design features of the units in relation to exterior (sun, highway, soud, familiar orientation); (4) Location in relation to exits, elevators, lights, and so on; (5) Availability of equipment: tubs versus showers, stove or oven type, call system to staff.

Grouping may also occur in the daily programs offered by a congregate residence or senior center. Currently, the National Council on the Aging, for example, is delving into a number of questions related to providing senior centers for a broader range of users referred to as those at risk or frail older people (Jacobs 1980). I visited one setting where a formula for "leavening" had been adopted. "Of 350 daily participants, we allow only fifty who are disabled," noted the social worker whose job it was to keep this order. In that center, the formula was arbitrary, based upon staff preference, noted another staff member.

The difficulties for gate-keepers in programs and residences are the questions of judgment. What is disabled? Is a person diagnosed as having all sorts of moderate limitations but appearing to cope with them independent? What about one who takes medication or is trying to overcome a bout of falls? (Hiatt 1981a).

The following case studies demonstrate the dynamics of two approaches to the issues of admissions policies and population mix.

Case Study 1: An Example of Regrouping

These days, many organizations are concerned with the clusters of people who already occupy buildings or attend community programs. The Jefferson (a fictitious name) illustrates a set of problems that result from an organization that naturally outgrows an image of the initial population.

The Jefferson was built under the original HUD 202 program (U.S. Department of Housing and Urban Development 1979; see U.S. Senate 1974, for an explanation of the specific funding program). This means that it was built in the late 1960s, with many of the amenities, such as group dining, we associate with today's congregate-care housing. The Jefferson was erected on a large tract of land already occupied by a vintage home-for-the-aged and a nursing home that had been expanded twice.

While there was some involvement of older people in the planning of the Jefferson, they typically reacted to various plans and illustrations rather than actively help to define services or design the apartments.

From the start, the Jefferson was promoted by its nonprofit sponsors (an alliance of churches) as housing for independent elderly. This was viewed as necessary to, in the words of one planner, "overcome the stigma of the nearby health-care facilities." The sponsors were determined to provide one required daily meal, partly out of their concern for nutrition and partly as a security system to keep track of tenants' capacities, but few other programs were initiated by the sponsors. Several rooms were intentionally left unfinished to allow tenants the necessary space to develop facilities appropriate to programs of their own planning.

Tenants formed their own council and committee structure shortly after the building opened and before it had actually filled up. Managers did not attend these meetings unless invited to report, though the managers occasionally requested that the residents' council officers schedule them at an upcoming meeting for some specific request or report. All programs were established by the tenants, though a staff member was available to process admissions, assist in relocation, and provide back-up in program details requiring maintenance, transportation, or equipment. The manager also surreptitiously attended to personal needs.

Tenants had recommended admissions criteria. They had requested that management, from the earliest days of operation, deny admission to anyone who required a wheelchair or walker. Tenants also voted that wheelchairs were unacceptable in the dining room—effective if not formal eviction. The management struggled with these policies; yet long waiting lists and continued commitment to the independent decision making of tenants allowed management to fill vacancies with able-bodied older people. The availability of nearby accommodations in health-care facilities circumvented what would otherwise have created serious problems of where to place an individual, but with each successive year after opening, the issue of independence seemed to be increasingly difficult to manage.

First, there were the difficulties in coordinating building design with occasional resident needs. The tenants had no call system in their apartments and no resident-to-resident security system had been installed. "This place is for the independent. I would only have put a phone in my own home," voiced one tenant when the possibility of devising some voluntary security system was suggested by a manager. Then, six years after the opening, a tenant was discovered in her apartment, seriously injured from an accident of three days earlier. Within forty-eight hours, a mutual-aid, tenant check-in program was adopted.

The call-system issue was only one of the problems arising between the fifth and sixth years of operation. By the sixth year, the service manager indicated that there were many drop-outs, people who were hiding their needs. She acknowledged that some neighborly assistance schemes had been devised. One person was helped to walk with the aid of two others; without such assistance she was virtually immobilized. There were a few who were reminded of meals or seated where their shakiness during eating was less noticeable, but the manager felt responsible for many others who were not receiving informal assistance.

Nearly two thirds of the original tenants were still present, but, she argued, at least half of these needed some aid to live safely and comfortably. Could it be that some were actually becoming more disabled through inactivity and the prohibitions against prosthetic devices (Hiatt 1981b)?

Nothing happened until later that year when one of the staunchest proponents of the stringent independence requirements had a stroke. By laws of her own making, she should have been relocated, but instead she became the focal point of an overall program-restructuring which took nearly four years and resulted in more options and more widespread neighborly assistance.

Comments

While these details may be specific to one residence, such situations are not unique. Entire retirement communities like Sun City, Arizona have undergone changes in the late 1970s to meet the needs of an aging population which indulged in unrealistic expectations of independence. It is a mistake to assume that the initial population and programs will bear any resemblance to possible constituent populations and their demands over time. It is risky to lock programs into policies and designs which will not be able to accommodate the changing needs of populations—in spite of any efforts made to maintain some homogeneity in resident/tenant capabilities. Waiting lists may sometimes provide older people with a social-insurance policy; it has been found that in some communities as many as half of those who initially express an interest may have no intention of making an immediate move. In fact, people on waiting lists may be more capable than those who actually seek housing once a building is available for occupancy.

The problems then, may not be how to affect the reformation of subgroups, but how to build flexibility into the services. The sponsors of the Jefferson have developed newer residences, taking care not to over-market the independent-without-exception theme. Other sponsors have taken the spirit of independent housing and tenant involvement a step further, creating cooperatives for older people (Wilner, Pease and Walgren 1978). The cooperative elevates the significance of tenants' councils from concern with social programs and selected policies to a strong position of management. One such building has carefully crafted features that would allow the conversion of storage closets to communication centers and the creation of apartments where health staff could reside and be electronically tied in, as needed, to several apartments without having to live-in. Arcane policies preclude such flexible design in many states, but we look ahead to this as a more meaningful way of keeping people at home and preventing unnecessary institutionalization. Interestingly, it is my understanding that the tenants cooperative council was not aware of the building's convertible features, since there was some concern by the sponsor that this might discourage potential buyers.

Behavioral scientists have recently taken a great interest in what has been called the micro-environment, emphasizing the importance of technology and space layout in compensating for minor changes in vision, hearing, mobility, agility and even memory (Faletti 1981; Hiatt 1981*b*, Fozard and Popkin 1978; Howell 1980a). The crux of their thinking is that we can probably extend the potential of people to function independently if we make minor adaptations in the visual, auditory, tactile, climatic, and physical environments (Hiatt 1978). It is not the name of the residence (apartment or nursing home) nor the height (high rise or low rise), nor even the population density of older people that will be emphasized in the future. Probably far more significant are the equipment, furnishings and hardware which, if appropriately selected—often from existing and available products—could greatly increase the abilities of older people to maintain a household on their own.

Case Study 2: Grouping that Begins during the Informal Planning Process

A planning committee had been formed from members of several churches and leaders in business and county government to develop an apartment residence for older people named The Vernon (another pseudonym). Twelve people had met for about six months to explore funding options, consider sites, discuss their hopes for the housing (often drawing upon personal or family experiences), and to share information on the requirements of various zoning, planning and funding agencies. When the group had just about decided upon a site, the leader contacted an architectural firm. It was at that point that I was asked by the architect, on behalf of the group, to provide an informational workshop.

The Vernon planning process was much like many others my colleagues and I have observed or participated in over the years (Hiatt 1979). There were participants to who had seen other residences and were quite knowledgeable about certain programs and funding mechanisms, and there were those who were newer to the process.

First on our workshop agenda, we asked participants to describe their fondest hopes for the new program and to list any particular questions that they might have about the possibilities or the process. We quickly learned that the members of the planning committee envisioned many different needs being served by an apartment residence. Participants also found it useful to know that there were some differences of opinion among the members regarding whether they should begin with an apartment residence, nursing service, or specific services to meet some special local needs; what the structure was to look like; and what services should be included.

As a group we established a short-term decision-making process, one which we agreed to respect during our two-day planning meetings. First, all aired their ideas, making sure that the differences of opinion were at least clearly articulated and adequately represented. Then, major questions were posed and discussion of some options for how problems would be resolved, and when, were set. One of the first discussions focused on how to decide who could be served or admitted.

Some members had subordinated their project hopes and dreams to the requirements and prerequisites of various sources of funding. Indeed, some of the funding programs were written in language that seemed to preclude choices or to limit building-design features. Participants had to weigh the alternatives between developing what they really wanted, recognizing that their dreams and goals did not fit the prerequisites of existing federal or state funding-programs, and taking longer time and some risk in developing a program with several funding sources that might more closely fit their needs.

There were members on the committee who spoke eloquently about the advantages of a formula project, urging quick decision making with convincing arguments about rising construction costs, and recommending that the design of a nearby project be copied on their proposed site.

Equally committed participants asked why they sould build for the sake of building, copy without understanding, and commit their time and energies to something that would fall short of the needs they had identified.

To move the discussion, we made a list of the givens, the firmly established, unchangeable tenets that would be respected throughout the planning process. This resulted in a meaningful discussion of some diverse perceptions of just what was set and what was still open to discussion and input. The site was the crux of much concern. It would cost money just to hold an option on it; time and money are nearly always scarce commodities and too early a commitment to any piece of land would force the group onto a time schedule. We also recognized, however, that the urgency to option a specific site was self-imposed. The availability of one particular site had begun to dictate programs, schedules, and even design. The members decided to shift the order of their decisions, even if it meant losing the site.

We then viewed color slides of various geriatric centers and programs around the United States. These slides had been taken as part of numerous studies and similar planning sessions that my architect colleagues and I had been involved in. The program was short, but it helped to put the group on equal footing regarding the possibilities and the decisions which are common to communities and planning groups such as their own.

At this point the group had been meeting for nearly three hours. We began the most critical discussion of the entire planning session: the definition of the people to be served and the services to be provided. Even though marketing studies had been commissioned and were available through resources of the area agency on aging, each group generally has some special insights into a particular population group, or access to people who represented a certain set of needs. (For information on conducting marketing studies, see Pease 1979; Murakami, Pellman and Sterrett 1979). This point is critical, because it is here that the decisions about people and their groupings are made, and it is here that we begin the process of negotiating and matching who is to be served, in which ways, and where, with the realities of funding and the prerequisites of the sponsoring group.

To organize our conversations, three questions were placed on three large pads of paper: (1) Who would we serve? (in conjunction with the marketing study completed); (2) What would we offer? (3) What were the design and funding implications of this?

Discussions were alternately heated and friendly as the group began to really get to know each other and to learn more about existing funding: programs and available community services. We adopted an if-then approach to working out disputed points: "But, if we were to do this, how would it affect . . . ?" "And, if we did do that, could we still accomplish our objective of . . . ?"

As outsiders, the architects and I served as resource people and offered options. We did not see our role as decision makers, since the project was clearly the province of this community. The group's regular chairman led the discussion.

Other specific topics addressed throughout the weekend were geographic drawing area; age or prerequisites of admissions; whether we would aim to serve individuals, couples, or small families of older people; racial, ethnic, religious or affiliation criteria for entry; economic target group; range of income levels of group to be served (present income and lifelong socioeconomic status); and health.

The discussion was particularly enlivened through the comments of several participants who saw themselves as potential residents. Frank confrontations were played out between some who were commited to providing for "people like us" and others who urged "meeting the *real* needs and priorities of the community." Throughout these conversations, a long list of questions was developed about topics requiring more input along with any brainstorming we had about who should be contacted for the necessary information.

At the end of two days, we had many notes, which my staff and I converted into a planning document. It summarized not only the formal presentations (for future members of the planning session), but also the decisions fairly well made and the questions needing further information. This document was treated as a perpetual draft and was revised several times as we integrated new possibilities with out list of items. Throughout the process, it served as a resource guide in review, for working with consultants and designers, in public relations, and even for staff training.

High on our list was the need to move from the marketing study and our own ideas about who should be served to those of a larger advisory council. We set up a group of potential clients, tenants of nearby buildings, professionals in health, welfare, and social services, as well as community leaders from services for older people, and transportation and clergy. This larger subcommittee was formed to develop (1) a plan for who could be served; (2) admissions policies and procedures; and (3) a program of public information. One of the subgroup's earliest meetings and several "pep-up" sessions involved thinking ahead to who the tenants would be three years after the opening (rather than focusing all their energies on the people who would be there opening day) (Lawton et al. 1980). The group also dealt with ways of serving people on the waiting list and with establishing procedures for people who were not best served by this residence.

Potential tenants began meeting nearly two years before the opening, participating in program and design planning and forming self-help and informational groups that have continued to function now that the building is operating. A major breakthrough occurred on issues involving admissions when, during the two years prior to opening, several of the committee members themselves experienced changes in financial status and health needs. Recognizing through their own experiences how physical and economic changes do not necessarily signal total incapacity, the committee opened its own membership to people more representative of the fuller range of anticipated tenants, including several individuals who had never served on such groups before.

Comments

The Vernon planning process illustrates one of several approaches to planning (Gelwicks and Newcomer 1974; Hiatt 1979; Howell 1976; Lawton 1975, 1980; Sanoff 1978; Thompson 1978; Wilner, Pease and Walgren 1978).

A planning process may either fix decisions or allow some flexibility for the unknown or indeterminate. If the initial group had followed its initial plan, a building would have been created for middle income, totally independent older people from a narrowly defined geographic area of the community. Through the combined experiences of older inhabitants of other residences, visits, consulting with their own friends and neighbors, combining this information with that of professionals, and broadening their representation, they were able to develop and fund a residence that met more than the first impression of needs.

Why Provide Opportunities for Association by People of Differing Characteristics?

Value of Role Models and Social Learning

Over twenty-five years ago, Leon Festinger, a social psychologist, posed a theory of social behavior he called "social comparison" (1954). The crux of this theory is that when people experience many changes (as during adolescence) and when there are no clear-cut criteria for determining how successfully one is managing one's life throughout these changes, peers become an extremely important source of information.

Although Festinger's initial research related to adolescents, the concepts seem to have equal validity for later life. Gerontologists have recently begun to pay greater attention to the significance of social learning for older people

(Howell 1980a, 1978). It has been suggested that the life-style and problem-solving skills necessary for coping with social, physical and economic issues of aging might be acquired through greater involvement with peers who have successfully dealt with similar concerns. The narrower one's associations or the less available the role models for coping with inevitable facets of aging, the more limited one's opportunities for such learning (Langer, 1980; Langer and Rodin 1976).

One of the concerns raised by residence or services for restricted types of users is the possible denial of important role models—models that suggest that there are numerous ways of aging and that all changes are not debilitating.

Recently, a great deal of attention has been focused upon self-help and mutual-assistance programs as a basis for adult learning. The assumption of these programs is that there are experiences that can be valuably shared by people of similar interests. Self-help groups have not been widely adopted for issues of aging, though they are increasingly supported in the literature (Butler et al. 1979-1980). The same question raised by theorists in self-help can be raised by theorists in housing: what is the balance of similarities and differences that best contributes to a meaningful, useful, learning experience?

There are some differences in points of view on the value of social learning that suggest the need for additional research. Atchley (1980) is among those who argue that, by the time one reaches late adulthood, the self-concept is typically fixed and complete, and that little that others say or do can shake or change one's self-concept in old age. The issue is whether human development and learning continue to occur all through life despite a multitude of factors ranging from age itself to physical and mental condition. There is increasing evidence to support the idea that, given adequate social and environmental stimulation, such development is not only possible, but likely (Fozard and Popkin 1978).

Limiting the individual's social contacts to those of fairly similar abilities may also limit the variety of roles one plays, the demands placed on behavior, and, therefore, limit the factors that motivate cognitive growth.

Fallacies of Assessment

Despite the number and variety of methods available for assessing the health and condition of older people, few of these adequately predict functioning (Raskin and Jarvik 1979; Hiatt 1981a). For example, we can measure eye sight or the presence of eye diseases, but this tells us all too little about the older person's ability to independently negotiate a particular type of home or to perform activities of daily living.

One set of complications emerges because such evaluations are typically made in clinical settings and do not relate to experiences confronted in actual community programs or residences. Other difficulties arise because a person may appear independent or capable when judged. We simply do not have reliable, valid measures widely available and regularly readministered to adequately reflect the capabilities of older people. Therefore, most assessments are very gross approximations which do not take into account the older person's abilities to learn to cope, given adequate time and training. As a result, very specific and concrete cues to independence become the norm, even though they may have little to do with actual performance. Many of the admissions criteria that are most easily stated are the most difficult to meaningfully implement (Thompson 1978). For example, age, use of special prosthetic devices as wheelchairs, or history of institutionalization may all be faulty predictors of present day capabilities.

Some organizations have developed transitional living programs such as trial residencies or training services. Then give a more realistic picture of competencies in relation to the demands of the environment and activities to both the older person and the staff.

Concerns about the Effects of Relocation

Other factors suggesting less stringent segregation by ability level include the recent concerns over the effects of relocation, especially moves forced upon people who are in the midst of health or emotional crises or are unwilling to be relocated (Shultz and Brenner 1977; Borup, Gallego, and Heffernan 1979). The stricter the policy of grouping people and the more the options for transfer, the more possible the pressure to move people arbitrarily. Such moves, when made for staff convenience without consideration of the interests and feelings of the individual older person and family, can be particularly disruptive. At the very least, concern over relocation should involve some policy for apartment maintenance during short-term hospitalization, development of relocation-preparation programs, and maximization of the potential for some continuity with previous residences through social contacts with staff and residents, and the retention of personal possessions.

Understanding the Reticence of Older People

Many older people are vehemently opposed to sharing space or activities with people whom they do not know or who are different. Why? Is it arrogance? stress? fear of change? Some of the factors that may contribute to the preference for residing and interacting with peers are quite reasonable when considered from the point-of-view of older people:

Tradition

Today's elderly have lived in communities where grouping by ethnicity, income, and religion were commonly accepted ways of life.

Uncontrollable Social Change

Many social, economic, and environmental developments occurring recently have wrought visible changes to the social compositions of neighborhoods. Each additional request to accept new or unfamiliar people challenges the sense of command and, hence, competence with the surroundings (Lawton 1972).

Financial Stake

Those who are now seventy and eighty were raised during an era when public attention was directed toward improving health care and the problems of the mentally disadvantaged. These elderly contributed the dollars to construct institutions that were supposed to serve the physically ill and mentally needy. The concept of caring for less-able people at home seems at odds with social policy and a financial investment made.

Shifting Philosophies of Preservation and Recovery

This generation of older people was reared during the era of tuberculosis sanataria, when a prevalent philosophy of care for chronic diseases was good food, rest, relaxation and separation from the public. Is it any surprise that this notion is applied to chronic disabilities of aging or that the less vigorous retreat from more adept peers or strenuous activity on the assumption that this will conserve their energies? Older people are seldom privy to gerontology.

Confusion of Aging, with Disease

There seems to be a subtle belief-system among many older people that disabilities associated with aging may, in fact, be contractable and rather shameful.

The potential benefits of integrating more impaired residents include a more stimulating environment and opportunities for modelling adaptive behavior. ... Yet, fear of contagion on the part of those who are less impaired or the emotional impact of associating with those who have functional impairment has been an overwhelming deterrent to greater utilization of housing facilities in the long-term care component. (Kahana and Coe 1975, p. 547)

Sometimes, this is expressed as a fear of transmission of forgetfulness by association. More attention should be paid to meaningfully shared spaces or actions; one of the deterrents to interaction among people of different capabilities is that one group is expected to behave in the mode of the other. Recent research has suggested circumstances where interaction among alert and memory-impaired people may benefit both the more and the less capable (Cross et al. 1979; Rathbone-McCuan and Levinson 1975; Lawton, Nahemow, and Yeh 1980).

Inexperience in Mainstreaming or Integration

Today's children, who have been schooled alongside those who have sight loss, speech impairments, are slower learners, or are in a wheelchair may someday view older peers who have diverse abilities somewhat differently from today's older people who had neither experience with disabled peers not exposure to a social philosophy aimed at maximizing capabilities and underplaying physical handicaps. Even sexual, racial, and economic integration were incorporated as social policies long after today's seventy-year olds arrived at the age of majority.

All of this suggests the importance of engaging opinion leaders and older people in the social learning and decision-making process far in advance of facility opening. The hope that the residence itself will resolve conflicts among people of different backgrounds and abilities is foolish and stressful to both staff and program participants.

Innovation and Creative Grouping Using Environmental Design

The features of the buildings and sites themselves may be helpful in facilitating participation by people of varying abilities and interests. This is an idea that is hard to discern from existing policy or site visits to existing housing. Often too little attention is paid to features of the micro-environment that would maximize the individual and participatory potential of older people (Fozard and Popkin 1978; Fozard 1980). One particular shortcoming of community facilities and retirement residences continues to be their technological design and equipment. Much more is known about how to create a functional building than is actually being put to use (Hiatt 1978, 1981b).

For example, is one congregate-housing complex, both younger and older disabled people were served under one roof. However, social exchanges were rife with conflict, insults were freely hurled among older and younger. A look at the design of the facilities indicated that the building's acoustics and layout reinforced intergenerational hostilities (Snyder and Bowersox 1976). The older people were particularly irritated when engaged in table games, because the acoustics of the multipurpose room were abominable. Voices were lost in the echoes, hard surfaces, and the cacophony of sounds. Part of the competing noise resulted from the stereo of the younger people. With only one space to gather in, the two groups were constantly contesting for control over the use of the place in order to meet their individual acoustical needs. Design also intruded upon privacy. Many of the older residents retired early and were uncomfortable about the visitors of the younger ones who roamed shared hallways at night. In other buildings, where the entry, social areas, and acoustics are more supportive of the legitimate passtimes of each group, such conflicts are exceptional (Pastalan and Moyer 1969).

Lack of information about design precedents may also limit creative environmental planning for diverse populations (Architectural Design: Housing for the Elderly, 1981). Several years ago, I was involved with a congregate housing project designed to have *some* moveable walls. The goal was to be able to create adaptable apartment interiors that could serve one or two occupants of either similar or different abilities, to allow personal flexibility in design depending on possessions or preferences, and to minimize the need for apartments to be specified as either handicapped or nonhandicapped. The project met with a series of objections in the planning stages in spite of the fact that costs were kept in line with conventional construction figures. Local housing authorities asked how a mortgage-value could be arrived at. The funding agency set mortgage rates according to the number of rooms and anticipated number of occupants. Did this space system mean that the unit was a two-person, one room dwelling? Or, should the value be computed on the basis of a one-person, two room or studio apartment? Other programs set mortgages on the basis of unit square-footage which was an important point in resolving the regulatory agency's dilemma. There were practical concerns as well. Who would move partitions? Where would they be stored and would that be within the maximum storage allocated in the funding program? What about insurance? Working through questions such as these takes time, the involvement of officials who accept a participatory rather than adversarial relationship with planners, knowledge of other similar or related efforts regardless of funding sources, and the availability of research conducted by disinterested parties.

Staffing Considerations

Staff also have strong convictions about the propriety of grouping people according to various criteria. Some describe tightly matching groups of people of similar abilities as the right way to provide services most equitably, "We can specialize in their needs; we give better services when people are all of fairly similar capabilities."

Yet there are those administrators who connect the practice of working with similarly described older people with high staff turnover rates, noting:

> We grouped people this way because staff thought it best, but, the burnout rate with 'that group' is very high. All of the people are so similar, it's a drain. And, then I think we've developed a status system. It's more prestigious to work with the more capable than with the chronically impaired even though the pay's the same. (Administrator)

> It's as if staff resent changes in the conditions of their familiar clients, for better or worse. Maybe everybody's a little afraid of unknown replacements. (Manager)

There is a great need to air the pros and cons and perhaps develop staff-assignment systems that encourage rotation and continuity among clients and services if ability grouping among the older people is the norm.

There are models of integration by abilities. In many rural, typically county- or community-sponsored facilities I have visited in the South and Midwest, the population is sufficiently small that very diverse people are served in institutional facilities. I have observed integration of people in recreation and dining, informal social gatherings (on porches or in dayrooms) and in living quarters. Staff seemed to provide powerful role models and there was a strong local community support in such facilities. It appeared that if the staff encouraged shared activities, ranging from walking to cooperative tasks such as grooming to table seating, then such interactions seemed rather natural. This is not to say there were not clutches of people who gathered to share similar interests, be they age, generational, religion or hobbies. There were. There was also an effort to respect preferences for roommates or corridor neighbor preferences. What seemed to be different was the sense of bonding despite differences rather than association solely on the basis of physical and mental similarities.

Conclusions

A primary question is whether we are excluding a powerful source of social learning, of self-help, of mutual assistance, by extensive partitioning of people into ability groups.

Design features and misconceptions about aging and disease may be strong pressures toward simplistic, rigidly defined admissions policies, which then serve as the basis for daily social contacts.

The pressure of existing policies may result in artificial distinctions between the design of apartments, congregate residences, adult homes, homes for the aged and even intermediate-care facilities. While some of these distinctions are based on real provisions of different types of staff in supervisory and care-giving roles, in practice we find difficulties in maintaining a match of people and rigorously differentiated levels of care. This, in turn, raises some questions about whether the strictures of independently mandated funding sources (HUD, Medicaid, Medicare, Administration on Aging, Title XX, and Mental Health) might not contribute to the need to differentiate services and residences in order to help the sponsoring agencies maintain a clearer understanding of their own differences. With the move toward block grants in the 1980s, it will be interesting to learn from states taking the opportunity to more flexibly respond to aging as a variable process rather than as a fixed category of abilities and develop some new and more responsive programs and facilities.

Dahlin (1980) has conducted research on changes in family life from 1900 to the present day. She concludes that, at the turn of the century, lifestyles of the old were indistinguishable from those of the middle aged. Could it be that rigid separation of populations, by age and then by abilities within age groups, alters not only older people's perception of aging, but the views held by the general and professional public as well?

Since the substance of this chapter rests upon experiential evidence and current literature rather than tight, comparative surveys, the conclusions are presented in a form that permits additional, more systematic research:

1. There are more financial incentives for segregation by ability level than for integration of services for older people.

2. Grouping older people becomes a problem when the groups cannot in fact be maintained; grouping is deleterious to the overall program objectives; groups are the basis for the majority of social contact available to older people and those people are either not mobile or otherwise unable to interact with others; architecture, equipment, design, and arrangement do not maximize the functioning of individual sub-groups; grouping is implemented by one group and maintained by others and those responsible for maintaining membership are unclear as to its bases or their freedom to deviate from such a grouping; or when moving out of a subgroup is decided upon by someone other than the target individual or without his/her knowledge.

3. There are administrative complications imposed by strict grouping: measurement techniques necessary to make decisions about overall functioning abilities are either not available, not satisfactory, not widely used or too costly to use; entrance requirements may conflict over time with the aging of the overall client-group, raising difficulties for management credibility and requiring flexible services and facilities.

4. Older people have not been adequately involved in deciding among various options for association.

5. Building technology is such that we could adapt settings to more diverse users (vision impaired, hard of hearing, those impaired in mobility, agility, endurance and even in memory), but there are few operating examples with available longitudinal data to support their existence.

6. There are few advocates of comingling older people of different abilities, even on a short-term basis such as in dining programs, recreation or informal social activities.

Without the policy or funding sources to promote more integrated programs, the burden for innovation will be left to advocates or to the public who support the concept that people should be encouraged to age within a familiar system or residence. Mainstreaming in public education has taken years. It is not a solution for everyone (Lapidus 1980). By offering more opportunities for geriatric mainstreaming, we may similarly become better versed with the situations, individuals, and factors involved. We may learn more about when individualized attention should be given to a specifically defined group of similar individuals. Much of the same type of community involvement, thinking, preparation and adventure that has characterized mainstreaming in education may be expected to produce similar results in gerontology. The fact that it will take time, that some individuals will be best served through existing, parochial systems, should not deter those who would like to see options for integrated service-delivery systems in their own lifetimes.

References and Additional Resources

Architectural Design: "Housing for the Elderly," 1981. *Progressive Architecture* 62, 8, 59-75.

Atchley, R. 1980. "Changing Perspectives in the Behavioral Sciences," symposium presentation made at the 26th Annual Meetings of the Western Gerontological Society, Anaheim, Calif.

Batelle's Columbus Laboratories. 1977. *Study and Evaluation of Integration the Handicapped in HUD Housing.* HUD, Office of Policy Development and Research. Washington, D.C.: U.S. Government Printing Office.

Berkowitz, M.; Hiatt, L.; De Toledo, P.; Shapiro, J.; and Luria, M. 1979. *The Role of Health Care Institutions in Satisfying the Reading Needs of Residents With Print Limitations.* New York: American Foundation for the Blind.

Borup, J.H.; Gallego, D.T.; and Heffernan, P.G. 1979. "Relocation and Its Effect on Mortality," *Gerontologist,* 19: no. 2, 135-149.

Butler, R.N.; Gertman, J.S.; Oberlander, D.L.; and Schindler, L. 1979-1980. "Self-Help, Self-Care and the Elderly," *International Journal of Aging and Human Development,* 10: no. 1, 95-110.

Cross, D.; Mattson, L.; Gray, K.; Pyrek, J.; and Carroll, K. 1979. "The Impact of Integrated Groups of Alert and Confused Elderly," paper presented at the 32nd Annual Scientific Meetings of the Gerontological Society, Washington, D.C.

Dahlin, M. 1980. "Perspectives on Family Life of the Elderly in 1900," *Gerontologist,* 20:99-107.

Davis, R.H., ed. 1973. *Housing for the Elderly.* Los Angeles: University of Southern California, Ethel Percy Andrus Gerontology Center.

Faletti, M.V. 1981. "The Normal Elderly at Home: Capabilities, Limitations and Interpretations Leading to Products and Technology," paper presented at the National Research Conference on Technology and Aging, a Joint Project of the Gerontological Society of America and the Western Gerontological Society.

Festinger, L. 1954. "Motivations Leading to Social Behavior." In *Nebraska Symposium on Motivation,* ed. M.R. Jones. Lincoln, Neb.: University of Nebraska Press, 2:191-219.

Fozard, J.L. 1981. "Person-Environment Relationships in Adulthood; Implications for Human Factors Engineering," *Human Factors,* 23: no. 1, 7-28.

Fozard, J.L., and Popkin, S.J. 1978. "Optimizing Adult Development: Ends and Means of an Applied Psychology of Aging," *American Psychologist,* 33: 975-989.

Garza, J.S. 1979. "Ethnic Lifestyles and Housing Policy," *Western Gerontological Society Generations,* 3: no. 3,32-33,37.

Gelwicks, L.E., and Newcomer, R.J. 1974. *Planning Housing Environments for the Elderly.* Washington, D.C.: National Council on the Aging.

Greer, D.S. 1978. "Housing for the Physically Impaired." In *Housing and Environment for the Elderly,* ed. T.O. Byerts. Washington, D.C.: Gerontological Society, 117-122.

Hiatt, L. 1978. "Architecture for the Aged. Design for Living," *Inland Architect,* 23:6-17.

———. 1979. "Reflections on an Environmental Psychologist's Roles in Design and Architecture for Older People." In *Environmental Design: Research and Applications,* ed. A.D. Siedel and S. Danforth. Proceedings of the 10th Annual Conference, Environmental Design Research Association, 233-247.

———. 1981*a.* "Aging and Disability," In *America's Retirement Population: Prospects, Planning and Policy,* ed. N. McClosky and E. Borgotta. Beverly Hills, Calif.: Sage.

———. 1981*b.* "Technology and Chronically Impaired Elderly: Interpretations Leading to Performance Demands and Products in Institutions and in Community Care Systems," paper presented at the National Research Conference on Technology and Aging, a joint project of the Gerontological Society of America and the Western Gerontological Society.

Howell, S. 1978. "Aging and Social Learning of a New Environment." In *Recent Advances in Gerontology. Proceedings of the XI International Congress of Gerontology,* ed. H.O.K. Shimada. Tokoyo, Aug. 20-25:371-376.

Howell, S. 1980a. "Environments and Aging." In *Annual Review of Gerontology and Geriatrics,* ed. C. Eisdorfer, 1:237-260.

Howell, S. 1980b. "Environments as Hypotheses in Human Aging Research." In *Aging in the 1980's,* ed. L.W. Poon. Washington, D.C.: American Psychological Association, 424-434.

Jacobs, B. 1980. *Senior Centers and the At-Risk Older Person.* Washington, D.C.: National Institute of Senior Centers.

Kahana, E., and Coe, R.M. 1975. "Alternatives to Long-Term Care." In *Long-Term Care: A Handbook for Researchers, Planners and Providers,* ed. S. Sherwood. New York: Spectrum, 391-454.

Langer, E. 1979. "Old age: An Artifact?" *Biology, Behavior and Aging.* Washington, D.C.: National Research Council Publication.

Langer, E.J., and Rodin, J. 1976. "The Effects of Choice and Enhanced Personal Responsibility of the Aged: A Field Experiment in an Institutional Setting," *Journal of Personality and Social Psychology* 34:2,191-198.

Lapidus, H.P. 1980. "Let's Get Serious about Mainstreaming," *Journal of Learning Disabilities* 13:9,500-502.

Lawton, M.P. 1972. "Assessing the Competence of Older Poeple." In *Long-term Care,* ed. D.P. Kent, R. Kastenbaum and S. Sherwood. New York: Behavioral Publication, p. 122-143.

Lawton, M.P. 1976. "Competence, Environmental Press and the Adaptation of Older People." In *Theory Development in Environment and Aging,* ed. P. Windley, T. Byerts, and F. Ernst. Washington, D.C.: Gerontological Society, 13-84.

———. 1980. *Environment and Aging.* Montery, Calif.: Brooks/Cole.

———. 1976. "Homogeneity and Heterogeneity in Housing for the Elderly." In *Community Planning for an Aging Society,* ed. M.P. Lawton, R.J. Newcomer and T.O. Byerts. Stroudsburg, Penn.: Dowden, Hutchinson and Ross, 131-180.

Lawton, M.P.; Nahemow, L.; and Yeh, T. 1980. "Neighborhood Development and the Well-Being of Older Tenants in Planned Housing," *International Journal of Aging and Humand Development,* 11:13,211-227.

———. 1975. *Planning and Managing Housing for the Elderly.* New York: John Wiley & Sons.

Lawton, M.P.; Greenbaum, M.; and Liebowitz, B. 1980. "The Lifespan of Housing Environments for the Aging," *Gerontologist* 20:1,56-64.

Murakami, E.; Pellman, K.; and Sterrett, J. 1979. "Service Inventory Analysis Techniques." In *Planning for the Elderly: Alternative Community Analysis Techniques,* ed. V. Regnier. Los Angeles: University of Southern California Press, 70-89.

Nahemow, L.; Fulcomer, M.; and Lawton, M.P. "A Study of Race, Racial Integration and Social Contact Using Multiple Regression and Orthogonal Contrasts," peper presented at the 29th Annual Scientific Meeting of the Gerontological Society, New York.

Newcomer, R., and Frise, L. 1979. "Housing in the Continuum of Care," *Western Gerontological Society Generations* 3, no. 3:13-14.

Ostrander, E.R., and Reizenstein, J. 1976. *An Evaluation of Housing for the Severely Disabled in the Context of a Service Delivery System.* U.S. Department of Housing and Urban Development Research. Washington, D.C.: U.S. Government Printing Office.

Pastalan, L.A., and Moyer, L.N. 1960. *Vistual Manor Demonstration Housing for the Physically Disabled.* Springfield, Virg.: U.S. Department of Commerce, National Technical Information Service.

Pease, J. 1979. "Getting Started in Developing Facilities for the Aging: Market Analysis and Feasibility Studies," paper presented at Successful Capital Financing Workshop, American Assn. of Homes for the Aging Sponsorship, Orlando, Fla.

Raskin, A., and Jarvik, L.F., eds. 1979. *Psychiatric Symptoms and Cognitive Loss in the Elderly.* New York: Halsted Press.

Rathbone-McCuan, E., and Levenson, J. 1975. Impact of Socialization Therapy in Geriatric Day-Care. *Gerontologist* 15:4,338-342.

Sanoff, H. 1978. *Designing with Community Participation.* New York: McGraw-Hill Publishing Co.

Sanoff, H.; Adams, G.; Andrews, R.; and Walker, C. 1979. *Senior Center Design Workbook.* Raleigh, N.C.: North Carolina State University/Community Development Group, Division of Aging.

Schutz, R., and Brenner, G. 1977. Relocation of the Aged: A Review and Theoretical Analysis. *Journal of Gerontology,* 32:323-333.

Snyder, L. 1972. "Environmental Challenge and the Aging individual," *Exchange Bibliography,* 254: (Council of Planning Librarians) 43 pp.

Snyder, L.H., and Bowersox, J.L. 1976. "Report of Four Case Studies of Federally Sponsored Housing for the Elderly and Disabled." In *Residential Environments for the Functionally Disabled,* ed. T.O. Byerts. Washington, D.C.: Gerontological Society, 159-212.

Snyder, L.H., and Ostrander, E.R. 1974. *Research Basis for Behavior Program, New York State Veterans Home, Oxford, N.Y.* Ithaca, N.Y.: Cornell University, Department of Design and Environmental Analysis.

Snyder, L.H.; Ostrander, E.R.; and Koncelik, J.A. 1972. *The New Nursing Home: A Response to the Behavior and Living Style of the Aging.* Proceedings of the Conference for Nursing Home Administrators' Continuing Education Licensure, New York State College of Human Ecology. Ithaca, N.Y.: Cornell University.

Thompson, M.M. 1978. *Assisted Residential Living for Older People,* A Guide to Tenant Selection and Preoccupancy Planning. Washington, D.C.: International Center for Social Gerontology.

Urban Systems Research Engineering, Inc. 1976. *Evaluation of the Effectiveness of Congregate Housing for the Elderly, Final Report.* U.S. Department of Housing and Urban Development, Office of Policy Development and Research. Washington, D.C.: U.S. Government Printing Office.

U.S. Department of Housing and Urban Development, Office of Policy Development and Research 1979. *Housing for the Elderly and Handicapped: The Experience of Section 202 Program from 1959-1977.* Washington, D.C.: U.S. Government Printing Office.

U.S. Senate, Special Committee on Aging 1975. *Developments in Aging:* 1974 and January-April, 1975. Washington, D.C.: U.S. Government Printing Office, pp. 70-82.

U.S. Senate, Special Committee on Aging 1978. *Developments in Aging:* 1977, Part I. Washington, D.C.: U.S. Government Printing Office, 106-111.

Welford, I.H., and Struyk, R.J. eds. 1978. *Occasional Papers in Housing and Community Affairs,* vol. 3, U.S. Department of Housing and Urban Development, Office of Policy Development and Research, Washington, D.C.: U.S. Government Printing Office.

Wilner, M.A.; Pease, J.A.; and Walgren, R.S. 1978. *Planning and Financing Facilities for the Elderly, A Resource Handbook.* Washington, D.C.: American Association of Homes for the Aging.

Zeisel, J.; Epp, G.; and Demos, S. 1977. *Low Rise Housing for Older People: Behavioral Criteria for Design.* U.S. Department of Housing and Urban Development, Office of Policy Development and Research. Washington, D.C.: U.S. Government Printing Office.

4

Placement and Location: The Elderly and Congregate Care

Elizabeth W. Markson

There is an old Russian proverb: A boat trip on the Volga is soothing to the nerves. What is meant, of course, is that a change of scene in which usual role responsibilities are reduced, modified, or abandoned, has a therapeutic impact on the overstressed person. As we consider the phenomena of placement and movement of the elderly into congregate facilities especially designed to meet their needs, it is worthwhile to dwell upon this proverb for a moment, asking the question: What makes such a transition a good trip instead of a rocky voyage? The focus of this chapter addresses this broad query. Specifically, the following topics are discussed: (1) some basic issues pertinent to the elderly and congregate housing, especially stress, congruency, and continuity; (2) the characteristics of people most likely to enter congregate care; (3) preparation for placement and relocation; and (4) some negative effects of relocation.

Congregate housing, as Carp (1977) has pointed out, is not a new concept, means the clustering of housing units in close proximity; yet some question remains about what is to be congregated—old people, services, or units. As commonly used, congregate housing implies all three; for example, Lawton (1976) has described it as "housing that offers a minimum service package that includes some on site meals service in a communal dining room, plus one or more medical/nursing services, personal care or housekeeping." In a variety of definitions, emphasis is on a semi-independent life-style that inhibits premature institutional care.

The process leading to choice of assisted independent living in congregate housing is complex. To some extent, it is analogous to choosing and entering a college; both congregate residences for the elderly and colleges for the young adult have certain socio-structural similarities in that they may be usefully viewed from the perspective of the typology of total institutions developed by Goffman (1961). While "total institution" has come to have a pejorative connotation to most of us, its properties are not bad or good in themselves; rather, the term denotes a series of social and structural patterns. As described by Goffman, total institutions are facilities in which the usual barriers separating work, leisure and sleeping are absent. While, for most of us, these three activities are carried out in different contexts and locales and thus are somewhat socially and spatially isolated from one another, in the total institution all aspects of life occur in the same place and under the same authority. Diverse needs and wants are handled by a bureaucratic organization that promotes group living rather than individual preferences. Batch living (Goffman 1961), where people are required to adapt to activities scheduled by the institution and thus to do things in unison, also characterizes this type of social structure.

Obviously there are not only different types but different degrees of totality among institutions. Jails, monasteries, summer camps, the military, nursing homes, congregate-care facilities, and hospitals are some different types. Within, as well as among, these categories, the amount of conformity expected of residents, the degree of social segregation and geographic isolation, and the extent of regimentation will vary. The common denominator among that disparate people-serving organizations is an underlying design which requires adaptation and resocialization from idiosyncratic norms and life-styles to group life and norms.

The relevance of the concept of total institutions to congregate housing is that it provides a useful frame from which such housing may be viewed. Although congregate tenants live in far more open settings than to residents of nursing homes, they are, nonetheless, members of a geographically, spatially and normatively demarked community—more so than residents of traditional housing. The provision of common services for all residents alters the social structure so that congregate housing for the old more closely resembles residential-college campuses than age-integrated neighborhoods. Put differently, while monasteries obviously differ from college campuses, and a residential congregate-complex for those sixty-five and over is distinctly different from a skilled-nursing facility, all have more common facilities, rules and regulations, social norms, and encourage closer contact with other residents than does traditional community living. Because congregate housing is a relatively self-contained system, it is important to ask if this type of facility (and this specific place) are congruent with the expectations, choice patterns, and life-style of the newcomer.

Choosing and entering congregate housing, however, is a far different process from selecting a college. The choice of Harvard University versus a community college or a technical school indeed has lasting implications; not only may the quality of instruction and the facilities vary, but both career options and informal social-networks after graduation may differ. With a college, one chooses a series of possible, albeit not binding or obligatory, options for a variety of life-courses. With congregate housing, one is choosing a life-style permitting less deviation but greater support, possibly for the rest of one's life. Briefly put, the dimensions of freedom and latitude vary.

The concept of freedom, while dear to our hearts and to the discourse of philosophers, has rarely been studied empirically. Dudley and Hillary (1977) focused on the differences in concepts of personal freedom in a variety of quasi-total and total institutions, including college dormitories, monasteries, military academies, communes, boarding schools, cooperative boarding homes, and homes for the aged. Distinguishing among three concepts of freedom—(1) ego or hedonistic, (2) disciplined or self-sacrifice and reciprocity, and (3) conditional or bound by the norms of the group—they found that residents in homes for the aged espoused either hedonistic or conditional ideas of freedom. These elderly were also the most likely group to report feelings of deprivation of freedom and of alienation. Apparently these residents were required to adjust to the social situation of the homes in which they resided; the degree of adjustment required was, however, not congruent with their own definitions of personal freedom.

Much has been written about the need for person-environment congruence. As Turner, Tobin, and Lieberman (1972) pointed out almost a decade ago, many psychological traits that are functional for community living do not necessarily promote adaptation to congregate or institutional living. In the specific facilities they studied, a "vigorous if not hostile narcissistic style" prior to admission was most conducive to intact survival one year after admission. Not only does the extent of freedom vary from home to congregate care but the person-environment congruity and personal continuity vary also.

Moving, Stress, and Continuity

Moving at any age is probably a stressful experience, even when the move is viewed as a positive change. The idea that both positive and negative life-events exact a toll on the individual has been substantially supported by a number of investigators (Rahe, McKean, and Arthur 1967; Dohrenwend and Dohrenwend 1974; Bramwell et al. 1975). Indeed, in one commonly used stress index that is highly correlated with the incidence of physical illness, changing one's residence and substantial change in living conditions have scores equivalent to such negative events as being eligible for a job promotion but being passed over or trouble with superiors (Rahe, McKean, and Arthur 1967). That a physical move itself is upsetting is commonly accepted folk-wisdom.

For the elderly, then, it is not surprising to expect that moving is a stressful experience. At any age, we are all creatures of habit who enjoy predictability and strive to reduce dissonance. The elderly, too, dislike change. In general, investigators have reported that the old are more rigid, more dogmatic, and have a lower tolerance of ambiguity than younger people (Riley and Foner 1968). This lack of flexibility and need for constancy may reflect duration in the role; that is, as older people accrete more experience in a role, they are less likely to want to relinquish its patterns. Recent longitudinal work (Maas and Kuypers 1974) has suggested that we strain for constancy and equilibrium throughout our lives. In old age, expansion and reflection of what has begun earlier in life take place.

The now-old are also more restrained, conforming, and passive than the young (Riley and Foner 1968), especially in new situations. Whether these are intrinsic characteristics of the old or merely of today's old is moot; those now sixty-five or over were socialized prior to World War I, a more predictable, less affluent era in which traditional family roles, values, and power relationships were far more clearly delineated than since World War II, Dr. Spock, Vietnam, and the Women's Movement.

The major point here is that moving to congregate care, like any other major life event, threatens the *behavioral system* of the individual. The behavioral system of any of us consists of several components: (1) the individual; (2) the close interpersonal environment or network of primary-group relationships; (3) the relatively impersonal or special-interest associations in secondary groups such as clubs, formal organizations, and other segmented roles (shopper, bridge player, weight watcher, and so on); (4) social norms and values; and (5) the physical environment (Lawton 1970). A change in any component part of this behavioral system threatens one's sense of continuity, and thus has a quintuple negative potential. As Cumming and Cumming noted:

> Both Federn and Erikson emphasize the importance of a sense of continuity for maintaining identity feeling. . . . Ego identity itself incorporates the idea of continuity and expectation of sameness, or predictable change, as part of its definition. The individual stands at a nodal point between his past and a future that he expects to be recognizable similar to the present, or, more precisely, reconcilable with his projected identity. (Cumming and Cumming 1962, p. 94)

The move to new housing—especially the move from an age-integrated to an age-segregated locale—is, thus, not only a physical but also a social and a psychological transition.

An important factor in alleviating stress is the individual's perceived or actual control over the event. Generally, the greater the perceived control one has over a situation, the less likely one is to feel stressed. A wide range of studies has indicated that old people who voluntarily relocate in the community fare well (Carp 1968; Wittels and Botwinick 1974; Storandt and Wittels 1975; Bell 1976; Shulz and Brenner 1977). They also make rational decisions when they are able to change dwelling units voluntarily in the community (Struyk 1980).

With respect to voluntary moves from traditional to more service-rich environments specifically for the old, one investigator has noted that low-to-moderate income, socially isolated elderly who applied and were admitted to a multilevel-care facility had higher morale and were happier at follow-up than they had been prior to their move; nonapplicant control-group members exhibited little change in morale or happiness, although they were initially at a higher level (Gutman 1978). Tenants in congregate housing have also been reported to improve in their general life-satisfaction and small-scale social relationships but to decline in community participation, a pattern of passive contentment not found among those in traditional community-housing (Lawton 1976).

However, among those elderly who voluntarily move from a relatively high personal-control setting to one in which they have less influence, the fact that the move was voluntary has less impact. For example, elderly who move into traditional retirement homes have reported lower levels of life-satisfaction than those who chose retirement villages, presumably because the traditional home offers fewer options for continuity and control of old behavioral systems (Wolk and Telleen 1976).

When both control over the decision to move and probable relative continuity of life-styles in the new setting are considered, the results are bleaker still. Although studies on the relationship between extent of control over the decision to enter a facility often do not adequately consider differences in the physical and mental statuses of movers and nonmovers, the results are nonetheless provocative: involuntary moving to a high-level-care setting has been associated with higher mortality rates (Ferrari 1963; Blenker 1967; Kasl 1972; Tobin and Lieberman 1976; Bourestom and Pastalan 1981). That paternalistic concern is more dangerous than the permission of individual choice and continuity of old patterns, is the implication.

It is useful to consider the process of choice of congregate housing from the perspective of the consumption disequilibrium used in studies of why younger people move (Rossi 1955). Briefly, this approach suggests that individuals generally decide to relocate because of dissatisfaction with their present housing. Depending on the extent of dissatisfaction, the degree of expected satisfaction with an alternative, and costs associated with moving, one will decide to leave or stay in present quarters. It is all very neat and, as Struyk (1980) has pointed out, those old who do move within the community (from house to house, house to apartment, and so on) indeed fit this rational model. This model is one that ensures both choice and probable continuity of the individual's behavioral system. Generally, the greater the functional independence, wealth, and level of personal autonomy, the broader the range of choices. However, many old people who have unsatisfactory housing, or who need assistance to maintain themselves outside of a nursing home, also have few options. They are, when offered the opportunity, ready to move into any housing environment, whether or not the nonshelter aspects of the housing match their own personal styles or needs (Lawton 1976). Congregate housing may not be one of several alternatives but the only alternative they see available.

The family of the old person often not able to pick and choose among environments either. York and Caslyn (1977), studying nursing-home patients (admittedly a more diverse group than congregate-housing tenants), reported that 51 percent of the families in the study did not visit the nursing home at all prior to the placement of their relative, perhaps because they were desperate to get any care at all. Placement decision were instead based on the availability of beds and location. Much less influential were such factors as quality of activities or physical care. The relevant match between the individual and the institution was not discussed; nor, in this study, had alternatives to placement really been explored or utilized.

Thus it is probably unlikely that many people, especially those with limited income, will have a wide range of options when they apply to a congregate residence. To the extent that they do not really choose the facility, they would be expected to exhibit stress. Their range of options is limited and their ability to control their futures is diminished.

At the same time, they may be aware that their physical or mental functioning is impaired and become even more distressed. Yet, as Lieberman (1974) has pointed out, much of the problem with relocation for elderly individuals lies not with its symbolic meaning but with the radical changes in the life-space and life-style required. The importance of continuity of the individual's behavioral system is critical. Changes in the total environment or behavioral system of an individual are extremely disconcerting and sometimes lethal (Bourestom and Tars, 1974), while changes in the physical relocation with minimal disjunction of other components of the person's social and personal environment are relatively easy passages (Lieberman 1974; Wells and MacDonald 1981). Those elderly whose behavioral patterns and adaptive styles fit into a new environment are most likely to fit well within that congregate care facility. A task in placement and relocation then is to try to match the individual with the environment, which is, alas, far easier to say than to do, as Kahana (1975) has pointed out.

For Whom Is Congregate Care Likely?

Residents in facilities for the aged during the 1970s and in the 1980s are older, more impaired in functional status, and sicker than those in the 1950s and 1960s (National Center for Health Statistics 1979; Riley and Foner 1968). Much of this is a reflection of increase in life expectancy.

As table 4-1 shows, within less than two decades, the number of years a white man who is sixty-five can expect to live beyond that age has increased

Table 4-1
Average Life Expectancies (Remaining Years of Life)
for Men and Women at Age 65, 1959-1961 and 1977,
for Whites and Nonwhites, United States

Race and Sex	Average Remaining Years of Life at Age 65	
	1959-1961	*1977*
Males		
White	13.0	13.9
Nonwhite	12.8	14.0
Females		
White	15.9	18.4
Nonwhite	15.1	17.8

Source: *Statistical Abstract of the United States* (Washington, D.C., U.S. Government Printing Office, 1980).

only nine-tenths of a year. Nonwhite men, whose life expectancy is generally lower, have made more gains and can expect to live 1.2 years longer than they could in 1959–1961. Women, whose life expectancy is greater than men's, have also increased their likelihood of surviving still longer. Between 1959–1961 and 1977, white women aged sixty-five added 2.5 years to their average life-expectancy and nonwhite women, who have shorter life expectancies than whites, have added 2.7 years. The net effect of increased longevity is that more and more people will probably develop chronic diseases that limit their functional capacity for independent living. These people will be prime candidates for the service-rich environments of congregate housing. Experience to date has indicated that those who move into congregate housing were significantly less active in organizations, less mobile, in poorer functional health, and older prior to the move than those who moved into traditional housing (Lawton 1976).

Not only are more chronically ill people going to be in the population, but also more old women than men will become the norm. In 1900, there were only 98 women to every 100 men 65+; by 1970, there were 139 women 65+ for every 100 men; in 2000, there will be 154! The data of longevity alone ensure that more women than men will dominate the ranks of the old-old.

Indeed, in 1977, the most recent year for which National Health Statistic data are currently available, 71.2 percent of the residents of nursing homes and personal-care homes were women; only 28.8 percent were men. Women are overrepresented in these facilities in comparison to their numbers in the general population, yet the National Health Survey data show that the reasons for which women seek care do not differ appreciably from those of men.

A very relevant factor in explaining some of the overrepresentation of women in institutional care is marital status. The most likely candidates for congregate care are people who are widowed or never married. Few married people seek congregate care; those who do are more likely to be physically impaired or dependent in some way than are the nonmarried (Wilson 1977). While congregate-care data are not available, current data from the National Health Survey indicate that only 5.6 percent of the nursing and personal-care or rest-home residents were married. Results from several sample studies (summarized in Barney 1977) indicate that not more than 10 percent of nursing-home residents were married, and these few died shortly after admission. Therefore, application to a congregate-care facility is likely to be postponed until widowhood or lessened capacity for self-care of both partners. When old men become ill, they may depend upon their wives (who are often a few years younger anyway) until the wife is no longer able to cope. Women, for whom the expectation of widowhood is much higher, have no such option. Elderly widows are thus likely to predominate in the congregate-care setting of the future.

Relevant to planning also is the fact that over one-half of the elderly widows in the United States currently live along or with nonrelatives; the older the widow, the more likely she is to live alone (Markson and Hess 1981). In New York City, for example, the highest proportion of single-person household in high-poverty areas is found among people in their 70s and 80s, many of whom are widowed. Not only are widows more likely to live alone, but they are also more likely to apply to a multi-level or congregate-housing facility, essentially because they do not have the social supports that exist among nonapplicants (Gutman 1978). Most of the elderly in urban public housing, too, are widowed women; old men who are alone apparently prefer the services, freedom and anonymity (and, perhaps, relative absence of women) provided by hotels and rooming houses (Stephens, 1977).

While elderly widows are the most likely candidates for congregate care, this is not, as current mythology would have us believe, due to uncaring children. Rather, coping mechanisms have either broken down, been exhausted, or overtaxed. Data on a frailer group, drawn from the National Health Survey in 1977, show that of the elderly in nursing homes or personal-care homes, the majority were admitted from a hospital or health facility (54.2 percent). Of the remainder, about one in every seven was living at home alone, about one in four lived with other people, and slightly over one in every ten lived with children. The congregate applicant of the future will probably be old-old, or young-old with some mild impairment, female, widowed, divorced, or separated, living alone or with unrelated individuals, and with few social supports within the community. It will be a population that needs shelter plus services in order to sustain itself as independently as possible. Ideally, congregate-housing environments will maximize people's capacities, permitting maintenance of individuality and productivity, thus alleviating the traumatic discontinuity of a new life-style.

Another group of candidates for congregate care includes elderly state-hospital or state-school residents who, prior to the recent trend toward deinstitutionalization, had "aged in"; that is, a long-term resident who entered an institution for the mentally ill or retarded when younger and who has no appropriate home to which to return. Used to the rules and regulations of institutional life as well as to its privilege system, former mental patients in relatively good physical health have been observed to improve or adapt well when placed in supportive, warm, autonomy-fostering, congregate care environments (Lieberman 1971; Marlowe 1974). Adult mental retardates who have been transferred into nursing homes, too, have generally demonstrated improved physical health and appear to be happier in the new setting. Those former mental patients who fail in community settings are most likely to be people with poorer physical health who are unable to meet minimal social-role expectations for appropriate behavior (Cumming and Markson 1975). Such variables as sex, chronicity, age, and psychiatric diagnosis of the patient are less important predictors of community adaptation than is environmental control. The former mental patient who is relatively intact apparently flourishes in settings permitting personal independence and control (Lieberman, 1971), and, in this sense, is not different from people who have no history of institutionalization. The best environment thus appears to be one permitting both continuity of old patterns of life and control over one's use of time, space, personal privacy, and skills.

Preparation for Placement

Both common sense and the results of empirical investigation indicate that preparation for placement in congregate housing increases the old person's sense of control and continuity and thus alleviates the stress of moving. At the time a decision is made to enter congregate housing, the prospective entrant must cope with a variety of impending problems, including not only the symbolic meaning of the move, but also such practical issues as disposal of property, changes in number and types of possessions, and the entry procedures of the new environment. The person who moves voluntarily, as noted earlier, is likely to have higher morale and to adapt better to a new residence than one forced into relocation. In either situation, the feelings of those elderly who move appear to be critical determinants of subsequent adjustment; those who are angry or philosophical about a move are more likely to adapt well than those who deny that change is taking place or who respond with depression or regression (Aldrich 1964; Miller and Lieberman 1965; Lawton and Yaffee 1974; Markus et al. 1971).

Prior to the actual move, involvement of the potential resident in the planning and decision-making process is crucial (Farrar, Ryder and Blenkner 1964; Yawney and Slover 1973; Liebowitz 1974; Locker and Rublin 1974; Brody, Kleban, and Moss 1974; Bourestom and Tars 1974; Bourestom and Pastalan 1973). Involvement is multifaceted; not only must the person-environment congruency dimension be explored by both facility personnel and the old person, but familiarity with the facility must be developed so that the environment is no longer unknown or unpredictable when the actual move occurs. Such techniques as portfolios presenting a view of the life-style of residents at the specific congregate-housing site, multiple visits, choice of apartment or rooms, meetings with various members of the staff and residents, and familiarity with the dining room and other on-site services have been found to ease transition. Opportunities to visit the prospective site several times seems to be more advantageous than a single tour of the facility followed by slides and information. Put simply, the greater the opportunity for exploration of the new environment prior to actually moving in, the greater is the likelihood that the older person will be prepared for the move and know what to expect. Anxiety about the unknown will be substantially reduced.

When possible, provision of a network of supportive services prior to relocation will ease transition as well; for example, the Philadelphia Geriatric Center provides continuing social-work services to assure appropriateness of placement, mobilizes community resources, and makes any appropriate medical or social-welfare referrals. Group counselling sessions have been used to ease placement and relocation (for example, see Hutchinson 1976), and family members have been involved in a variety of programs aimed at reducing their own anxieties or ambivalence about the relocation (Reuben and Byrnes 1977).

That relocation takes place without prior preparation has sometimes been the case, most often because there was inadequate lead time or personnel to implement a program for preparation (see, for example, Marlowe 1974; Borup, Gallego, and Heffernan 1978). Cost, too, is a factor; intensive and extensive preparations cost both time and money. To date, however, the limited evidence suggests that this expenditure is worthwhile.

What, then, is a good preparation program? Many have been developed, but, as in most human-service programs, there is no exact prescription to be slavishly administered. Basic to development of a good preparation program for residents is that the staff at all levels understand its own facility and have a clear idea of its goals and the types of residents it is currently serving. This is, incidentally, more difficult that it sounds, for putting the norms and values and goals that we take for granted out in the open is complex. As part of this self-examination process, staff need to delineate what they expect from people; what is a good resident? Congregate-housing staff who work with prospective applicants, then, are in a better position to help the newcomer decide if a particular facility is the best option available. Since moving is stressful whether or not the move is desired, staff must also assist applicants to work out their feelings about the move. Most important, preparation programs should be designed to permit the client to have as much control over the decision to move as possible, and to ensure as much continuity as possible between the behavioral system of the person throughout the transition.

Some Effects of Relocation

The dire effects of relocation have been widely reviewed in the literature and I shall not reiterate them in detail. Most frequently discussed has been what Lieberman (1974) has called one of our "near idiocies—overpreoccupation with the death rate," perhaps because we can quantify and measure the destructiveness of an environment better than the positive aspects. In general, there is considerable research on relocation and mortality among the elderly that suggests they may be at particularly high risk of dying upon relocation, although this is not always clear cut (Aldrich and Mendkoff 1963; Blenkner 1967; Killian 1970; Lawton and Nahemow 1973; Markus, Blenkner, Bloom, and Downs 1970, 1971, 1972; Markson and Cumming, 1974; Schulz and Brenner 1977). Whether the move is voluntary or involuntary, the attitudes of those moved to the relocation, the physical health and illness of those moved and their mental status, both psychological and organic, are variables that also have a demonstrated influence on mortality upon relocation (see, for example, Aldrich and Mendkoff 1963; Adlrich 1964; Bourestom and Pastalan 1981; Killian 1970; Lawton and Yaffee 1974); Goldfarb et al. 1972; Jasnau 1967; Ogren and Linn 1971). There are, the literature would suggest, certain types of people who are at excessive risk when relocated, no matter how good the preparation: those who are in poor physical health and are suffering from a severe, organic brain-syndrome. In short, they are already at a high risk and have little potential of controlling their environments or fates. Depending on their current life-situations, the risks of the move may outweigh the benefits.

Another high-risk group, about whom we are beginning to hear more and more but about whom there are few data, are people whose life-styles and personalities are not congruent with a congregate setting. In a recent pilot study of frail elderly in the community, I found several elderly women in this category. One women, aged eighty-six, who is severely disfigured and a social isolate, who receives "meals on wheels" and informal supportive services from neighbors, described herself as follows:

> No, I don't ever want to move. I've lived in this neighborhood almost all of my life. At home here I feel safe. I can do what I want when I want. There's nobody to bother me or tell me what to do. . . . Sometimes I get up at night and wander about because I hear noises and think somebody's getting in after my things. But I can't imagine moving [laughs].

Another eighty-four year-old woman, living in the same neighborhood, the victim of several minor strokes and severely crippled by arthritis, also lives alone. She stated:

> The one real fear is that I won't die before I am totally helpless. I am not afraid of death. But I am afraid of moving anyplace else and of having to be dependent on strangers. I can't afford it. But even If I could, I have watched too many of my friends who have gone to homes for the aged, nursing homes or the Mount Vernon Arms [a congregate-housing facility nearby which provides meals and housekeeping service]. No matter how nice these places look, they're not your own home. They're not *yours*.

This woman maintains her cooking skills, of which she is very proud. Unable to shop, she receives food deliveries from friends; cleaning and foot care are provided by a domestic. She is aware that her memory is failing and keeps a log, beginning upon arising each morning, of telephone calls, their content, and other daily events. In short, she is coping with her impairments in an idiosyncratic but personally congruent manner.

For old people as determined as these, who have been able to arrange alternative services that enable them to maintain themselves, minimally but placidly, in their own homes, relocation would perhaps be a risk not worth the benefits.

Rowles (1978) has suggested that there are four ways within which one interacts with one's geographic environment: action or physical movement, cognitive orientation or "mental maps," meanings that places in the environment have for us, and fantasy. These four dimensions of the geographic experience of older people are especially relevant to consider when placement and relocation are discussed. The types of interaction with a familiar environment, as well as the types of interaction most treasured by the old person, must be reckoned with if placement (or nonplacement and supportive services) are to be success-fully administered. These dimensions are also crucial to keep in mind in an era of diminishing financial resources available to the elderly and to their caretakers.

References and Additional Resources

Aldrich, C.K. 1964. "Personality Factors and Mortality in the Relocation of the Aged," *The Gerontologist* 5:92–96.

Aldrich, C.K., and Mendkoff, E. 1963. "Relocation of the Aged and Disabled: A Mortality Study," *Journal of the American Geriatrics Society* 11:194–195.

Barney, J.L. 1977. "The Prerogative of Choice in Long Term Care," *The Gerontologist* 17:309–314.

Bell, B.D. 1976. "The Impact of Housing Relocation on the Elderly; An Alter-native Methodological Approach," *International Journal of Aging and Human Development* 7:27–38.

Blenkner, M. 1967. "Environmental Change and the Aging Individual," *The Gerontologist* 7:101–105.

Borup, J.H.; Gallego, D.T.; and Heffernan, P.G. 1978. *Geriatric Relocation.* Ogden, Utah: Weber State College Press.

Bourestom, N., and Pastalan, L. 1973. *Relocation Report 3: Preparation for Re-location.* Ann Arbor, Michigan: Institute of Gerontology, the University of Michigan and Wayne State University.

Bourestom, N., and Pastalan, L. 1981. "The Effects of Relocation on the Elder-ly: A reply to Borup, J.H., Gallego, D.T. and Heffernan, P.G." *The Gerontologist* 21:4–7.

Bourestom, N., and Tars, S. 1974. "Alterations in Life Patterns Following Re-tirement," *The Gerontologist* 14:505–510.

Bramwell, S.T.; Masuda, M.; Wagner, N.N.; and Holmes, T.H. 1975. "Psycho-social Factors in Athletic Injuries," *Journal of Human Stress* 1:6–20.

Brody, E.; Kleban, M.H.; and Moss, M. 1974. "Impact of Intrainstitutional Re-location: Measuring the Impact of Change" *The Gerontologist,* p. 14.

Carp, F.M. 1968. "Effects of Improved Housing on the Lives of Older People." In *Middle Age and Aging,* ed. B.L. Neugarten. Chicago: University of Chicago Press.

Carp, F.M. 1977. "How Great is the Need for Shelter and Services among Older People?" In *Congregate Housing for Older People: An Urgent Need, A Growing Demand,* ed. W.T. Donahue, M.M. Thompson and D.D. Curver. Washington, D.C.: USDHEW, Pub. no. OHD 77-20284.

Cumming, J., and Cumming, E. 1962. *Ego and Milieu*. New York: Atherton.

Cumming, J., and Markson, E. 1975. "The Impact of Mass Transfer on Patient Release," *Archives of General Psychiatry* 32:804-809.

Dohrenwend, B.S., and Dohrenwend, B. 1974. *Stressful Life Events*. New York: John Wiley & Sons, Inc.

Dudley, C.J., and Hillery, G.A. 1977. "Freedom and Alienation in Homes for the Elderly" *The Gerontologist* 17:140-145.

Farrar, M.; Ryder, M.B.; and Blenkner, M. 1964. "Social Work Responsibility in Nursing Home Care" *Social Casework* 45:527-533.

Ferrari, N. 1963. "Freedom of Choice," *Social Work* 8:105-106.

Goffman, E. 1961. *Asylums*. New York: Anchor Books.

Goldfarb, A.I.; Shahinian, S.P.; and Burr, H.T. 1972. "Death Rate of Relocated Pursuing Home Residents." In *Research Planning and Action for the Elderly,* ed. D.P. Kent, R. Kastenbaum and S. Sherwood. New York: Behavioral Publications.

Gutman, G.M. 1978. "Issues and Findings Relating to Multi-Level Accommodation for Seniors," *Journal of Gerontology,* 33:592-600.

Hutchinson, J. 1976. "Preserving the Dignity of Life," *Challenge* 19:4-5.

Jasnau, K.F. 1967. "Individualized versus Mass Transfer of Nonpsychotic Geriatric Patients to Nursing Homes, with Special Reference to Death Rate," *Journal of the American Geriatrics Society* 15:280-284.

Kahana, E. 1975. "A Congruence Model of Person-Environment Interaction." In *Theory Development in Environment and Aging,* ed. P.G. Windley, T.O. Byerts, and F.G. Ernst. Washington, D.C.: The Gerontological Society.

Kasl, S. 1972. "Physical and Mental Health Effects of Involuntary Relocation and Institutionalization in the Elderly—A Review," *American Journal of Public Health* 62:377-383.

Killian, E. 1970. "Effects of Geriatric Transfers on Mortality Rates," *Social Work* 15:19-26.

Lawton, M.P. 1970. "Ecology and Aging." In *The Spatial Behavior of Older People,* ed. L.A. Pastalan and D.H. Carson. Ann Arbor: University of Michigan Institute of Gerontology.

Lawton, M.P. 1976. "The Relative Impact of Congregate and Traditional Housing on Elderly Tenants," *The Gerontologist* 16:237-242.

Lawton, M.P., and Nahemow, L. 1973. "Ecology and the Aging Process." In *The Psychology of Adult Development and Aging,* ed. C. Eisdorfer and M.P. Lawton. Washington, D.C.: American Psychological Association.

Lawton, M.P., and Yaffe, S. 1974. "Mortality, Morbidity and Voluntary Change of Residences by Older Poeple," *Journal of the American Geriatrics Society* 18:823-831.

Lieberman, M., et al. 1971. *The Effects of Relocation on Long-term Geriatric Patients*. Chicago: Illinois Department of Health and Committee on Human Development, University of Chicago.

Lieberman, M.A. 1974. "Relocation Research and Social Policy," *The Geron-tologist* 14:494–501.

Liebowitz, B. 1974. "Impact of Intra-Institutional Relocation: Background and the Planning Process," *The Gerontologist*, p. 14.

Locker, R., and Rublin, A. 1974. "Impact of Intra-Institutional Relocation: Clinical Aspects of Facilitating Relocation," *The Gerontologist*, p. 14.

Maas, H., and Kuypers, J. 1974. *From Thirty to Seventy*. San Francisco, Jossey-Bass.

Markson, E.W., and Cumming, J.H. 1974. "A Strategy of Necessary Mass Trans-fer and Its Impact on Patient Mortality," *Journal of Gerontology* 29: 315–321.

Markson, E.W., and Hess, B.B. 1981. "Old Women in the City." In *Women in the American City*, ed. C. Simpson et al. Chicago: University of Chicago Press.

Markus, E., 1970. *Post relocation Mortality among Institutionalized Aged*. Cleve-land: Benjamin Rose Institute.

Markus, E., et al. 1971. "The Impact of Relocation upon Mortality Rates of Institutionalized Aged Persons," *Journal of Gerontology* 26:537–541.

Markus, E., et al. 1972. "Some Factors and Their Association with Post-Relo-cation Mortality among Institutionalized Elderly," *Journal of Gerontology* 27:376–382.

Marlowe, R.A. 1974. "When They Closed the Doors at Modesto," paper pre-sented at the National Institute of Mental Health Conference, Where Is My Home?, Scottsdale, Arizona.

Miller, D., and Lieberman, M. 1965. "The Relationship of Affect State and Adaptive Capacity to Reactions to Stress," *Journal of Gerontology* 20: 492–497.

Ogren, E.H., and Linn, M.W. 1971. "Male Nursing Home Patients; Relocation and Mortality," *Journal of the American Geriatrics Society*, p. 19.

Rahe, R.R.; McKean, J.D.; and Arthur, R.J. 1967. "A Longitudinal Study of Life-Change and Illness Patterns," *Journal of Psychosomatic Research* 10: 355–366.

Reuben, S., and Byrnes, G.K. 1977. "Helping Elderly Patients in the Transition to a Nursing Home," *Geriatrics* 32:107–112.

Riley, M.W., and Foner, A. 1968. *Aging and Society, Vol. 1*. New York: Russell Sage foundation.

Rossi, P.H. 1955. *Why Families Move: A Study in the Social Psychology of Urban Residential Mobility*. Glencoe, Ill.: Free Press.

Rowles, G.D. 1978. *Prisoners of Space? Exploring the Geographic Experience of Older People*. Boulder, Colo.: Westview Press.

Schulz, R. and Brenner, G. 1977. "Relocation of the Aged: A Review and The-oretical Analysis," *Journal of Gerontology* 32:323–333.

Stephens, J. 1977. *Loners, Losers and Lovers: A Sociological Study of the Aged Tenants of a Slum Hotel*. Seattle, University of Washington Press.

Storandt, M., and Wittels, I. 1975. "Maintenance of Function in Relocation of Community Dwelling Older Adults," *Journal of Gerontology* 30:608-612.

Struyk, R.J. 1980. "Housing Adjustments of Relocated Elderly Households," *The Gerontologist* 20:45-55.

Tobin, S., and Lieberman, M.A. 1976. *Last Home for the Aged.* San Francisco: Jossey-Bass, Inc.

Turner, B.F.; Tobin, S.S.; and Lieberman, M.A. 1972. "Personality Traits as Predictors of Institutional Adaptation among the Aged," *Journal of Gerontology* 27:61-68.

Wells, L., and MacDonald, G. 1981. "Interpersonal Networks and Postrelocation Adjustment of the Institutionalized Elderly," *The Gerontologist* 21:177-183.

Wilson, R.W. 1977. "The Population to be Served." In *Congregate Housing for Older People: An Urgent Need, A Growing Demand,* ed. W.T. Donahue, M.M. Thompson and D.D. Curran. Washington, D.C.: USDHEW.

Wittels, I., and Botwinick, J. 1974. "Survival in Relocation," *Journal of Gerontology* 29:440-443.

Wolk, S., and Telleen, S. 1976. "Psychological and Social Correlates of life satisfaction as a function of residential constraint," *Journal of Gerontology* 31:89-98.

Yawney, B., and Slover, D.L. 1973. "Relocation of the Elderly," *Social Work,* 18:86-95.

York, J.L., and Calsyn, R.J. 1977. "Family Involvement in Nursing Homes," *The Gerontologist* 17:500-505.

Part II
Planning and
Development

There are no accurate generalizations about older people that hold true from individual to individual or from community to community. Untested notions of need and preference are a great handicap for planners of congregate or sheltered-housing. In each instance, planning should include a market analysis coupled with an inventory of resources currently available. One generalization that can be made about developing housing is that there should be considerable experience represented on the development team. No development is ideal, there will be trade-offs. Skillful developers define the trade-offs in the planning process. For example, in new construction versus rehabilitation, the flexibility in spatial relationships in the new might be traded for the more ample spaces in the old.

5

Programming for Alternatives and Future Models

Louis E. Gelwicks and
Maria B. Dwight

Forty years ago in an article, "Planning for Older Years," Ollie Randall pointed out the obvious. She said that the aged are individuals with varied needs and desires. "This means that there is no single plan or living arrangement suitable for a person just because she or he is old." She emphasized that the variables to be considered were personal choice, psychological, economic, social, and health requirements.

Over the intervening decades, a large body of gerontological literature has supported Ms. Randall's statements. Many of the researchers contributing to this book have already contributed greatly through their work, and we are pleased to be among them. As advocates of participatory planning and consumer-based programming, the firm of Gerontological Planning Associates has had the opportunity to survey and interview over 40,000 older adults in a wide variety of settings throughout the United States. We find that the pervasive public stereotyping of the elderly as physically and mentally dysfunctional, is false and damaging, in the planning and policy areas and to the elderly themselves.

Most of us are aware of the major demographic changes that will greatly affect the future of this country. As the elderly cohort increases, all phases of our society will be influenced. Demographics, however, should be more than body counts. We must examine who the elderly are, what their characteristics are, and how they are changing. We know that there are more elderly, but it is vital to understand their demands if we are to respond appropriately. If the congregate housing we plan today is to survive the life of its mortgage, it will have to meet the needs of persons who are thirty-years old today.

Many of the models for housing and services in place today are inappropriate and outdated. They do not meet the demands of the older market. An example of ill advised and unmarketable planning is the overbuilding of efficiency apartments; yet, well-meaning sponsors are still planning them, and unknowing mortgage lenders are still financing them.

There is a vital need to disseminate the data of the researcher and the market analyst to the sponsor and practitioner in the field. As the older market is discovered by the business world, competition will increase. Alternatives are being created, and the uninformed will fail. Bankruptcies of congregate-housing projects in both the proprietary and nonprofit field have increased alarmingly in the past five years.

What Is the Future?

In many ways, the future is here. Today we are confronted with a new generation of elderly that is better educated, more affluent, more mobile and more
selective than those preceding it. The stereotypical elderly lady, rocking and
knitting, is a myth. We are increasingly finding two generations of elderly in a
family. As we look at the statistics of the elderly population (sixty-five years
and older), we see that from 1953 to 1978 that population grew twice as fast as
the population as a whole. If mortality rates continue to decline as they have in
the past, the aged population will continue to increase more rapidly in the future.
Some estimates indicate that by the year 2003, the total population will increase
by 28 percent, and the over sixty-five generations will increase by 59 percent.
The most rapidly growing segment of the elderly group is the oldest, those over
eighty-five years of age. In the psst twenty-five years, this age cohort has tripled,
and it is projected that it will triple again in the next twenty-five years.

The age diagrams for 1960, 1970, and 2000 reveal the dramatic shift away
from an age pyramid.

As demographers project the future, their estimates are based upon the statistical past. This can be a risky business. The dramatic increase in life expectancy in the twentieth century (49.2 years in 1900 to a projected 76 years in
1990) is the result of a variety of factors including immigration and improved
health-status throughout the life cycle. Prognosticators hasten to point out that
great strides have been made in preventive medicine in the past, but little has
been accomplished in the area of curative medicine. We no longer have tuberculosis, smallpox, polio, measles, typhoid, and so on, but we do not yet have
cures for the leading causes of death among the elderly: diseases of the heart,
malignant neoplasms and cerebrovascular disease. Replacement parts for our
bodies are becoming more readily available, and many of us can expect to de-
part this life with one or two pieces other than those with which we enter. The
impact of this technology on life expectancy and the sought-for cure for cancer
would dramatically alter the projections of life expectancy in the near future.

The sex ratio among those sixty-five and older has also changed radically
within the past few decades. In 1960, the ratio was eighty-three men per hundred women. In 1975, the ratio was sixty-nine males to hundred women. Death
rates are higher for males, and the predominantly male, immigrant population
from before World War I has died. As a result, the difference in life expectancy
between the sexes at birth was only 2.0 years in 1900, but was 7.8 years in 1975.

Older men are much more likely to be married than older women. Approximately 77 percent live with a spouse, 40 percent of whom are younger than
sixty-five. Conversely, 53 percent of older women are widows. Over two-thirds
of women over age sixty-five (in 1975) and 40 percent of women over seventy-
five years lived alone, compared to 14 percent of the over sixty-five year males
and 18 percent of the men seventy-five years and over.

The statistical literature is voluminous and these highlights should send the
sponsor, programmer, and architect and marketer scurrying to the sources, for

the data have a myriad of variables that will affect production of goods and services in the future.

One of the primary reasons that the business world and Madison Avenue have suddenly discovered the elderly market, besides its magnitude, is its affluence. The older market is described in the advertising world as "potentially lucrative but relatively untapped." No matter whose statistics you accept, the poverty level among the elderly has declined over the past decade. The Department of Commerce (1975) estimates that 9 percent of the elderly live at or below the poverty level. Other agencies offer other percentages, up to as high as 16 percent. It should be noted that the total household income of the retired population was $142 billion in 1977.

Furthermore, the economic circumstances of the over sixty-five population are generally more favorable than the raw statistics indicate. In 1977, the per capita income of elderly households was greater than that of the under twenty-five and thirty-five-to-forty-four-year-old age groups, and equal to that of the twenty-five-to-thirty-four-year olds. This does not include hidden assets such as home ownership, investment, and savings. It is estimated that as many as eighty percent of the elderly own their homes and eithty percent of those are mortgage free. The over fifty-five-year olds represent eithty percent of all money in savings and loán institutions.

The disposable income of the elderly is greater than that of most segments of the population. The children are educated and the house is paid off. With a lifetime of experience in shopping around, the elderly represent a strong, but very selective, potential, market for housing, services, and a wide variety of goods.

We are experiencing a variety of social and economic events that are going to have a significant impact on future generations of elderly and/or their preferences, demands, and needs.

Women have been entering the work force in unprecedented numbers. It is estimated that in June 1979, 63 percent of the women between eighteen and sixty-four were employed. This means an increase in future retirement benefits and pensions. It also suggests that women with work histories will be far better educated and prepared as widows than their mothers were. A life experience of financial management, self-reliance and independent decision making will make the female market even more demanding than it is today. Values are changing and will continue to do so rapidly. For example, in 1967 a survey by Leo Burnett Company showed that 60 percent of the people agreed that a woman's place is in the home. In 1975, only 28 percent agreed to that statement.

Divorce rates are also on the rise. It is estimated that the 12 percent divorce rate among elderly persons in 1975 will increase to 22 percent by 2000.

Undoubtedly, one the greatest and relatively unheralded events that will have an impact on the elderly population is the tidal wave of military veterans who are approaching sixty-five years. Presently, there are only 2.7 million elderly veterans. By 1995, there will be over 8 million. In fact, by that year, 60 percent of all American men over sixty-five will be veterans. These older veterans and their families have been the recipients of major benefits throughout their lifetimes: home loans, educational grants, health insurance, employment preference, pensions, compensation pay, and so forth. These benefits, and the life experiences that they provided, greatly changed the socioeconomic status and the expectations of this cohort and its children. More educated, mobile and affluent than preceding generations, this new generation of elderly will put great pressure on society and the market place. It is doubtful that they will allow their benefits to be decreased, and their standards for facilities and services are high.

It should be further noted that there are 5.8 million Korean-conflict veterans (average age forth-nine) and some 11 million younger veterans of post-Korea and Vietnam who, if our forty-year mortgages are successful, are the potential residents of the congregate-housing and services we plan today. In the face of this, the debate over whether to allow a cocktail before dinner in the multi-purpose room will fade to insignificance. Our policies, fortunately, can remain flexible, but too many of our buildings are static, and our sites are immovable.

What do these statistics indicate to us about the programming and design of congregate housing now and in the future? How do the statistics interrelate with federal, state, and local policies, which also have bearing on our planning?

The statistics show us that the market will continue to grow, and, combined with current fiscal policies, the housing shortage which now exists will be exacerbated in the future. There will be a continuing increase in the old-old and in single-person households. The number of hosehold units will probably continue, throughout the population, to grow twice as rapidly as the population as a whole. The need for supportive services, both social and health related, should increase as the size of the older spectrum of the retired population increases.

When preparing a program of spaces and services, it becomes imperative that the sponsor take maximum advantage of national and state entitlements. This is good fiscal management that benefits both the corporation and the resident. Furthermore, national policies that affect reimbursement patterns for such services indicate that home-delivered services shall gain prominence as a more viable alternative to institutionalized services. The recent amendments to the Older Americans Act, the liberalization of Medicare regulations, and the bills before Congress all support this supposition.

The proportion of elderly people with activity limitations differs from a number of variables, of which age is the most important. Studies from 1977 show that only 42 percent of people aged sixty-five-to-seventy-four were limited as opposed to 56 percent of those seventy-five years and over. Women are less likely to be limited than men (40 percent to 50 percent) and, as income and education increase, limitation decreases. Those living alone or with a spouse are less likely to be limited in their activity than those who live with others, and elderly in the Northeast and in urban areas are less limited than those in less urban and southern regions.

Two debilitating chronic conditions cause 50 percent of activity limitation: heart disease (24 percent) and arthritis (23 percent). Orthopedic impairment

(10 percent), visual impairment (10 percent), and hypertension (9 percent) are other incapacitators.

Despite initial charges that Medicare is overutilized by many who do not need the services, statistics clearly reveal that medical services are utilized to a greater extent by people in poor health. When a sponsor or developer includes a program that is highly health-service oriented, he should expect to attract primarily those who are chronically ill, disabled, or in poor health.

Market Feasibility: Is there a Future for the Project?

Secondary data will give the planner an early advantage in establishing the market. How large is it? Where is it? What are its apparent needs? What are the trends in the specific location or region? What segment of the market is most appropriate for the project? What are the characteristics of that segment? What is the competition?

The use of secondary data (that is, statistics from the Bureaus of Agriculture, Labor, and Commerce—U.S. Census, Social Security offices, health-systems agencies, local planning departments and service agencies, studies and reports from area universities and colleges) is vital in establishing the groundwork for market feasibility. However, there are shortcomings inherent in secondary data; it can become quickly outdated. A primary concern is that, although these data may indicate need, they do not necessarily indicate demand. A market area could have 10,000 elderly capable of paying the rent in a congregate-housing project. Statistically speaking, on a national basis, somewhere between 8 percent and 18 percent of the older population are estimated to need congregate housing. The potential number of units to build might therefore be interpreted to be 1,800 (excluding consideration of existing units and the competition). Our marketing research reveals in some areas that less than 3 percent of those 10,000 elderly should be considered potential inmovers and only 1 percent will be convinced by a sound marketing program to relocate. Many local options, priorities and trade offs will govern the decision to spend and particularly to move. A range from 1 percent to 18 percent is too great to be assumed from secondary data.

There is no viable alternative to asking consumers (present and future) what they want and are willing to pay for. Generating primary data, which involves time, energy, and money, is the best indicator of feasibility and assurance of success. Need and demand are not synonymous. The older person wants to maintain the option of spending his dollars as he prefers and not as developers, sponsors or agencies see fit.

We have experienced many graphic examples of how the perceptions of the decision makers vary from the demands of their clientele. These differences occur over small details affecting the daily lives of the residents as well as over large policy issues regarding the inclusion of a health care facility on the site. For example, a comparison of the responses of the Board to those of the residents.

Top choices of the Board—those additions to the home that would appeal most to residents.

	Percentage of Board	*Percentage of Residents*
	Listing as Top	*Listing as Top*
Greenhouse	78	19
Card Room	47	23
Physical therapy	47	29

Top choices of the Residents

	Percentage of Residents	*Percentage of Board*
	Listing as Top	*Listing as Top*
Convenience grocery store	57	42
Gift shop	45	31
Whirlpool	39	42

In another project, 362 clergy were surveyed regarding their opinions of the needs and desires of their parishoners. In response to the question: "Would you prefer to have a skilled nursing unit on the site or would you prefer to have a skilled-nursing facility on a nearby site but affiliated with the retirement community?"

Sixty-three percent of the clergy, but only 37 percent of the inmovers preferred the skilled-nursing facility on site.

Many congregate housing contracts include three meals a day in the monthly fee. Our surveys across the country indicate that virtually no one (5 percent) wants to eat breakfast in a communal setting, and elderly single women, who are usually the primary market segment, want it least of all. The more affluent the resident, the less likely she is to want linen services included in the rent. The kitchen is an extremely important room to both males and females. Privacy in the dwelling unit is more important than availability of public spaces. Emergency care is far more attractive than inpatient care. Efficiency apartments have extremely limited appeal (7 percent) regardless of income, sex, or age. We could go on and on, lising findings that contradict much of what is being planned, programmed, and built today.

Our findings also support the statement that older people are becoming increasingly selective in choosing living environments. They are shopping around and doing their own research before deciding on relocation. They are considering the capital-gains tax advantages of buying rather than life-leasing or renting. They want far more than statements that the sponsor is doing well.

Frequently recurring written comments from residents to open ended questions include such poignant remarks as:

"When I applied here, they asked me all about my finances but told me nothing of their deficits."

"It may be that one of the main planning objectives should be to find a good balance between putting money into buildings and putting it into programs and services that would enable people to remain longer in their homes."

Living in a democracy I get many reports—financial, etc. In the YMCA Retirement Fund I get annual financial and other reports. As a member of this home, I have gotten nothing from the board."

"Physical change is built into our universe. If we do not change, then this 'universal process' will change us!"

A major national trend we have observed in our data is that religious or fraternal-order ties grow weaker when the elderly consider congregate housing. In a community survey developed in October 1979 for a congregate project, religious affiliation was rated seventh out of seven variables as a factor in selecting a retirement community. It was rated seventh out of eleven variables by residents of an extremely successful church-related home.

Consumer research must have a strong influence on the many components of congregate housing. This includes building plans, service programs and, certainly on site selection. A neighborhood considered satisfactory by a sponsor or developer is often perceived as undesirable by the elderly population. The financial success of a project depends on its ability to meet the demands of the market. Consumer-based planning translates those requirements into a physical product (the building) and into services. The process must begin and end with the consumer if the sponsor is to minimize risk and maximize success in a cost-effective manner.

Geographic Location: Where Is the Future?

Older people represent a significant social and financial resource in most communities. When employed (and many remain so), they are a reservoir of experience. As volunteers they fill vital gaps. Their taxes support local and state services and a couple over the age of sixty-five has more disposable income to purchase goods and services from the community than the under thirty-five-year-old couple. Unfortunately, many states in the Northeast and Midwest are losing their elderly to areas with more favorable tax advantages, temperate climates, and more appropriate housing. If a community is to halt its "brain drain", it must look to creating environments for living that will meet both the needs and demands of its elders.

Based on the long-range projections of Chase Econometrics, the ten most attractive states to retire to in the next ten years are, in ranked order, Utah, Louisiana, South Carolina, Nevada, Texas, New Mexico, Alabama, Arizona, Florida, and Georgia. These rankings are based on cost of living, taxation, and available housing and services. The least desirable is Massachusetts, because it has the highest cost of living for retired persons, high taxes, high utility bills, and a scarcity of housing. All of New England, New York and New Jersey fall among the bottom ten rankings for similar reasons.

If sponsors/developers in the Northeast are to offset the negative features as described in this economic analysis, they must design innovative and cost-effective programs for payments, service and facilities to attract the market.

The Market: Who Will Be Served?

Congregate housing has been described by some as a panacea for the older generation's housing needs. It is one solution. It is important to identify the segment of the older market that is attracted to such a milieu, as well as the segment that can best be served. There is an inherent danger in building for such a broad spectrum that no portion is attracted. It can be compared to designing and producing an average shoe that fits no one. Market segmentation is as valid for the elderly population as it is for any other market.

There are many methods of segmenting the elderly market. One popular description is the young-old, the old, and the old-old. Another is "empty nester", preretired, active retired, and disengaged. There are multiple variables to consider when segmenting the market to match appropriately with a congregate-housing model. Socio-economic status, income ranges , trends in affluence, health status, sex and life experience are only a few. The sponsor/developer must decide which market segment is the target, and plan accordingly. Each segment should be considered prior to programming for alternatives and future models.

Homes for the aging, which have historically been congregate-living facilities, attract a very small percentage of the total elderly market. The residents are traditionally older (eighty-two years), predominantly female (80 percent) and are usually in need of extensive support systems. This may be the result of the existing programs and accommodations attracting this segment of the market. New programs and facilities will attract other segments.

The Competition: Who Will Do the Serving?

The HUD 202 Section 8 program and FmHA 515 program, in conjunction with HEW, have recently funded several demonstration projects in congregate housing. These projects are targeted to the lower-and-middle-income elderly. Despite this interest and effort, the federal government can be expected to fulfill the congregate-housing needs of only a minute portion of the population.

The private sector, which many years ago developed the Leisure World model, has recently discovered the congregate-housing market of middle-and-upper-income elderly. Proprietary developers are aggressively moving into the field. Condominiums, cooperative ownerships, life leases, and monthly rentals are offered as payment options and services range from cocktail-room service to nursing care. The resident can pick and choose from a variety of services, and pay for them as they are rendered. There is no paternalistic attitude, as is sometimes found in church-related homes. There are no long lists of restrictive rules and regulations. There is an emphasis on creative leisure rather than on health care. As the younger, more active elderly seek out a recreational oriented facility, the health-oriented housing will attract the oldest and most frail segment of the market. This is the most expensive population to service and manage.

The plethora of new sponsors and developers making the competition more intense includes a major billion-dollar food-service corporation. This corporation delivers millions of dollars of meals each year to seniors at home, owns over 20,000 nursing-home beds, and is actively completing its continuum with congregate housing.

Competition is also increasing within the health-related segment of the market. Hospitals are actively developing housing and services for the elderly, thereby strengthening their market for their underutilized acute-care beds and amortizing existing ancillary services (as food and housekeeping) over a broader population-base. They can provide services at lower costs than can a self-contained unit.

The continuum of care, from independent living to preinpatient care can be provided within the program of congregate housing. With contractual options allowed, there can be a range of services within individual buildings, but the successful project must be cost competitive, service responsive, and demand oriented.

Sponsors and developers of congregate housing projects have many motivations. Some may undertake the projects to serve a human need; others are interested in financial investment and return. No one can afford to fail, regardless of the motive. To succeed, the sponsor must take advantage of reimbursement mechanisms, private and public programs, and innovative services. As the competition increases, success will rest on the ability to attract and continue to attract the specific market. Appropriate programming is the key to long range viability in a competitive market.

What Do the Elderly Want?

The elderly want to be heard, just as everybody else. Our market surveys have had phenomenally high response rates throughout the country.

Elders are demanding information about the fiscal health of the sponsor/developer. Recent bankruptcies among nonprofit sponsors have made them wary. They want alternative options for payment mechanisms and service provisions. They want independence and self-determination.

The target population may statistically need to relocate to congregate housing, but to create the demand for it is something else. Most older people prefer to remain in their own homes as long as it is financially and physically feasible. The move from the private environment of one's own home to a more communal life-style can be a traumatic experience. Congregate housing must match the client demands if it is to induce him to relocate.

What does this older market want? Here are a few of our results, collapsed from a number of surveys from across the country. The average age of the respondent was 69.5 years, the mean income $14,000 in 1978 dollars.

When asked what facilities were important in a retirement community, the response was (1) a small convenience grocery-store, (2) a library/reading room, (3) a beauty/barber shop, (4) a pharmacy, and (5) a room for special programs. Of the respondents sixty years and older, couples, males and younger elderly showed a stronger preference for recreational facilities such as swimming pool, whirlpool, exercise room, card room, Craft room, and area for private entertaining.

When asked about utilization of central dining-facilities, 53 percent indicated that they would take one meal and 25 percent that they would take two. Seven percent wanted three meals, and 15 percent were not interested in the idea of control meals. Increased age correlated with the increased number of meals desired. However, the sample felt strongly that kitchen facilities should be available within the dwelling unit: must have—88 percent, not necessary but nice—10 percent, would not want—2 percent.

An emergency call system within the unit was also considered important with 77 percent saying they must have one and 23 percent considering it not necessary, but nice.

Housing that was residential in character was preferred by the majority of the sample: building height: one-story—55 percent; two-story—20 percent; three-story—13 percent; High-rise—11 percent, for building type the responses were as follows: townhouse—8 percent; cottage—28 percent; two-bedroom 20 percent; one-bedroom 34 percent; efficiency—7 percent.

It is important to note that different communities had significant differences in responses. For example, in a northeastern urban area, increased income correlated with decreased interest in moving to a retirement community. Conversely, in the midwestern agricultural area, increased income indicated increased interest in planned-retirement living. Age of potential inmovers also varied from community to community, as did their expressed desires for facilities and services.

The percentage of the population that would be potential inmovers varied considerably among communities. Whether the sponsor's existing facility is perceived to be for high, middle, or low income residents appears to strongly influence the response rate among inmovers and noninmovers.

These few examples emphasize the need for individual studies in specific areas. Each community and each elderly population has its own individuality. The value of primary data from a community survey is the delineation of those responses that significantly differ from the norm, analysis of the underlying premises and their translation into appropriate programs, services and building spaces for the specific population to be served.

The Program: More than Shelter

Once feasibility has been established, the market defined, and consumer preferences determined, the next major task is to translate this information into a written project-program.

Many sponsors of congregate-housing projects have had the unpleasant experience of devoting several years to planning, design and construction only to discover that the final results were below their expectations and very different from what was envisioned when the planners and architects first began. There are many reasons for the disappointments and surprises, but, in most instances, the results can be traced to an inadequate program.

Planning is advanced thinking as a basis for doing. *The program is a planning tool used to determine desirable ends before we become involved with the means.* We need to establish where we want to go before we can work out the most efficient ways of getting there.

The architect's success at the synthesis stage of the design process will depend as much on the quality of the program as on his ability to design. One of the most powerful techniques we can develop is the ability to state our goals so clearly that the statement itself indicates a direction and a possible solution. If one is able to define a goal succinctly, he is usually well on the way to achieving it. Creating and managing the housing environment is a process of synthesis, and we must determine early in the process what principles should have the greatest influence.

During the early stages of preparing the program, the sponsor or developer, the planner and the architect will decide (either consciously or subconsciously) whether they intend to deal with symbols or with people. Very few building programs deal with people (the market) and describe the characteristics of the prospective residents. Unfortunately, we normally start by writing down the physical spaces we think the future residents should have. A sound building program should clearly define the many facets of the environment and serve as a prime source of information and communication. A complete program should develop systematically to establish the true needs and goals of the elderly and to shape and order these goals so they may be incorporated effectively during the synthesis stage to follow.

The housing needs of the elderly are acute and extremely complex. We cannot approach the program for congregate housing in total isolation from the housing situation in general. As the New York State Housing Element states, "In order to satisfy the projected need for new housing units, over 2,100,000 additional housing units will be required by 2000, with the private sector being expected to provide 80 percent of these units."

In our efforts to close this housing gap, we must maintain a concern for the quality of the housing as well as the quantity. It is imperative that we recognize that the living environment is far more than shelter. It is a complex interrelationship of many factors, which include not only the physical, or built environment, but also the social and psychological perceptions of the milieu, and the impact of local, state, federal and administrative policies. The latter may well determine the use of space and the satisfaction of the resident.

In simplistic terms, the living environment, as diagrammed in figure 5-1, is a chain with many links. The significant factor is that for the older person, each link is vital. The chain must be continuous to produce its maximum effect. When a younger person is confronted with a missing link, she can ignore it, leap over it, rebel, avoid it, or adapt to it. The older person is least able to undertake any of these coping behaviors. The details of each link become very important.

The attention paid to the myriad of details and the manner in which they are incorporated in the initial program often makes the difference between a successful environmental experience and a stressful one for the elderly individual. An excellent example of an oversight of meaningful detail is the rapid transit system that spent millions of dollars to redesign buses to accommodate frail older people. The buses were never fully utilized because the company neglected to put benches at the bus stops. The cost effectiveness of a well-designed kitchen for the elderly is drastically reduced if the housing is located in an area where the older person is either too far from, or afraid to go, shopping.

The environment is rarely neutral. It will either be an integrating force in the life of the older person or a disintegrating force. We must avoid the condition where the older person is required to spend more of his energies in maintaining his relationship with the environment than using them in a productive way to satisfy his needs and goals and to maintain his health. Housing must support the older person by removing environmental barriers, encouraging independent functioning, and allowing him to relate to the experience with dignity and increased self-esteem.

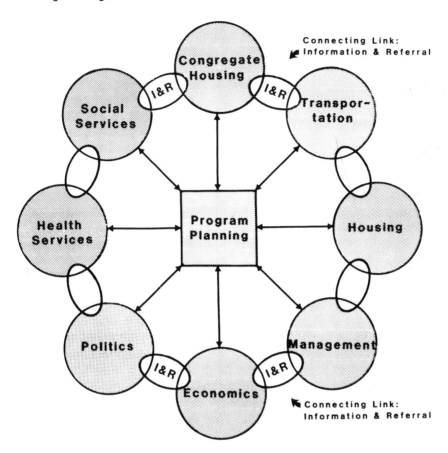

Source: Louis E. Gelwicks and Maria B. Dwight, Santa Monica, Calif. Gerontological Planning Associates.

Figure 5-1. Environmental Chain

Professionals in human behavior have studied the interactions between humans and the environment for several decades. They recognize that our health, well-being, and way of life are dependent on the environment. The balance between it and ourselves is quite delicate. In the past, the elderly housing resident has been expected to adjust to the existing environment. Recently, efforts have been made to reduce problems, not through treatment of the person, but through treatment of the environment that shapes the resident. An environment can be created which will enhance the capabilities of individuals or groups and enable them to more fully realize their objectives. It may also be designed to expose individuals to new stimuli that enable them to develop potentials that otherwise might have remained untapped.

Housing is one of many links in the environmental chain. Its relative importance in the continuum varies but the fact that the elderly person needs assistance in connecting the links that relate to housing is constant. Our approach to design and operation must have a broad perspective on the total housing environment and establish the connectors, or glue, to assist the elderly person in keeping the environmental chain intact.

As we develop congregate housing, it appears reasonable to establish a program based on the basic environmental needs of the older person. We interpret these needs as: information, competence and control, options, change, and finally, marketing.

Information

Our survey of the desires and needs of older people in more than thirty-six states has led to the overriding conclusion that what older people need most is information. In spite of an acute shortage of services and facilities for the elderly in many areas, there are many which go underutilized because the older person is either unaware of their existence or lacks information on how to reach or use them.

An environment must contain information that is relevant to the interests and needs of the user. The process of obtaining essential information favors those people who are most skilled in seeking and utilizing it (the younger or stronger person). This leaves those most in need least likely to come in contact with the informational resources that could help them cope successfully. Information may become the connecting link or glue in the environmental chain of which we spoke.

A certain amount of assertive and aggressive behavior is necessary to successfully obtain crucial information and most older people are not comfortable engaging in this type of behavior. A readily accessible information and referral source (a person as well as a booklet) should be available so that older people may obtain answers to questions about their housing and the surrounding community.

A recent statewide survey showed that three out of every four older persons who expressed dissatisfaction with their housing or neighborhood will find it very difficult to locate a new place to live. Of those who are dissatisfied with their housing, 71 percent desire help in obtaining better housing. They need information.

However, the elderly resident is not the only one who needs information. The policymakers, service directors, planners, architects, all the individuals serving the elderly need information. It should be emphasized that the greatest need is to present the program information in a form that will be clearly understood by the variety of disciplines involved in developing a congregate-housing project.

This brings us to a final consideration of factors influencing the interpretation and application of the information contained in the program. A person who is directly and financially accountable for his decisions may apply information from a different perspective from that of one who is not. The developer in competition is not about to gamble $200,000 on a design feature that may not sell. The administrator must be able to keep his operating and maintenance costs within the limitations set by the projected income. He will be held accountable long after the planner, developer and contractor have left the job. The prospective resident is viewing the congregate housing as the home in which he or she must spend the last few years of life.

In short, different people bring different perspectives to the situation. This was well illustrated (in fact, burned pleasantly but indelibly in our minds) during a visit in 1978 to a House of Respect in mainland China. This is a home for about seventy-five elderly men in Manchuria. The name itself, House of Respect, is something to think about. While visiting their small apartments, we found that the men lived three to a room. Suddenly we came upon a very small room for one person that had been made by closing off the end of a corridor. For years, we have advocated private rooms, so it naturally struck us that this man must be important to have such a privilege. We asked the gentleman why he had a private room. He replied, "Because three people won't fit." As owners, administrators and planners, we would do well to remember that the user perspective may vary from our own.

Competence and Control

The ability of a person to function within any housing setting depends on the individual's capabilities and the characteristics of that setting. The relationship between these two elements determines his environmental competence. This relationship becomes particularly critical for the older person in an unfamiliar or transitional setting such as a new housing project.

If an individual is to be and feel competent, the environment must provide both direct physical and psychological supports. Three important components in this regard are security, orientation and control.

The sense of security, of being able to move about day or night without being accosted or robbed, is a paramount concern to older persons who know they are very susceptible to crime of all types. We must reevaluate our program input and standards of not only what is, but also what apperas to be, a safe environment. Personal security for the older person transcends the fear of mugging in a dark parking-lot. Worn steps, highly polished floors, narrow, steep stairwells, wobbly benches, all present potential physical hazards to an older person. Ice, snow, uneven walkways and unrestrained dogs are inhibiting factors the younger person takes for granted that may create a feeling of insecurity for the older person.

There are few fears greater than that of being lost. The unpredictable may be a challenge to youth, but uncertainty is a cause of anxiety among the elderly. Understanding one's surroundings is of great importance to one's ability to function effectively and to one's general sense of well-being. For older people, the ability to successfully navigate the environment will lead to this sense of control and well-being. There is, of course, no better way of developing a feeling of control than allowing the elderly to play a direct role in the planning and programming process.

Options

Aging has been defined as the process of closing out life's options. We would prefer to extend this definition by suggesting that it is a process of attempting to avoid closing out life's options. This effort creates the stress that in turn contributes to the aging process.

In view of escalating construction and money costs, it is unlikely that there will be national policies providing large quantities of housing within a price range the elderly can afford. Nevertheless, we must not be so misled by the crisis of decreased production that we overlook the increasing need for quality and options. It is true that when an environment does not satisfy an individual's needs, the human being has shown a remarkable ability to adapt. However, as Rene Dubos has so well documented, it is our very adaptability which may do us in. Adaptability to an inappropriate environment consumes energy and personal resources better put into enhancement of life, or goal reaching. Not all people are capable of such adaptability and one pays a price to adapt. Our policies and planning efforts should aim to sustain the individual, to fit the setting to the person, not the person to the setting.

Change

Change, ironically, appears to be a constant factor in the efforts to create congregate housing. Tomorrow's elderly will be different from today's, whether the housing is well planned or not. With a sound planning process and well documented programs, the alternatives and future models can reflect more directly the needs of the users. When initially developed, a project may provide readily accessible, high quality environments relevant to the interests and needs of the users. However, as composition and characteristics inevitably change (as people and neighborhoods do), there will be a need for continuing environmental planning and evaluation.

The role of the environmental-planning team is to shape the environment in such a manner that it will be interpreted as a place that welcomes and assists older people, and that it will remain viable in the future. Relevant questions we should try to answer include Will the older residents find the kinds of information they need? Is it comprehensible? Does its use have significant and constructive consequences? If the environment does not perform properly, it must be changed. With good planning it should be possible to identify the changes that are needed well before the housing environment reaches the point of producing stress, alienation, inefficiency and failure.

Marketing

For the proprietary-housing developer or service provider, marketing is a key component of any project or service. Millions of dollars are spent to inform the public about a single product. Unfortunately, many marketing personnel are still using the approach used to sell the eighteen-to-fifty-year-old segment of the population. This is changing as the marketers realize that a different (but not more costly) approach is needed to attract the older, selective customers.

On the other hand, the majority of nonprofit sponsors of congregate housing, who have worked with the elderly for years, often neglect the marketing function. This, too, is changing. As Philip Kotler has pointed out in his book, *Marketing for Non-Profit Organization,*

> In recent years, marketing has become a subject of growing interest to managers of public and private nonprofit organizations. The concepts, tools, and models that have worked so effectively to manage products and services in the profit sector are becoming increasingly relevant to the management of products and services in the nonprofit sector. Nonprofit organizations face a host of problems that would be analyzed as straightforward marketing problems if found in the profit sector. Museums and symphonies have a difficult time attracting sufficient funds to carry on their cultural activities. Blood banks find it hard to enlist enough donors. Churches are having difficulties attracting and maintaining active members. Many colleges face serious problems in attracting a sufficient number of qualified students. Police departments are hampered by a poor image in many communities. Family planners face formidable problems in selling the idea of "zero population growth." Safety councils seek more effective ways to persuade motorists to wear their safety belts. National parks such as Yellowstone are plagued with overdemand and are seeking ways to discourage or "demarket" the parks. There is hardly a public or private nonprofit organization in existence that is not faced with some problems stemming from its relations to its markets.

The elderly not only need information about what is or will be provided, they need to be informed of its merits and value. We are not referring to a Madison Avenue pitch, but a sound marketing program to inform the older population of the options available.

The world will not beat a pathway to our congregate-housing doors unless we market the total program. A selective consumer expects a reasonable and direct marketing effort, particularly one which provides the necessary information to make critical decisions.

Marketing information is the first phase of a chain which develops awareness to knowledge, knowledge to interest, interest to desire and desire to action. Each of these links may be evaluated by consumer reaction; for instance, the request for a brochure, a site visit, application for residency, etc. A responsive and successful organization should. (1) Learn the needs, perceptions, preferences, and satisfactions of the consumer and utilize systematic information collection. (2) Encourage inquiries, suggestions, opinions, and complaints and create formal systems to facilitate feedback. (3) Take positive steps to adjust services, policies and procedures to respond to consumer desires. (4) Evaluate the adjustments for cost-effective consumer satisfaction.

The benefits of sound marketing can be twofold, as Kotler states:

> When systematic marketing is introduced into an organization, two distinct benefits may be achieved. First, the organization may increase the satisfaction that it delivers to the target market as a result of understanding its needs better and developing better-matched products and services. Second, the organization may improve the efficiency of marketing activities through a better knowledge of how to formulate prices, communications, and distribution.

> Finally, the administrator is concerned with ethical questions raised by marketing. Critics may charge that marketing is a waste of money, think it is intrusive, and that it is manipulative. It is important for administrators to be sensitive to these criticisms and avoid marketing practices or expenditures that cannot be defended. At the same time, marketing is an efficient way of accomplishing communication and distribution tasks facing organizations; it researches people's attitudes primarily to serve them better; and it usually advances causes that are in the public interest.

Certainly congregate housing for the elderly is in the public as well as private interest, but the future success of congregate housing lies in our ability to adjust to changing market-demands. Past buyer behavior is one basis for developing and marketing a product. It can be disastrous in a market that is changing as rapidly as the current generation of elderly.

If we are to successfully plan, program, design, develop and market congregate housing to new generations of elderly, we will need the talent and teamwork of the variety of disciplines represented in this volume. The creation of successful living environments for and by older persons is well beyond the capability of any one discipline. Let us direct our efforts toward working together.

Reference

Kotler, Philip. Marketing for Non-Profit Organizations (Englewood Cliffs, N.J.: Prentice-Hall, 1975).

Key Steps in the Development Process

Edward H. Marchant

To many prospective housing-sponsors, the development process often appears to be complex and confusing. Based upon my experiences at Greater Boston Community Development, Inc. (GBCD), a nonprofit corporation that serves as development consultant to community-based, nonprofit sponsors of subsidized housing, I would agree that the housing development process is complex. Unfortunately, it appears that little can be done to reduce the complexity of the process. In fact, given current economic conditions, the process is likely to become more complex as it becomes increasingly more difficult to develop economically feasible projects.

The housing-development process can, however, be made more understandable. This chapter will introduce prospective housing-sponsors to the development process by identifying the key steps in this process. Given the complexity of housing development and the significant financial and organizational commitments required, an inexperienced sponsor is well advised to proceed on a step-by-step basis. It is often unwise and sometimes impossible to proceed to the next key step without completing the one preceding it.

The key development steps are as follows (following each step is a statement a sponsor should be able to make before proceeding):

Step 1. Review of Organization's Overall Agency Corporate Objectives and Establishment of Its Housing Objectives. After reviewing our organization's overall objectives and resources, we feel it makes sense for us at this time to commit staff and financial resources to seriously explore a potential role as a housing sponsor.

Step 2. Selection of Development Consultant. Given our organization's limited familiarity with the housing-development process, we have retained a qualified development consultant to guide us through the process.

Step 3. Preliminary Review of Available Funding Programs. We are aware of the odds of receiving funding and our ongoing level of staff and financial commitments reflects our understanding of these odds.

Step 4. Site Selection and Site Control. We have site control of a site that satisfies our selection criteria.

Step 5. Funding Application. Development team and its qualifications; site information; preliminary design information; preliminary feasibility study. Our funding application has been approved.

Step 6. Intermediate Processing. Development work schedule and timetable; seed money schedule; design development drawings and construction-cost estimate; feasibility study. At this stage we have a feasible project. Based upon our own feasibility studies and the financing agency's concurrence, we are willing to incur a significant financial liability by authorizing the architect to proceed with the preparation of working drawings.

Step 7. Advanced Processing. Working drawings have been completed, final construction costs are within budget, all municipal approvals have been received; the project remains feasible and we are ready to borrow the funds necessary to construct the project.

Step 8. Construction. Construction is scheduled to be completed within (six) months.

Step 9. Implementation of Management and Social-Service Operations. Initial rent-up of our project has now been completed. Management and social service programs have been implemented.

Step 10. Evaluation.

For the first five key steps, this chapter briefly explains each step and then outlines a series of questions a housing sponsor and/or its development team should consider during its completion. The next four key steps are again briefly explained. For these four steps, the development process is more directed. Basic questions have already been answered and now the primary issue is one of implementation: completing architectural drawings, preparing final cost estimates, securing all required municipal approvals, maintaining project feasibility, having a construction loan closing, completing construction, and managing the property. The final step, one that is rarely done with as much seriousness or objectivity as is necessary, is evaluating the housing-development process and its results for each sponsor and project.

It should be noted, of course, that no two sponsors, sites, or projects are alike. The generalized explanation of the housing development process presented here must be tailored to the specific objectives and resources of each sponsor and to local funding opportunities and housing-development practices. In some projects a different ordering of tasks would be appropriate based upon specific sponsor and project characteristics. It should be noted, also, that this explanation of the housing development process is oriented toward a non-profit organization with little or no prior experience as a housing sponsor.

Step 1: Review of Organization's Overall Agency/Corporate Objectives and Establishment of Its Housing Objectives

A critical, but often overlooked step in the housing-development process, is the establishment of a sponsor's housing objectives based upon a thoughtful review and careful understanding of the organization's overall objectives. Before an organization can meaningfully establish its housing objectives, it should become familiar enough with the housing-development process to be able to decide whether it should seriously explore a potential role as housing sponsor. The best way to get a quick education in the housing-development process may be to meet with sponsors of housing projects similar to that which you think your organization might want to sponsor.

For example, if your particular interest is congregate housing, you should visit several congregate-housing projects, as well as traditional elderly housing designed for independent living. Call the HUD Multi-Family Housing Representative for your geographic area and ask for an explanation of the various HUD elderly-housing programs. Ask also for the names of some successful housing sponsors and project locations. Check with public-housing authorities and with state housing-finance agencies. Talk with the sponsors of this housing. Ask them to describe the steps they went through to get the housing built, how long it took and what problems they encountered during the process. Talk with the residents and the management agent to understand how this project is being operated. It is also useful to meet with some potential sponsors whose development efforts were not successful. Try to determine why their efforts were unsuccessful and learn from their mistakes.

In general, contact anyone whom you feel would be able to supplement your understanding of the process. Talk with development consultants, architects, general contractors, and lawyers who have helped produce the type of housing in which you are interested. After your organization develops a basic familiarity with some representative housing sponsors, programs, and projects, it should have answers for the following questions:

1. What type of housing does the organization want to sponsor? Why? Approximately how many units of housing would you want to develop? Is this type of housing a logical first step?
2. What staff, management, social service, political, financial and/or land resources does your organization now possess that could be committed to a housing-sponsorship effort?
3. What additional resources could be mobilized by your organization if it decided to become actively involved as a housing sponsor?
4. What risks will be incurred by your organization as a housing sponsor?
5. What rewards does your organization expect to get as a housing sponsor?
6. If your project is successful, how will your organization be affected?
7. If your project is unsuccessful, how will your organization be affected?
8. Are there methods of achieving these perceived rewards without incurring the perceived risks? For example, should your organization assume a role as advocate rather than sponsor?
9. How do these risks/rewards relate to your organization's present and future overall objectives?
10. Does the undertaking of such a housing venture make sense for your organization at this time?

Step 2: Selection of a Development Consultant

The development of any type of housing requires the input of a wide range of professionals working together to achieve the development objectives. Direction of the individual members of a development team, as a conductor leads an orchestra, is the development consultant's job. An effective development consultant is familiar with all of the steps in the development process and, more important perhaps, knows how the different steps in the development process are ordered and relate to each other. The development consultant's expertise is not architecture, construction, or property management. Although familiar with each of these specialties, the development consultant's primary purpose is to coordinate the entire housing-development process in order to insure an economically feasible project that satisfies the sponsor's development objectives.

It is critical that sponsors make their development objectives clear to prospective development consultants. It should also be made clear that the development consultant works for the sponsor. Final policy decisions rest with the sponsor. Assuming that a satisfactory working relationship exists between sponsor and development consultant, an understanding of the level of decision making at which a sponsor wants to become involved should evolve naturally. My experience has been that sponsors assume different roles: some are actively involved on an almost daily basis while others leave all but the major decisions (for example, selection of other members of the development team) to the development consultant. In interviewing prospective development consultants, a sponsor should review the role it intends to play in the development process and make sure that the development consultant finds such a working relationship acceptable.

In searching for a qualified development consultant, a sponsor should consider the following questions:

1. What individual or firm has provided development-consultant services for projects similar to the one which your organization would like to undertake?
2. What individual(s) will be working on your job? Has the development consultant's work been satisfactory? Be sure to get detailed references from prior clients, funding agencies, municipal officials, etc.
3. Does the development consultant understand and feel committed to your organization's development objectives and understand that his/her role is to assist the sponsor in achieving these objectives?
4. Is the development consultant willing to make a satisfactory time commitment to the project?
5. What services will the development consultant provide? What is the development consultant's fee schedule? Is the development consultant willing to work on a contingency basis for any period of time?

6.   Do you feel comfortable dealing with this development consultant? Do you respect his/her judgment?

Step 3: Preliminary Review of Available Funding Programs

The development consultant chosen should possess a working knowledge of existing local, state, or federal housing-funding programs. One of the first services to be provided by your development consultant might be to answer the following questions:

1.   What existing local, state federal mortgage loan, mortgage insurance, and rental assistance housing programs are suitable and available given the sponsor's development objectives?
2.   If government subsidy programs are used, what strings are attached?
3.   How intense is the competition for these housing program funds? Can you assess the likelihood of receiving a funding commitment assuming an acceptable application is submitted?
4.   What type of project is most likely to be funded? What features would give our project a priority for funding? What site locations would be most attractive to funding agencies?
5.   When are applications for these funding programs due? What materials must be submitted? How much will it cost and how long will it take to put together an application?

Given the extreme scarcity of rental-assistance funds today and the nearly absolute need for these funds for any housing development designed to serve low- and moderate-income prople, it is important that potential sponsors who lack their own funding be aware of the odds of receiving such funds prior to making any significant staff and financial commitments. In some cases, sponsors should not be surprised if their development consultant advises them that there are no funding programs currently available. Given such a circumstance, a sponsor should discuss with its development consultant whether any further development efforts should be undertaken until there is at least a possibility of competing for funds.

Step 4: Site Selection and Site Control

Assuming that suitable funding programs exist and that a potential sponsor wishes to compete for such funds, a critical component of the funding application is the quality of the site and evidence that the sponsor has site control. A sponsor does not have to own the site. Normally, a contract between a land owner and a sponsor in which the sponsor is given an option to purchase the site at a certain date for a specified price constitutes satisfactory evidence of site control.

Given the critical role that location plays in any housing project, it is important that the sponsor and its development consultant carefully establish site selection criteria consistent with the type and size of housing proposed by the sponsor.

Answers to the following questions should establish threshold site-selection criteria:

1. What location is preferred by the sponsor? Why is this particular location preferred?
2. What market requirements for renting apartments are there likely to be?
3. What commercial, social, recreational, transportation, health and municipal amenities are required?
4. What are the minimum and maximum number of units the sponsor expects to build? (This question will help define what size site is needed. The actual number of units that can be built on any particular site is dependent, of course, upon zoning requirements, building use and design, soil conditions, and so forth.)
5. Is rehabilitation or adaptive reuse of an existing building a potential alternative to new construction?[1]
6. What land or building purchase price is feasible for the type of housing proposed?
7. By what date must the sponsor have site control? How long must the term of the option period be?

In reviewing those sites that meet the sponsor's threshold criteria, a number of other factors should be considered: (1) How attractive will this site be to funding agencies? Does the site satisfy the agency's site and neighborhood standards? Has the agency funded other projects near this site? Is such prior funding a disadvantage to the sponsor requesting funding approval? (2) Is it likely that necessary neighborhood, zoning, and other municipal approvals will be granted at this location? Can a feasible real-estate tax agreement be negotiated for this site? Are municipal officials generally supportive of the type of development that would be proposed for this site? (3) Is the site or building suitable for the type of construction proposed? Are there any unusual site or building conditions which will cause extraordinary construction cost problems? (4) What utilities are available at or near the site? (5) Are there plans under way by other potential sponsors to build in this area? Is this competition likely to have any adverse impact on the likelihood of the sponsor's proposal being funded or on eventual operations?

A few final points relevant to site selection are worth noting: (1) Do not overlook the possibility that some sites might be available to a non-profit sponsor at a reduced or nominal cost. For example, a municipality or institution might make a land parcel or building available at a below market cost to a credible nonprofit sponsor. (2) Sites with significant residential or commercial relocation requirements should be avoided.

Step 5: Funding Application

Although each funding agency has its own submission requirements, the primary requirements for an initial funding-application normally include a description of the development team and its qualifications; a description of the site and evidence of site control; a description of the type of housing proposed, including preliminary architectural drawings; and a preliminary feasibility study.

Development Team and its Qualifications

Funding agencies are naturally interested in reviewing the qualifications of the development team organized by the sponsor and its development consultant. Although a sponsor might not have any direct experience in housing development, the funding agency will want to review the sponsor's current operations, staff, board of directors, and financial statements. The funding agency wants to be sure that the sponsor understands its responsibilities. Having made a judgment that the organization appears to be a viable potential housing sponsor, the funding agency will review the qualifications and prior experience of the development consultant to determine whether they can provide the sponsor with the technical expertise necessary to produce the proposed housing.

Architect. Experience shows that it makes sense to delay selection of an architect to this point. By this time the sponsor will have a better understanding of the housing development process. Also, by this time, the sponsor will have had an opportunity to more clearly define its housing objectives, identify potential funding sources, and select a site.

In selecting an architect, a sponsor should ask questions similar to those asked when interviewing the development consultant. The architect and engineers will play a major role in the housing-development process. It is important that good working relationships be developed among the sponsor and its development consultant, architect and general contractor.

A sponsor should try to select an architect who has successfully completed projects comparable to its proposed project. For example, if the sponsor is considering rehabilitation or adaptive reuse of an existing structure, it is preferable that the architect have prior experience with such projects. If state and/or federal funding programs are being used, it is preferable that the architect have experience with the requirements of these programs and prior experience in working with the personnel at these agencies.

It is important to select an architect who is committed to producing a feasible design and who understands the balance between design and feasibility.

General Contractor. Again, the critical factor is that the sponsor select a general contractor with experience in constructing comparable projects. It is important to inspect the general contractor's work and carefully check references. The sponsor should know which subcontractors the general contractor normally uses and should make sure that the general contractor has adequate bonding capacity to build the job.

Lawyer. A lawyer experienced with the housing-development process will be necessary to provide a wide range of legal services. The sponsor's development consultant should review with the sponsor the scope of legal services required and the timing and potential cost of such services.

Management Agent. Funding agencies are particularly interested in the qualifications of the proposed management agent. Once construction is completed, the management agent serves as the sponsor's agent in coordinating the operation of the project. During earlier steps in the development process, the management agent must prepare an acceptable management plan with a realistic operating budget. It is possible that some sponsors have staff members who are qualified to serve as property managers themselves or could possibly be trained to assume these responsibilities at a later date. Self-management gives a sponsor the greatest possible understanding of and control over its housing.

Site Information

The funding agency requires a description of the site and evidence of site control. If rehabilitation is proposed, certain engineering evaluations of the building may be required.

Preliminary Design Information

The funding agency will want to review preliminary architectural drawings which present the general scale of the development and include a preliminary site-plan, elevations, and typical unit layouts.

Preliminary Feasibility Study

The funding agency will require a preliminary feasibility-study indicating that the proposal appears to be within normal feasibility guidelines. The development consultant's primary responsibility throughout the housing-development process is to coordinate the sponsor's development efforts in a manner that will result in a feasible project. Feasibility studies are discussed in greater detail later in this chapter.

Step 6: Intermediate Processing

Notification that a sponsor's funding application or other financing has been approved triggers a number of events.

Development Work Schedule and Timetable

Based upon his general knowledge of the housing-development process and the particular requirements of the proposed project, the development consultant prepares a detailed work-schedule listing the tasks to be completed by each member of the development team. Realistic target dates for the completion of each task are included. This work schedule is the primary management control device used by the development consultant and the sponsor. This can also be descriptively referred to as the critical path if it defines the controlling time factors and/or tasks.

Seed-Money Schedule

Housing sponsorship almost always requires a financial investment by the sponsor. The development consultant should prepare a seed-money budget. For example, funds are normally needed to pay for land options, development consultant fees, architectural fees, legal fees, property surveys, test borings, and funding-agency application fees. The development consultant should be familiar with certain charitable corporations or agencies willing to loan seed money funds to qualified nonprofit sponsors who do not have sufficient working capital to cover such costs themselves.

Design Development Drawings/Construction Cost Estimate

Under the direction of the sponsor and the development consultant, the architect prepares more detailed architectural drawings and specifications than those prepared for the funding application. The drawings should be done to a sufficient level of detail to allow the general contractor to prepare a meaningful construction-cost estimate. The general contractor should receive actual bids from subcontractors to make such an estimate valid. The development consultant and the general contractor should work closely with the architect during the preparation of these design development drawings.

Feasibility Study

The development consultant must now complete a more detailed feasibility study. Simply stated, a feasibility study is an exercise that attempts to determine whether or not a proposed project is feasible—does the project generate sufficient income through rents and/or third party subsidy payments to pay for all of the expenses of the development: debt service-costs, operating costs and real estate taxes?

Having received the general contractor's construction cost estimate, the development consultant must then estimate certain development costs in order to undertake his feasibility study. Development costs normally include the following items: architectural and engineering fees; interest, real estate taxes and insurance during the construction period; financing and application fees, legal fees; development-consultant fees; initial marketing costs, sponsor overhead; contingency; and land costs.

The sum of the construction costs and development costs represent the total cost of the proposed project. With knowledge of the estimated total cost of the proposed project, the development consultant can project the total estimated debt service payments required based upon his understanding of the details of the particular funding program involved.

The development consultant, with input from the proposed management-agent, must then estimate the operating costs of the project. Examples of normal operating costs include property management fees, advertising, office expenses, fuel for heat and hot water, electricity, water and sewer, repairs, maintenance and social service payroll, janitorial materials, accounting and legal fees.

Next, the development consultant estimates the projected real estate taxes for the project. Sometimes a nonprofit sponsor, even if legally not liable for taxes, may wish to negotiate a voluntary payment in lieu of taxes to assure municipal approvals.

Finally, the development consultant must determine whether sufficient rental income can be generated to cover these three categories of cost: debt service, operating costs, and real estate taxes.

If the projected income is sufficient to pay all expenses, the project is determined to be economically feasible.

Step 7: Advanced Processing

Assuming that the feasibility study is positive and that no problems that could unreasonably delay or halt the project are anticipated, the sponsor authorizes the architect to prepare working drawings and specifications. At this point the sponsor probably incurs its greatest financial liability. Working drawings are the detailed drawings used by the general contractor to construct the housing. Once the working drawings have been completed and reviewed by the funding agency, the general contractor prepares a final construction-cost estimate and a final feasibility study is prepared by the development consultant. Meanwhile, while working drawings are being prepared, the lawyer has the primary responsibility for securing necessary municipal approvals, negotiating a real estate tax agreement, and making preparations for a loan closing at the funding agency. After the closing attorney at the funding agency reviews the closing documents, a closing date is scheduled and the initial closing occurs.

It should be noted that the description of the advanced processing step provided above has been greatly simplified given the scope of this chapter. It is inevitable that delays will be encountered during this step.

Step 8: Construction

Once a mortgage-loan closing has been completed, construction can proceed. The sponsor, through the architect and development consultant, monitors construction progress and quality. Periodic payments to the contractor are made based upon requisitions submitted by the contractor and approved by the sponsor's architect and the funding agency's construction inspector. Construction progress is primarily a function of two variables: the competency of the general contractor and subcontractors and the quality of the working drawings and specifications prepared by the architect. Even under the best circumstances, there can be numerous difficulties during the construction period; therefore, it is absolutely critical that a sponsor select a competent general contractor and architect. These two members of the development team, along with the sponsor's development consultant, must attempt to minimize any potential design and/or construction problems through careful attention to design and construction details prior to the signing of a construction contract and the sponsor's approval of final architectural documents.

Step 9: Implementation of Management and Social-Service Operations

As indicated earlier, basic planning for management and social-service operations must occur during an earlier phase of the housing development process. For example, a competent management agent must be selected, an acceptable management plan with a feasible operating budget must be prepared, and suitable spaces for required social-service programs must be planned early in the development process. Successful management and social-service operations are highly dependent upon such early efforts.

However, actual implementation of management operations does not normally begin until six months prior to the completion of construction. At this time initial rent-up and tenant-selection program activities begin. Given that initial rent-up and tenant selection are often key concerns to a housing sponsor, a sponsor should work with its development consultant and property management agent to establish a rent-up and tenant-selection policy consistent with both the sponsor's objectives and any applicable rules and regulations of funding agencies. The sponsor should clearly define the role it wants to play in the tenant-selection process. From a cash-flow perspective, it is important that tenants are prepared to move into the new building as soon as construction is completed and occupancy permits are received.

It should be further noted that the actual timing for implementation of a rent-up and tenant-selection program should be based upon the expected requirements of such a program. For example, if a congregate facility for the frail elderly or special housing for the physically handicapped is being constructed, the implementation stage for rent-up and tenant selection should probably begin earlier than six months prior to the completion of construction, especially if special funding of social-service programs are required.

Implementation of ongoing management and social-service operations should be based upon a management/social-service plan and budget prepared by the management agent and approved by the sponsor. Input from building residents should be solicited and incorporated into the management/social-service plan. When appropriate, consultants with practical experience in particular social-service program areas should be used to supplement the more traditional maintenance and financial management skills of the property manager. Management and social-service operations should be closely monitored by the sponsor. In particular, the sponsor should be thoroughly familiar with the monthly financial operating statements prepared by the management agent and be able to use these statements as a means of evaluating the financial status of the project and the performance of the management agent.

Step 10: Evaluation

Having reached this stage in the housing development process, the sponsor should evaluate the experience, particularly if sponsorship of additional housing is being considered. The following questions should be addressed:

1. Has the sponsor achieved the housing objectives originally established?
2. Have the rewards justified the risks involved?
3. How has the sponsor's overall organization been affected by the development of this project?
4. How could the sponsor's housing development experience have been improved?
5. Could certain mistakes have been avoided?
6. Has the sponsor been satisfied with the services provided by the members of its development team: development consultant, architect, general contractor, lawyer, and property manager?
7. Does the housing meet the needs of its residents?
8. How could the housing be improved from a design and construction perspective?
9. Given the sponsor's experiences with this particular project, does the sponsorship of additional housing make sense at this time?

7

Housing Production: New Construction versus Rehabilitation

Chia-Ming Sze

The design and development of housing is a complex process that must respond to basic human, site, and economic factors. Although the end goal of producing quality housing remains the same, the basic approach in rehabilitation and new construction projects is, by necessity, different. In new construction projects, a program is established and a new building is then designed for that program. In rehabilitation projects, an existing building is found and the program adapted for that building. As one might expect, both approaches have positive and negative tradeoffs.

Only recently has there been a strong trend toward rehabilitation and preservation of buildings in this country. In the past, when the economy was stronger and the country more confident, the American preference seemed to be for new things over old. There was little hesitancy in tearing down perfectly adequate old buildings to build new ones in their place or to create parking lots. Recently, due to a weakening economy and an awakening preservation movement, the situation has changed with the result that existing buildings have become valued and much sought after for renovation and adaptive reuse.

Housing has been one of the major areas demonstrating that, properly rehabilitated, existing buildings could become as attractive as new buildings and, in many cases, more appropriate. In New England, where a large supply of old, underutilized industrial buildings and schools existed, the building recycled into housing use has become one of the conventional means of providing housing. Churches, hotels, and even prisons are being converted to housing. Because of community preference for elderly housing over family-housing developments, almost all of the rehabilitated buildings for housing have been for the elderly. A majority of the elderly housing built has been subsidized with federal and state rent-supplement programs, under which the residents pay only 25 percent of their income. Most existing buildings to be rehabilitated are located in dense, older parts of a community and are multistoried buildings more suited to elderly than family housing.

National policy implemented by HUD and state housing agencies has placed financing priorities on rehabilitation over new construction. While in the past the movement for rehabilitation and preservation was largely an aesthetic and historic one promulgated by a sophisticated, elite group, it has now become a venture of both profit-motivated developers and nonprofit community and religious groups eager to produce housing. For existing buildings qualifying for certification as

103

historic properties, rehabilitation costs may be amortized over five years and depreciation accelerated under the Tax Reform Act of 1976. A developer who tears down a historic property cannot deduct demolition costs. This tax incentive has been designed to encourage preservation and rehabilitation.

Rehabilitation projects start with a feasibility analysis and inventory of an existing building's dimensional configuration, code adaptability, and structural soundness. For housing, unit depth for corridor apartments generally should not exceed thirty feet, with twenty-five feet ideal. With allowance for a corridor width of five to six feet, the average desirable building width for a double-loaded-corridor apartment building falls between fifty-five to sixty feet. Should the width exceed these dimensions appreciably, it may be possible to introduce an atrium space or courtyard and design a single-loaded-corridor solution. This alternative is usually quite dramatic, but unfortunately quite costly also.

The structural condition of an existing building is probably the single most critical checkpoint in building evaluation. If structural soundness does not exist, the project will not be economically sound. Housing-development budgets rarely can support this extra burden. The necessary clear span for housing units is usually twenty-five to thirty feet but can drop down to ten to fifteen feet by making the dividing wall between bedroom and living room structural. These dimensions easily adapt to structural grids found in existing buildings. Very often they can fall into an existing structural system to reinforce it.

One of the earliest problems encountered in rehabilitation projects was the reluctance of building code and fire department officials to approve rehabilitation projects that did not specifically meet each item of the code. For many projects this was difficult, if not impossible, because most codes were written with new construction in mind. Achieving code compliance for renovation projects can become a lengthy, complicated process requiring numerous appeals and variances from numerous boards. Fortunately, the leading model code authority, Building Officials and Code Administrators Association (BOCA), has recently adopted a special section on historic buildings and renovations that provides for a more flexible interpretation. Sometimes code difficulties can be eliminated by providing a full sprinkler system in a renovation project, even though that degree of precaution might not be necessary. The added cost can offset the cost of delays and red tape necessary to obtain code approval.

Because rehabilitation deals with an existing infrastructure, it can save on some building materials and is more labor intensive during construction. There are advantages to a community in using existing utilities, not taking up undeveloped land or open space, and not destroying familiar local landmarks. Very often, existing buildings are found to have been built with details, materials, and craftsmanship superior to present-day building. Many old buildings, constructed before central-heating systems, have been found to be very energy efficient with thick masonry-walls, small window-openings, and ideal solar orientation.

Older buildings are usually located in an established, central part of a community near existing services. This makes them ideal for housing, which should be near community resources. Saving an existing building in a community, assuming that it is worthy of preservation, can have several positive benefits. Preservation of an old building retains the overall historic time frame of a community's past for future generations. In some rehabilitation projects where former schools and mills have been turned into housing, past students and mill hands have returned as apartment dwellers. It is generally easier to obtain community acceptance for a popular rehabilitation project than for a new construction proposal, because the building to be rehabilitated exists and can be visualized, whereas the new building represents an unknown and requires some imagination and good faith for acceptance. In the design of a rehabilitation project, there is no need to make basic decisions as to style, scale, and siting as there is in new construction. These design decisions are among the most difficult that an architect and client make.

One of the major benefits of housing rehabilitation and adaptive reuse is the greater space allocation that can result. Since the building program is tailored to an existing volume, rehabilitation projects that deal with large volumes such as schools, mills, and churches or similar large-spaced buildings will have larger-sized apartments, higher ceilings, larger windows, and more available storage space. They will have more areas to provide large community spaces. If existing features and detailing such as period ornamental woodwork, hardware, and fixtures can be preserved, then there is an uniqueness produced specific to that project. Rehabilitation projects in housing generally result in a less conventional approach to interior-space design and can produce a more unique project.

There have been some misconceptions about the relative economics of rehabilitation projects and new construction. Rehabilitation projects for housing are only more economical than new construction if the building in question is in excellent condition and dimensionally suited to housing use. The larger the existing building, the more likely that there will be savings from an economy of scale. Buildings with repetitive structural bays and few interior partitions such as mills, factories, and schools are particularly suitable. Existing residential structures such as hotels or outdated apartment houses are relatively easy to renovate into new housing units. Larger buildings can allow for a greater number of units to spread out the cost of renovation. If the exterior envelope, foundation, and structure can be reused, and the size of the building is large enough and appropriate, then renovation can be more economical than new construction. The project will have started with its basic volume complete and ready for adaptation and will not be dependent on good weather or subsurface site conditions to be built. These are two important cost factors in construction.

In a new-construction situation, programmed spaces and their organization are established from the start. There is the opportunity to create a totally new building with its own spatial relationships, expression, and style. The project can be directly tailored for a specific situation inside and out. Finally, there is little doubt that all materials are new and in good condition, since they can be inspected before they are built into the project. Symbolically, the newly constructed building is an expression of newness and progress in a more obvious sense than a rehabilitated structure.

It is important to note that the constraint of economic feasibility places many restrictions on the design of new housing. The designer must meet per-unit-cost constraints established by a lending agency's standards. There is little room to deviate from these limits unless the developer chooses to pump in additional sums of money over the lending agency's standards. The allowable unit cost for elevator buildings will be higher than for non-elevator units. HUD's Minimum Property Standards (MPS) will be the governing rule for establishing room sizes, materials, specifications and program elements. The experienced housing designer soon learns that there are certain rules of thumb he should be aware of if he is to design a project within normal housing budgets for subsidized and non-luxury housing. Some of these suggestions are as follows:

1. Housing should be designed to achieve an efficiency ratio of 65 to 75 percent, if possible, in order to meet normal cost constraints.

$$\text{Efficiency Ratio} = \frac{\text{Total Residential Units Net Sq. Ft.}}{\text{Total Building Gross Sq. Ft.}}$$

2. Single-loaded corridors are less efficient and therefore more expensive than double-loaded corridors. They should be used sparingly and only in special situations.
3. Stacked and back-to-back plumbing chases for bathrooms and kitchens will result in large overall savings.
4. Repetitive unit-types will result in economies, as will fewer different unit-types.
5. Balconies in the Northeast are not cost effective for elderly housing. It is better to provide larger-sized units instead.
6. Keep buildings under seventy feet in height, if possible, to save on sprinkler and other fire-protection costs. Building codes require a fully sprinklered building over seventy feet in height.
7. Plan details with simplicity in mind and use stock, factory-made products wherever possible. Custom-made, special items are costly. The factory wage-scale is far lower than on-site labor wage scale.
8. Modular, prefabricated design-solutions can save in very large projects. In small projects more conventional construction methods will be less costly.
9. The larger the project, the greater the room for cost savings. Agencies allocate per-unit costs to establish an overall budget. All projects, large and small, have similar basic costs such as utility tie-ins, elevators, and stairs spread over the entire project budget.

10. Because elevator buildings are given more dollar allotment per unit, there will be a larger budget to work with in an elevator project than in a non-elevator project. This fact may result in more latitude to resolve a complex development problem.
11. Building-corridor lengths are governed by fire-stair distance. The economical use and placement of stairs will result in significant cost savings.
12. Corners, jogs, and step-downs in massing are expensive; they should be used sparingly and for maximum effect.

Cost containment should not be the only objective in the design and production of housing. It is equally important to maintain qualitative standards that can make the difference between a well-designed, humane living-environment and a routine, restricting and ordinary project. Some of the more important items to consider might be the following:

1. Povide natural light and views to the outside at all corridors, elevator lobbies, and stair whenever possible.
2. Design circulation spaces, lounges, and community spaces to encourage casual meeting and sociability.
3. Provide visual security and surveillance of elevator lobby, front entry, and parking area.
4. Provide secure, comfortable outdoor seating areas directly accessible from the building with views out to the community.
5. Avoid placing family units in high-rise buildings.
6. Design and situate housing close to community services, and establish relationships with them to encourage interaction between housing and community.
7. For elderly housing, provide a vehicular drop-off and a covered front-entrance.
8. Units should be designed with furnishability in mind.
9. Community rooms and public community-spaces within housing should be programmed and designed with flexibility for future and varied uses in mind.
10. In larger housing projects, residential units should be broken into clusters to scale down the overall project.
11. Use colors to differentiate areas and add variety to interiors.

Because a new construction solution establishes as much building area as is needed for a specific program, it will usually have smaller-sized spaces than a rehabilitation project. However, it will be easier to control costs and to predetermine those costs in a new construction project than in a rehab. A rehabilitation project encounters many unforeseen conditions during construction. A 5-10 percent cost contingency should be carried in a rehabilitation project if possible. Rehabilitation work is generally better performed by a patient contractor experienced in that type of work. There is some question as to whether the public bid-process is suitable for rehabilitation. A system that allows the pre-qualification of contractors and a negotiated maximum price is a better way to execute rehabilitation projects.

Two recent projects illustrate some of the situations encountered in designing new construction and rehabilitation projects in housing.

Woodbourne Housing for the Elderly, Jamaica Plain, Boston, Massachusetts

New construction housing under the HUD 202 program. Nonprofit developer: Woodbourne Community Housing Corporation. Seventy-five units in three buildings on three adjacent sites. $2.2 million. Completed in 1979.

The site contained six vacant apartment buildings on three adjacent sites. Existing buildings were three-and-a-half story masonry bearing wall and wood frame built at the turn of the century and containing large three and four bedroom units. The buildings almost totally covered the sites so that there could be no off-street parking spaces. The first floors of these buildings started a half story up from the grade and were entered directly from the sidewalk, making it difficult to provide access for the handicapped. Building analysis indicated that the masonry-bearing walls, while in good condition, limited the flexibility for converting the three and four-bedroom units into one and two-bedroom elderly units. Cost analysis showed that rehabilitation of the structures would not be more economical than new construction. Because the buildings were blighted and had been a symbol to the community of deterioration, there was strong community sentiment for a new building that could be designed to community specifications. From numerous neighborhood meetings, it was ascertained that the new buildings should be pitched roof and low rise, have brick exteriors, off-street parking, and relate to the residential setting behind them rather than the four-lane artery they fronted. The neighborhood insisted that all three sites be developed and contain housing. No site was to be used only for parking.

This was a situation that only a new-construction approach could satisfy. The added cost of building three separate buildings instead of one put pressure on the construction budget. After several alternatives had been examined, it was found that designing two simple wood-framed walk-up buildings, each containing four identical townhouse units would be an economy. The remaining sixty-seven units were put into a steel-framed and masonry elevator building that stepped up from three to four stories and contained all the common-community spaces. A multi-purpose community room that could accommodate a meals program and neighborhood meetings and activities was provided along with a game room, health office, administrative office, and laundromat. The ground floor was designed as an interior street along which these spaces were threaded

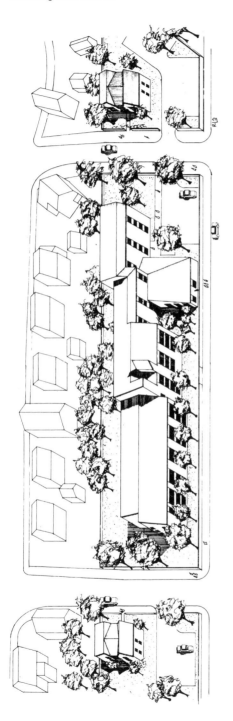

Woodbourne Housing **For The Elderly**

Jamaica Plain, Boston, Massachusetts
Greater Boston Community Development Inc. Boston, Mass.
HUD PROJECT NUMBER 023-EH-012 / MA06-1155-202

Architects & Planners

Chia-Ming Sze Architect Inc.
Cambridge, Massachusetts

Figure 7-1. Woodbourne Housing for the Elderly

Source: Chia-Ming Sze Architect, Inc. Cambridge, Mass.

and which also contained numerous lounge areas and access to outdoor court-
yards, terraces, and a garden area for residents. The interior street connected all
three sites.

Tapley School Housing for the Elderly, Danvers, Massachusetts

Adaptive reuse and new-construction addition. Forty units, $1.4 million. Dan-
vers Housing Authority and Massachusetts Department of Community Affairs.
It was completed in 1981.

An historic eight-room elementary-school building constructed in 1896 was
selected for conversion to elderly housing. The building was a distinctive neighborhood landmark and there was strong sentiment for preservation. The existing
building was found to be in good structural condition except for the large center-
portion, which had been used on each floor as a gymnasium area and was de-
flecting there. The building contained a large attic-area with huge heavy-timber
trusses. Spatial analysis showed that the existing building could accommodate
only twenty-six units out of the housing authority's state allotment of forty
units. The first floor of the school was a half story above grade and entered by
large interior stairs.

The design solution placed a simple addition containing sixteen units on
the existing structure. The addition was designed to be as straightforward as
possible so as not to compete in stature with the distinguished existing building
and to realize per-unit cost savings, which could be transferred to the complicated existing building. In the existing building, the basement floor was raised
two feet to give units there a better view to the outside. The existing attic-
trusses were adapted to allow for four dormered units. The center of the existing building, which was structurally unsound and could not accommodate
apartment units, was removed to create a four-story, skylighted, central com-
munity-space at the heart of the building. The building is entered under the link
of the new addition at grade where handicapped access could be accommodated.

The apartment units in the existing building are larger and more unique than
those designed in the new addition. Building costs for the existing building were
significantly higher than those for the new addition. However, a neighborhood
landmark was preserved. The funding for the project was the result of a state
policy encouraging the preservation of existing outdated community-buildings.

It should be clear that in the design and production of housing, both rehabilitation and new construction are viable routes to take. The question then
is not whether one approach is better than the other, but rather which is more
suited for a specific situation. The end goal is to produce more and better housing to meet a critical nationwide shortage.

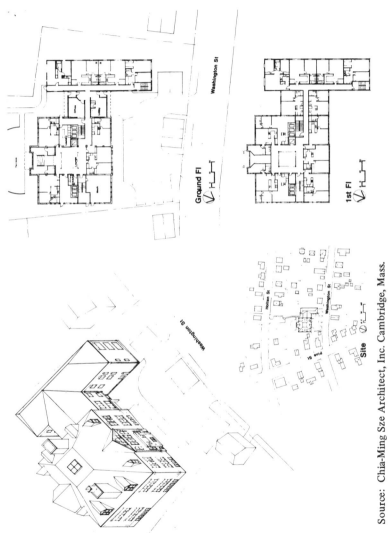

Source: Chia-Ming Sze Architect, Inc. Cambridge, Mass.

Figure 7-2. Tapley School Elderly Housing (Site, Ground, and First Floor)

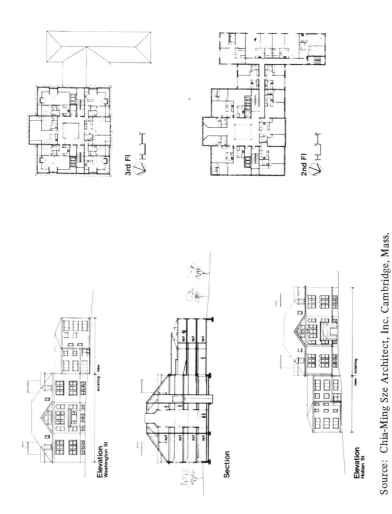

Source: Chia-Ming Sze Architect, Inc. Cambridge, Mass.

Figure 7-3. Tapley School Elderly Housing (Elevations, Section and Second and Third Floors)

References and Additional Resources

Cantacuzino, S. 1975. *New Uses for Old Buildings.* New York: Watson-Guptill Publications.

Green, I.; Fedewa, B.; Johnston, C.; Jackson, M.; Deardorff, H. 1975. *Housing for the Elderly, The Development and Design Process.* New York: Van Nostrand-Reinhold Co.

Kirschemann, J.C., and Muschalek, C. 1980. *Residential Districts.* New York: Whitney Library of Design.

Macsai, J.; Holland, E.; Nachman, H.; Yacker, J. 1976. *Housing.* New York: John Wiley & Sons.

Massachusetts Department of Community Affairs. 1977. *Build to Last.* Washington, D.C.: The Preservation Press.

National Trust for Historic Preservation. 1976. *Economic Benefits of Preserving Old Buildings.* Washington, D.C.: The Preservation Press.

Schmertz, M.F. 1981. *Apartments, Townhouses and Condominiums,* 3rd edition. New York: Architectural Record Book, McGraw-Hill Book Co.

Urban Land Institute. 1979. *Economic Analyses of Adaptive Use Projects.* Information Series.

Zeisel Research; Epp, G.; and Demos, S. 1978. *Low Rise Housing for Older People,* 023-000-00434-8. Washington, D.C.: Government Printing Office.

8

Nonprofit Housing for the Elderly: A Primer for Sponsors

James N. Broder

One of the clear developmental implications of the aging-process is the need to assume that a tenant coming into a building while still very physically active will be less able to handle his physical environment as time passes. He will need more support services. Therefore, a building must be designed not only for a tenant who is seventy today, but for that tenant when he is eighty and older. Well-planned congregate housing will continue to meet the needs of an increasingly frail elder within the facility and thereby delay or eliminate the need for traumatic moves.

Well-designed elderly housing can increase healthy lifespans. Because of social involvement, emotional and physical security, and the services that can be provided, people occupying such housing tend not to deteriorate in many of the ways associated with aging. Residents of such housing tend to live more active, healthier lives and require less institutionalization. These considerations have important design-implications.

If a sponsor intends to serve elders who are physically able to live independently, the expense of a congregate-dining room may not be necessary. If the sponsor hopes to serve a broad range of older people, a congregate-dining facility should be designed into the building. If the proposed facility is physically related to an institution such as a nursing home or a campus-type environment where many different levels of care are colocated, a sponsor may be able to limit services in one building while providing them in another. The very complex process of developing housing for the elderly can be conceptually simple if one focuses on the people to be served. Assume that in ten years today's tenants will still be tenants. A sponsor must foresee their needs.

One must also consider that the elderly of today, both demographically and educationally, are not the elderly of tomorrow. The elderly of tomorrow will be primarily American-born and English-speaking, and well educated in relation to their counterparts today. Consequently, the kinds of services provided today, such as ceramics and Bingo, may be inadequate in ten years. Programs for the future may include computer terminals for tenants to learn history and French and other continuing education programs. A sponsor must consider, during the design process, the kind of elderly it wishes to serve in the community of the future. One must design a physical structure with the flexibility to provide the services needed now and contemplated in the future. This problem is often manifested during the mortgage-processing stage of development.

If a development team indicates that the common dining room will cost $100,000, putting the project over budget, and suggests that the dining room be dropped, the situation should be considered carefully. How long can it be postponed? Future construction will be complex and even more expensive. That is why it is critical, before entering the design process is begun, to know what is wanted: what is important, what can be tolerated and what can be forgone. There may be a mortgage on this building for forty years. The decisions that are made— whether to cut $20,000 or $30,000 or $50,000, or whether to take an element out or leave it in—should not be looked at from a narrow perspective. The sponsor should know what it wants, what it is willing to fight for, and how it is willing to structure its whole effort to obtain its goal.

Assessing the Need

The best indication of need may grow out of involvement in the community, the perception of the local needs, and the goals of the organization. Objective criteria are used to prove this need to whomever will provide financing.

First, it is necessary to look at existing facilities within the community. Is there a facility such as one funded under the HUD Section 236 program that primarily serves the elderly, or a public-housing facility that has no congregate social-service facilities? Is there a need for sheltered congregate-housing or for independent housing? If there is an existing facility with a long waiting list, it is best to note when that list was updated last. The sponsor can also make some design decisions from a survey of existing facilities. Sometimes efficiency apartments in rural areas will stand vacant, even when there is strong demand for other larger units. Occasionally one hears of elderly who are afraid to use elevators and are afraid of a high-rise building. While this is an often-expressed sentiment, it is not likely to present a marketing problem. In any elderly building that is over one story there should be an elevator—stairs can be an insurmountable barrier.

It is also important to look at a needs assessment. This is performed by most local governments as a matter of course under HUD's Community Development Block Grant program, a revenue-sharing program to urban counties and cities. As a condition for receiving assistance, communities must submit a Housing Assistance Plan (HAP) to HUD. The HAP sets forth a survey of existing housing conditions. It indicates how many people are underhoused, how many people live without plumbing, and where people needing assistance live. The HAP is reviewed annually and completely updated every three years.

If the HAP shows that demand for the specific proposal is not reflected in the goals or locational preference, it is time to begin the process of amendment. The best site in town and a HAP calling for one thousand units of elderly housing, will mean nothing if the HAP shows that assisted housing may only be built in the west end of town and the selected site is in the east end. The project will not be approved unless the HAP is changed. The sponsor should approach elected officials and explain what it wishes to do and why. Then it must do its best to make sure that goal is reflected in everything the community does with respect to community development and to housing. It may be critical to build a political constituency as early as possible in the process. There can be nothing worse for a sponsor than a politician ignored, but nothing better than one who can claim credit for a project.

Two local mechanisms are most often used to prevent developments: zoning and taxes. In a zoning matter, a project can be turned down without the true reasons ever having to appear on the record. The project may ostensibly be rejected because it is too tall or may overburden public facilities. Any number of planning excuses can be raised that actually mean a community does not want federally assisted housing. The other obstacle is tax abatement, since a tax-exempt organization may be taking land off the tax rolls. Possibly a payment in lieu of taxes can be negotiated and fit into the project budget. Rarely can a project afford full taxes. Rarely can you go through the whole development process without going to the community for some special request or concession.

Organizational Structure

The ways to organize are as many and varied as the organizations that sponsor housing. The sponsor does not necessarily need a developer or an architect to direct the project. It is more important to have leadership willing to spend an enormous amount of voluntary time and effort for the three-to-five years from concept to the time the doors are opened. The problems will range from finding a site and obtaining zoning to coping with 1,000 applications for 100 units. The more educated the leadership is to the risks and to the process itself, and the more the board has an idea of what it wants at the outset, the easier the process will be.

It is a good idea to formally incorporate a subsidiary on the specific project. It gives the members of that board a sense of belonging to something with a very specific mission. The next step is to apply for a tax exemption under 501(c)(3) of the Internal Revenue Code, creating an entity that can receive tax-deductible donations, bequests and endowments. Consideration must be given to the creation of a membership organization where, in lieu of stockholders, the corporation has members. Elected from that group is a board, with diversified talents. Each member pays dues, providing some seed-money. A staff is not needed in the early stages, since the staff of the parent organization, or consultants, can generally provide whatever support is needed.

Selection of Development Team

One of the greatest risks of the development process is that the finished project will not generate enough rental income to cover the expenses of the building. In the past, that has been the downfall of assisted housing, primarily because, under the Section 236 program, the subsidy was based on the mortgage and not on the rent. After 1974, when sponsors could not raise rents fast enough to keep up with utility bills, project after project went into default. Under the Section 202/8 program, or any project assisted by Section 8 rent subsidies, when rents are set properly at the initial stage of processing, and when automatic subsidy increases reflecting the utility and tax increases in the market area are provided, the danger of default is minimized.

The Section 202/8 program is unique. Normally, under Section 8, rents are determined on comparability. Comparability means determination of rent levels in similar existing projects in the area, insuring that the proposed project is not out of line with the rents tenants are paying in a comparable market rate building. Under Section 202/8 the determination is totally different; the rent is based on the debt service and the approved operating-cost, within the fair-market rent limit.

With these aspects in mind, a basic development team consisting of the consultant, financing team, architect, attorney, contractor and management agent must be chosen. There is one criterion for selection that is overriding—experience.

The consultant, in the nonprofit context, is the developer. This is the person who interfaces with the sponsor and the other members of the development team. He assists in the selection of the other development team members and in structuring the entire project.

Because the Section 202/8 program provides a direct loan from the government, the financing team is HUD. In the profit sector there might be a limited partnership with limited partners as investors in the project. The participation of bankers and counsel for various parties would also be required.

The architect designs the structure and supervises the construction. He must also work closely with HUD to negotiate acceptable amenities and with the contractor on pricing. The attorney will perform a wide variety of services including zoning, title, corporate work, tax matters and the closing of the HUD loan. Under the 202 context, the builder is really a construction manager. He is not a developer and does not work for an interest in the building. He simply receives a fee for doing his job.

Let the for-profit developers, who stand to make money, train people. Most nonprofits are not in the business of venturing risk capital. They are in the business of providing a service for people. It is incumbent upon you to reduce your risk as much as possible. The best way to reduce your risk is to get a proven product, and experienced employees.

Each one of the team members has a role to play in the process. The decisions made during the development process will establish how successful operations are, how good a building there is, and what kind of maintenance problems will be encountered in the future.

The Development Consultant

The best indicator for the success of a development consultant is the percentage of his projects that have actually been built. In addition, of the ones built, how many required significant sponsor contribution and how many were built with a minimum sponsor contribution?

It is important to have a consultant who is independent of the architect and builder. Though in some cases the project attorney provides consulting services, it is sometimes difficult to distinguish between the consultant who negotiates the contract and the lawyer who writes it. The consultant's role is to lead the development team.

In reviewing a consultant's HUD experience, examine previous participation certificates (FHA Form 2530). There are no standards set by HUD for who may act as a consultant. Check with the HUD offices in the specific jurisdiction for a reference. A consultant should not be afraid, however, after having done a project with a particular HUD office, to have that HUD office never want to work with him again. It is the development consultant's responsibility to be the irritant. He is going to anger the architect when he has to cut the design; he will anger the builder when he has to cut costs; and he will anger the sponsors when he says they cannot afford to include special amenities. He must be willing to antagonize everyone.

The Architect

Do not retain a firm or individual with no previous experience in elderly-housing development. For a HUD project an architectural firm should be willing, and of the size and capacity to financially carry the project work and expense until such time as the HUD mortgage-closing occurs and the fees are paid. A real concern for the elderly and their housing needs should be evidenced. Some firms have made a dedicated commitment to work in this area. On the other hand, there is a caution, something known as an FHA architect. This is the firm that designs the box that HUD wants and never takes a risk. Every building he does is accepted quickly, but there is little concern for the special needs of the tenants.

The architect should be willing to carry some of the risk. Unfortunately, most groups developing assisted housing do not have the cash to carry the project on a daily basis. Consequently, the professionals wind up bearing some of the risk. Architects who do not have the capacity to bear that risk should not enter the field.

Of course, not all projects involve government subsidies. A sponsor with substantial assets or income, or a plan where middle-to-upper-income residents can contribute capital in some way, or support from a foundation or financing source, may make the development process more predictable and controllable.

The Builder

The process of selecting a builder is determined by his position on the development team. Generally, projects are developed on a negotiated basis, meaning the design process includes a pricing component at each step, rather than a bid process when plans are complete. A builder might be paid for his estimates and early input, and then allowed to bid against other qualified builders to help assure the lowest cost.

The telling factor in a no-bid situation is how early in the process a builder will commit himself to a firm price, how firm that commitment is, and how long he will hold the price.

The Manager

Many nonprofit organizations self-manage, or build into their organizational structure a management entity. Others manage by hiring an outside management-agent. There are management resources, that can provide training for the organization's own staff. The manager should be consulted during the development process and be made part of the development team to assure that the building design works well from a program standpoint.

Site Control

A sponsor should consider several, often overlooked, technical areas in site selection. When selecting a site, a sponsor should first examine the title to the property to make sure there are no restrictive covenants preventing the site from being used for elderly housing or limiting the scope of development. Then the property should be examined in relation to the standards set by the agency financing the project. It is necessary to examine the price of the land in relation to the overall cost of the project. Under most circumstances the option must extend long enough to allow time to go through the entire processing period before closing. This period can be up to two years.

Sponsors can benefit from public agency participation in Section 202/8 housing proposals through the reuse of land inventory not otherwise in demand. This can assist agencies in meeting basic urban-renewal goals including the re-population of downtown areas and the alleviation of relocation demands by dis-placed persons.

Option agreements, board resolutions designating a nonprofit corporation as developer of a reuse parcel, or simple letters of intent from urban renewal authorities are proven site-control mechanisms. One public body made such a parcel generally available to all qualified applicants, binding itself to convey the parcel to the successful applicant chosen by HUD. At least in theory, a public body could hold a competition among potential redevelopers and, upon selec-tion, place full support behind such an application for ultimate selection by HUD.

In providing land to nonprofit sponsors, public bodies should consider two significant constraints, time and money. HUD advertises for proposals from non-profit sponsors for Section 202/8 fund reservations once each fiscal year. The application period is approximately ninety days. Allocations of funding are made on a fair-share basis in conformance with Section 213(d) of the Housing and Community Development Act of 1974. However, allocation areas within HUD area-office jurisdictions are often aggregated in order to provide at least one viable project; thus, funding availability and priorities shift from fiscal year to fiscal year. Potential sponsors tend to wait until allocation areas are announced before beginning the search for appropriate sites. Consequently, the speed in which legally sufficient site-control can be obtained becomes a critical matter. Several states, such as Oklahoma, have provisions of law that allow ex-pedited, negotiated sales or urban renewal reuse parcels to nonprofit corpora-tions. Other states, such as Iowa, demand time-consuming, expensive, and cumbersome public notice and competitive-bidding procedures. Moreover, po-tential nonprofit sponsors, primarily religious, community, fraternal or labor groups, do not have risk capital available to pay the large deposits often re-quired. Waivers of this requirements are often sought and often granted.

There are also opportunities for creativity on the part of public bodies. The use of air-rights over city or agency-owned property is such an example. Air-rights above land owned by parking authorities in center-city areas, even when encumbered by bonded indebtedness, have been successfully utilized in Miami Beach, Florida, resulting in two 126-unit structures above two parking lots along Collins Avenue. Each site is under one-half acre in size. In addition to providing much needed low-income housing in an especially needy area, the parking lot, with the exception of several spaces now being used for building supports, re-mains committed to its intended use. In addition, the city is receiving substantial revenue in the form of annual air-rights rent. The purchase of air-rights in fee simple has also been approved for Section 202/8. However, both leases and fee purchases can present difficult appraisal problems.

Figure 8-1. Council Towers: Air Rights 202/8 Project Developed over a City-Owned Parking Lot

In making urban-renewal sites available to nonprofit sponsors, public bodies often must bear the burden of obtaining planning approval, rezoning, alley closings, street dedications or releases, and relocation. However, this process gives public agencies the opportunity to impact on design decisions. In one instance, the city of Chicago made a portion of a former tuberculosis-sanitorium site available to a nonprofit sponsor by lease at nominal rent. It coordinated this development effort with a new senior center and a broad range of service programs.

Risk Factors

The financial requirements of developing housing for the elderly should be examined in relation to risk. The period of greatest risk is prior to initial approval. The second period of risk is from initial approval to construction start. The third period of risk is during construction.

During the riskiest stage, prior to initial approval, the sponsor must obtain site control. This cost is as variable as the market condition. As soon as word gets out that someone is proposing a federal project on a parcel of land, the price tends to triple. There must be discretion. Rezoning may be required in this initial stage and the sponsor will have to retain an architect to provide certain design studies. Another expense prior to initial approval may be the development-consultant fee.

Once initial approval on a HUD project has been received, a sponsor has eighteen months in which to begin construction. This eighteen-month period includes completion of design development, definition of management requirements, the completion of final plans and specifications, a construction contract, clear title, and final zoning changes. The difference between expenses in the first and second stages is that many second-stage expenses will be repaid out of mortgage proceeds. For a typical project of 150 units it is ideal to have seed money of $100,000 available. There are many ways to raise this money most of which do not involve a sponsor committing its own resources. HUD has a seed-money loan program used in conjunction with Section 202/8 financing that provides sponsors with up to $50,000 interest free.

Architects generally require some compensation during the stage prior to construction, although some architects will wait until construction commences and look only to HUD for their fees. The HUD seed-money loan program provides funding for a maximum of 25 percent of the design fee. Typically, the architect receives approximately $25,000 to $40,000 in seed money. Site engineering, including surveys and soil borings, will also be required at a cost of between $5,000 and $7,000. The sponsor will also incur development-consultant and legal expenses during this period. Most, if not all, of these expenses are recoverable during this period from loan proceeds. One of the responsibilities of the consultant is to make sure that monies expended from that seed-money loan are in fact recoverable. Before the sponsor expends funds, he should check with the development consultant, who should monitor the project's cash flow carefully.

Construction

The biggest risk to the sponsor is that the builder may not build the project for the contract price. Under the Section 202/8 program there are several built-in protections. The construction contract the sponsor signs with the builder is based on the cost of construction plus a fixed fee up to an upset limit. If the builder has not performed well in estimating the project cost and if he stands the chance of losing a great deal of money, he might default. A payment-and-performance bond is required to cover such a contingency. The bond does not, however, cover cost overruns caused by omissions in the drawings, bad drawings, misapplication of the building code or changes that are made voluntarily. The best protection against such cost overruns is the competence of each member of the development team. An architect who has designed and supervised HUD projects before, with a record of minimal cost over-runs, is vital. Another protection is sufficient errors-and-omissions insurance coverage on the part of the architect to insure against possible loss. Another source, under Section 202/8, is the 3 percent contingency-allowance in the project budget. In a new construction project, HUD allows 3 percent above the development cost for contingencies. If, in fact, this 3 percent is used for cost overruns, there will not be funds for furnishings in the building. If cost overruns were caused by substantial errors in HUD processing, substantial changes in conditions, inflation, intervening laws, or even a strike, HUD might grant a mortgage increase.

Conclusion

As the proportion of elderly in the population increases, the federal commitment to housing for the elderly is decreasing. In the face of such shrinking resources, it is incumbent upon government and sponsors alike to develop cost-efficient proposals to serve the greatest number of elderly constituents. However, this need for economies must be tempered by a level of quality that creates appropriate environments for the elderly.

There is no clear consensus on what that appropriate level should be. The sponsor can assist in developing such a consensus through dedication to serving the needs of the elderly with a clear understanding of the risks and limitations attendant on the process of meeting their housing and service needs.

Part III:
Design Issues

It is often shown that the construction cost of a building is miniscule when compared with the cost to maintain a building over its life. The cost of poor design in human terms is much more difficult to compute. Elder people tend to stay at home more due several factors. This increases the importance of the internal environment of sheltered or congregate housing. Designing the micro-environment, down to hardware, is often the last consideration in development, but, over time, may be the most significant aspect in terms of resident comfort.

The Congregate-Housing Model: Integrating Facilities and Services

Thomas O. Byerts

A clear need exists for better integration of housing and service programs designed to prevent the unnecessary and premature institutionalization of growing numbers of frail, older people. The recent support for model congregate-housing/service programs by the Department of Housing and Urban Development (HUD) and the Farmers Home Administration (FmHA) of the Department of Agriculture (following the lead of the private sector) should go much further to match the demand for both quality and quantity of housing with integrated services for those who would benefit from age-segregated, assisted, group living. Longitudinal research and European examples suggest innovative directions for the improvement and selective implementation of congregate-living arrangements as an important response to the frail elderly who must move from their own homes but do not require institutionalization.

Housing can become a particularly acute problem as people grow frail and have to choose between remaining in their home, moving in with relatives, or seeking new living arrangements and/or necessary services that may be scattered throughout the community. If there is a loss of spouse or onset of physical conditions requiring environmental modification, assistance, or relocation, major sets of personal and social issues and stresses are raised. Therefore attention in this chapter is focused on expanding the spectrum of choice for the vulnerable elderly who constitute a significant and growing group in the community.

At the same time, some of the older group-housing settings (nonprofit-sponsored housing, public housing and retirement hotels) are experiencing the aging of their building along with the mass aging of their residents. Coupled with this is the concommitant rise in the need for selective intervention of services, and the adaptable environments that can be provided in the congregate settings are alternatives to the threat of relocation to an institution.

In addition to critical social-policy and housing-production issues, the inhibiting or facilitating role played by the physical environment in aging is often overlooked. This continues although researchers and advanced practitioners recognize the increasing influence the physical environment has with advancing age and disability. Therefore, particular emphasis is focused on this important aspect of housing designed for the aging process—recognition of the environmental conditions of aging and changing over time. Selected issues, including attention to a more flexible approach to the design of housing environments and related services, are discussed and alternatives suggested. A case for

127

further research, continued exchange of ideas, and expanded support for programs that link housing and services is made in this chapter.

Background

Industrial societies are beginning to fully realize the dramatic growth taking place in both the number and percentage of their older populations. The United States is moving toward the more mature-population pyramids of the European countries. The past population figures and projections for the United States, for instance, are dramatic. Based on federal government statistics for 1979 (U.S. Department of Health and Human Services 1980), the elderly population rises from 3 million (or 4.1 percent of the total population) over sixty-five years of age in 1900, to 24 million in 1978 (or 11 percent) to a projected 32 million (of 12.1 to 12.9 percent) in 2000. Stated another way, over 4900 people reach the age of sixty-five daily in this country, while some 3300 die each day. This produces a net daily gain of over 1600 new older people or approximately 550,000 people turning sixty-five years of age each year.

The field of gerontology is progressing in knowledge and sophistication. Social scientists are exploring the similarities and differences of the preretired, the young-old (generally sixty-five to seventy-five) and the old-old (generally over seventy-five). The great diversity of the older population is being fully recognized and research on the parameters of normal aging (as opposed to the past emphasis on disease and problem states) is beginning to bring forth new views about the great capacity for life possessed by so many older people.

The old-old is the fastest growing segment of our population. It has grown to 2.6 percent in 1976 and is projected to more than double to 5.9 percent by 2020 (U.S. Bureau of the Census 1979). This group is considered to be the most vulnerable. It consumes the largest per-capita share of health-care services and represents the highest percentages of widows, economically disadvantaged, transportation-dependent, and poorly housed older people. Congregate housing is a key alternative that can be applied in an expanded way to support many of these people in semi-independent group-housing environments linked to the community.

Dr. Bernice Neugarten (1968) who coined the terms "young-old" and "old-old" stressed functional age and not chronological age, though many fit the pattern of increased dependency and reduced function with advancing age.

It should be underscored that most (over 80 percent) older people in the United States are coping well, living independently in the community in their own homes or apartments. Another 3 percent of the elderly population live in planned-housing facilities for the elderly. These places range from fully independent housing to boarding homes, and from single buildings to retirement villages. Others, particularly those with family or access to special services, can remain longer in the community during their later years. However, about 5 percent of the over-sixty-five population, or over 1 million people, live in health-care institutions. While this figure runs contrary to the stereotype of most old people as sick and frail, one out of four older persons can expect to spend some time in long-term care institutions and many will remain in such facilities for long periods of time. Others could move back into the community from institutions if appropriate environments were available.

In a major international study, Shanas et al. (1968), found that 6 percent of the sample were housebound and 2 percent bedfast in the United States. Data from Denmark showed 8 percent housebound and 2 percent bedfast, while data from Britain showed 11 percent housebound and 3 percent bedfast. Additional attention to supporting those living at home or developing new living arrangements and improving neighborhood services could expand this population and prevent premature and costly institutionalization.

In one of the few longitudinal studies comparing movers versus nonmovers to a new public-housing facility for the elderly (with some services), Carp (1975) found that 38 percent of the movers and 26 percent of the nonmovers reported major problems with housing prior to the move. Complaints from those who moved into the new facility declined to zero. Meanwhile, the nonmovers experienced expanding problems with their housing. An eight-year follow-up demonstrated that the complaints of the control group (nonmovers) had clearly surpassed the baseline level of complaints raised by the original movers. In addition, Carp (1977a) found a 40 percent higher rate of organizational membership, a 33 percent increase in the number of close friends as well as substantial increases in morale and life expectancy among the in-movers as compared with community controls.

However, a one-year study (Lawton 1976) comparing two service-intensive Section 202 housing-projects for the elderly, and three typical Section 202 housing-projects for the elderly with few services, found mixed results. Residents in the service-oriented environments became more facility bound than those in fully independent housing, though the experimental group scored higher on morale, housing satisfaction and social-network dimensions than their counterparts living in typical housing for independent elderly.

The Physical Environment

Environments and aging, an emerging area of study, is concerned with the impact that the social, psychological, and physical dimensions of the environment have on older people. Perceived in isolation or viewed in ecological interdependence with the personal and suprapersonal context of a place, the physical environment can have a strong and even pervasive influence on the behavior of people of all ages. However, according to the Environmental Docility Hypothesis, advanced by Lawton and Simon (1967), as people become less competent through aging, illness, or accident, environmental factors have an increasingly greater impact on their behavior.

Decreased competence can accrue from the (gradual or sudden) accumulation of various combinations of sensory decrements: mobility reduction, loss of stamina, reduced social options, deteriorating health conditions, concerns about security and safety, and lack of motivation. These generally age-related changes represent passages through various life stages and are not necessarily negative. Many conditions develop gradually and adjustments are made successfully by the individual, the formal-service system, and the informal network. However, these adjustments often are made at some cost to the individual, consume more energy, and require greater reliance on outside factors or people.

A major and often overlooked factor affecting the ability to remain in independent living is the design of the dwelling unit itself. Interventions such as additional lever handles to tub/shower controls, removal of raised thresholds in doorways, or increased security lighting can extend individual independence and safety (Byerts 1979). Direct access to shopping and on-site services can permit the frail to remain longer in their housing (Regnier forthcoming), though institutions begin to develop as more and more services are available in the building.

Physical environments can be more or less supportive depending on how well the capabilities of the individual either fit or mismatch with the demands of each particular place. Creative use of new ecological approaches and expanded support of man-environment research are beginning to demonstrate from the micro scale (for example, furniture, room layout, and lighting) to the macro scale (for example, building form, site development and community services), how the physical environment shapes or reinforces levels of behavioral independence for various kinds of older people.

A new wave of educators and designers interested in working with social and health-service providers is more clearly articulating user needs, developing master plans, programming facilities, designing buildings and conducting post-occupancy evaluation (see Byerts 1977 for examples). However, these cases are exceptions and a great deal more needs to be done for this new wave to penetrate fully into the mainstream of professional practice.

Design for the elderly and handicapped can be a life-and-death stituation where death can happen as suddenly as a fall in the bathtub or as slowly as a decade of neighborhood decline, family neglect, and personal apathy. Behaviorally oriented planning is not just applicable to new buildings, but the results of remodelling or renovation should be made responsive to the full range of human needs.

Housing for the Elderly

When informal or formal support-systems cannot meet the needs of an older person in the community, a move to a more secure, service-supported environment may be considered. A sufficient number of appropriate alternatives and affordable settings linked into the life of the community must be provided. In addition, steps should be taken to minimize the trauma of relocation. The seriousness of this trauma generally increases as competence, autonomy and involvement in the decision making process is reduced (Pastalan 1973).

Some sponsors of housing organize a variety of alternative environments or levels of care on a single site. These campus settings or retirement villages often feature a full range of choices from small cottages to nursing-home rooms. These arrangements permit the aging individual to move from one level to another and back as health conditions change, while remaining within the same management/sponsorship pattern and social network.

A more common approach to purpose-built housing for older people is the development of single, age-segregated buildings. These environments include: elderly housing (age-segregated apartments for independent older people), congregate housing (all or some meals provided centrally plus various combinations of integrated recreational, social and health services are available in the facility), cooperative (occupants purchase shares in the corporation that owns and manages the facility), communal (share of public spaces and group decision making), retirement hotels (privately owned hotels with single rooms and central meal-plans), and public or private rest homes (where meals, recreation and personal care are provided, though residents are usually more frail and privacy/autonomy is reduced). An expanded discussion of housing options from the British perspective can be found in Madge (1969).

Focus on Congregate Housing

Congregate Housing, broadly defined as service-integrated group living, is an expanding option emerging between independent housing, living with relatives/ friends, and institutions. Lawton (1980) reports that the term was derived from one of three dimensions Kleemeier used to define the institutional character of the environment in which all residents do the same thing at the same time. Lawton further defines congregate housing as "having the single necessary characteristics of central kitchen and meal service, but in addition, it may optionally provide space for other social, housekeeping, and personal care services." This model will not meet the needs of everyone, but it can extend independence for those who need some structure and would benefit from group living. While demand for services in congregate housing may be low at first, need for services will increase with the aging of the population (Carp 1977b).

Various examples of congregate housing have been initiated in the private sector (both nonprofit and proprietary); they include converted hotels or housing with a set of services developed after occupancy or through agreements with other human-services agencies. However, only recently (1978–1980) have the HUD and FmHA begun to develop model congregate-programs. Formerly, HUD and FmHA viewed their role as one of housing finance and production with sponsors or other agencies responsible for service as necessary. Some softening of this position has occurred progressively since more amenities and space for service delivery and in-house activity have been permitted than before. More recently, the FmHA began a series of small (twenty-four unit) model-congregate projects located in small towns. HUD funded five-year service packages in conjunction with selected new Section 202 construction.

Service-intensive congregate-housing innovation was slow to develop in this country. This was due, in large part, to the categorical separation of housing, health, and social-service programs at all levels of government. Historically, many European countries combine these services and entitlements more closely. This combination produces a more integrated approach servicing a larger segment of the aging population in a more coordinated manner than does dealing with the independent in housing settings and the dependent in health-oriented institutions.

Thompson estimates that over 500,000 people are on waiting lists for planned housing for the elderly in the United States (Donahue, Thompson and Curren 1977). Further, the Urban Institute (U.S. Congress 1974) estimates that as many as 1,100,000 of the 23-million older people in this country would benefit from congregate housing with its integral services.

While age-segregated congregate-housing for the elderly should not be the only model proposed, significant unmet demand exists. Few who make the move express dissatisfaction, and fewer yet willingly move out. Nevertheless, new and traditional models of age-integrated as well as age-segregated living arrangements should be explored along with new models of community supports. In the long run, the maturing of society may lead to a restructuring that could, it is hoped, reduce the number of elderly impelled to seek age-segregated living arrangements.

Current problems will persist and could worsen unless comprehensive changes are tested and implemented. Further, because of projected individual variations and changing group characteristics (increasing education levels, better health, higher expectations, and so forth) the typical architectural tradeoff questions (for example, highrise versus lowrise, large versus small, traditional versus contemporary style, age-segregated versus age-integrated buildings or sites) have less importance at the extremes than how well each model is articulated and whether there are enough decent choices available to meet the demand.

Major Concerns

Four of the major concepts of concern to the growing interest in congregate housing are summarized below. A key reference is included after each point for further study.

> Housing should be conceived of as a service and planned as part of a comprehensive service-package tailored to the needs of today's residents, with flexibility for future individual or cohort changes (Carp 1977a).

The physical environment, in concert with the rest of the service package, should be responsive to an appropriate range of individual and collective group-differences as well as to the changing mix of abilities and aspirations of the users (Kahana, Felton and Fairchild, 1976).

Residents should be encouraged to utilize the physical and social environment outside as well as inside the facility where sufficient, appropriately located spaces should be provided to accommodate current and projected on-site service and activity programs (Lawton 1977).

Management should select new tenants in an attempt to maintain a stable population compatible with the fixed goals of the facility, or the program/ physical plant must adapt to accommodate the mass aging of the resident population and the potential inability to attract more active and independent residents (Lawton, Greenbaum and Liebowitz 1980).

A major accomplishment, particularly vital to the congregate-housing movement, is the demonstration to decision makers, consumers and professionals, that sensitive planning, adaptable physical plant, and a mix of appropriate and integrated services do make a difference and are cost effective.

Design Approach

Five major environmental attributes are proposed for consideration when developing or evaluating settings for the aging. These are legibility, accessibility, usability, adaptability, and choice/challenge/change. They are particularly relevant to congregate housing with its emphasis on assisting the aging to remain in the residential environment. Successful resolution of each of these should contribute to an enriched environment that can respond to changing needs and enhance the integration of vital services in housing for the aged. In addition, other planning and design issues are explored further in Gelwicks and Newcomer (1974), Green et al. (1976), Howell (1980), and Zeisel, Epp and Demos (1977).

A brief presentation of the five environmental attributes follows. An extended discussion of these issues, including illustrated examples, appears in Byerts, 1979. A key reference is included after each point for further study.

Legibility

Legibility is the ability of the environment to communicate a sense of place and to reinforce messages of orientation and direction. Legible environments can be achieved in a variety of ways, so people with various combinations of sensory loss or slower reaction times will perceive the cues. Building layout,

color and texture coding, signage/graphics, interior furnishings, window treatments, and staff dress are examples of elements to be considered. Legibility
is particularly important in congregate housing, where environmental communication can help residents orient themselves without burdening other residents
or staff, which, in turn, could build feelings of dependence (DeLong 1970).

Accessibility

Disabled and frail persons have the civil right to live as normal lives as possible.
Accessibility is the capacity of people to freely and independently enter and
egress the environment, ranging from the neighborhood, to the building to
the room. Section 504 of the Rehabilitation Act of 1973 has mandated that
all programs with federal support be accessible to the elderly and handicapped.
It is interpreted that not every space in a new or rehabilitated building need
be accessible but that the *full program be accessible*. This includes telephones,
drinking fountains, bathrooms and kitchens, as well as program spaces. Building
entry for a person in a wheelchair, for an example, should not be through the
loading dock nor via a service elevator. People must be integrated with dignity
into all or certainly the more important areas of the facility to be able to access
the program.
    Architects responding to the challenges of integrated, barrier-free design
recognize new opportunities for creative design solutions. The approach
advanced by a few, particularly for new construction, is to attempt to make
all units and areas barrier-free and adjustable to the widest range or capacities
as possible. The alternative, arbitrary quotas for the handicapped, breaks down
when overlapping needs exceed demands (Jones 1978).

Usability

Linked closely with accessibility is the aspect of usability or functionality of
the environment for older people who experience various conditions or limitations. The layout and detailing of a dwelling unit must be efficient and effective
for independent operation. Functional items should be handy, efficient and
safe. The physical environment should accommodate the scale of furnishings
and quantity of goods typically brought into the unit. The circulation and
public spaces should be inviting, and should reinforce orientation and provide
opportunities for various levels of social interaction (Howell, 1980).

Adaptability

Adaptability denotes the capacity of the physical environment—architectural
features, furnishings and equipment—to be adjusted to meet changing individual
needs. Findings from design research and new technology must be applied

more broadly to better meet the range of needs of the aged. The physical environment (countertops, cabinets, lighting levels, and so on) should be designed to suit a variation in occupant size, strength, bias (right hand versus left hand or hemiplegia, and so forth) or condition (restricted reach, confined to walker, and so forth). At the larger scale, whole floors could be designed for conversion to changing levels of support, or adjacent units could be converted from two-bedroom apartments into suites or efficiencies. Incorporating broader ranges of age groups into the program could also be considered (Koncelik 1976).

Choice/Challenge/Change

In order to minimize the institutional qualities of group living, a range of appropriate choices (providing alternatives and variety), manageable challenges (stimulating various levels of ingenuity and capacity), and ongoing change (expressions of seasons and special events) should be incorporated into the environment. These attributes should provide variety and continuity with the real world. Older people should be encouraged to remain engaged in and able to influence their environment as part of a total program of involvement in life, since people of all ages are so often dominated by their environment. Staff should help residents to maintain control over the facility and its environments to the extent their capabilities allow (Gelwicks 1970).

Cost

Of course, cost is a critical issue, but it should not limit the implementation of a good program and building design. Emphasis on cheap or insensitive solutions is self-defeating. Buildings are often purchased with forty to fifty-year mortgages. Only 5–10 percent of the total cost of owning and operating a building is attributable to the construction costs. Ongoing management, insurance, taxes, energy, repair and maintenance expenses dwarf the original purchase price.

Buildings must be built with safety and security in mind and with an emphasis on enhancing the quality of life of the occupants. The frantic last-minute elimination of key amenities and quality finishes/features in order to meet a tight budget should be avoided. Good anticipatory design should not cost more and should accrue a significant savings in physical plant, efficiency, and staff function, not to mention the impact of an accommodating design on resident morale and satisfaction.

Conclusion

The formula for producing a good congregate-living environment combines a capable architect, a knowledgeable client, a thorough understanding of the intended user, knowledge of various service/building options, and a reasonable

budget. With imagination and skill, these ingredients can be brought together
to produce a building/program that will serve the needs of a variety of elderly
occupants in an effective manner, enhancing their quality of life now and
into the future for as long as possible.

Some growth in developing new knowledge and adding to the congregate-
housing stock has been made in recent years in the United States and throughout
Europe. However, in this country, progress in both areas falls far short of recommendations made during the 1971 White House Conference on Aging and
further documented in the International Symposium to the White House Conference on Aging (Lawton with Rajic 1972). This later program and examples of
other fertile international exchanges such as (Donahue, Thompson and Curren
1977), research on the role of the British warden in sheltered housing (Heumann
1980), and visits comparing facilities in northern Europe (McRae 1976) can
further stimulate our thinking about new integrated-housing and service
approaches designed to improve the condition of a growing number of frail
elderly. Many of these people could benefit from living with their peers in
supportive environments with appropriate and integrated services linked to their
neighborhoods. Answers to the questions of who benefits, to what degree, for
how long, from which combinations of services and facilities, and at what cost,
need to be further explored. With these answers, a more rational expansion of
congregate housing can be developed that will provide an appropriate response
to accommodate a significant number of older people in settings of dignity.

References and Additional Resources

Byerts, T.O. 1979. "Toward a Better Range of Housing and Environmental
    Choices for the Elderly." In *Back to Basics: Food and Shelter for the
    Elderly*, ed. P.A. Wagner and J.M. McRae, Gainesville, Fla.: University
    Presses of Florida.
Byerts, T.O., ed. with P. Taylor, 1977. "Curriculum Development in Environ-
    ments and Aging," *Journal of Architectural Education* 31:1.
Carp, F.M. 1975. "Long-Range Satisfaction with Housing," *Gerontologist*
    15:1.
Carp, F.M. 1977a. "Impact of Improved Living Environment on Health and
    Life Expectancy," *Gerontologist* 17:3.
Carp, F.M. 1977b. "The Concept and Role of Congregate Housing for Older
    People." In *Congregate Housing for Older People*, ed. W.T. Donahue,
    M.M. Thompson, and D.J. Curren. Washington, D.C.: U.S. Government
    Printing Office.
Delong, A.J. 1970. "The Micro-Spatial Structure of the Older Person: Some
    Implications of Planning the Social and Spatial Environment." In *Spatial
    Behavior of Older People*, ed. L.A. Pastalan, and D.H. Carson, Ann Arbor,
    Mich.: University of Michigan Press.

Donahue, W.B.; Thompson, M.M.; and Curren, D.J., eds. 1977. *Congregate Housing for Older People*. Washington, D.C.: USGPO.

Gelwicks, L.E. 1970. "Home Range and Use of Space by an Aging Population." In *Spatial Behavior of Older People*, ed. L.A. Pastalan and D.H. Carson Ann Arbor, Mich.: University of Michigan Press.

Gelwicks, L.E., and Newcomer, R.J. 1974. *Planning Housing Environments for the Elderly*. Washington, D.C.: National Council on the Aging.

Green, I.; Fedewa, B.; Johnston, C.; Jackson, W.; Deardorff. 1975. *Housing for the Elderly: The Development and Design Process*. New York: Van Nostrand Reinhold Company.

Heumann, L. 1980. Sheltered Housing for the Elderly: The Role of British Wardens," *Gerontologist* 20:3.

Howell, S.C. 1980. *Designing for Aging: Patterns of Use*. Cambridge, Mass.: The M.I.T. Press.

Jones, M.A. 1978. *Accessibility Standards—Illustrated*. Springfield, Ill.: The Capital Development Board.

Kahana, E.; Felton, B.; and Fairchild, T.J. 1976. "Community Services and Facilities Planning." In *Community Planning for an Aging Society*, ed. M.P. Lawton, T.O. Byerts, and R.J. Newcomer. Stroudsburg, Pa.: Dowden, Hutchinson and Ross.

Koncelik, J.A. 1976. *Designing the Open Nursing Home*. Stroudsburg, Penn.: Dowden, Hutchinson and Ross.

Lawton, M.P. 1977. "Applying Research Knowledge to Congregate Housing." In *Congregate Housing for Older People*, ed. W. Donahue, M.M. Thompson, and D.J. Curren, Washington, D.C.: USGPO.

Lawton, M.P. 1980. *Environment and Aging*. Belmont, Calif.: Wadsworth, Inc.

Lawton, M.P.; Greenbaum, M.; and Liebowitz, B. 1980. "The Lifespan of Housing Environments for the Aging," *Gerontologist* 20:1.

Lawton, M.P., ed., with R. Rajic, 1972. "Housing," *Gerontologist* 12: no. 2.

Lawton, M.P., and Simon, B. 1968. "The Ecology of Social Relationships in Housing for the Elderly," *Gerontologist* 8:108–115.

Lawton, M.P. 1976. "The Relative Impact of Congregate and Traditional Housing," *Gerontologist* 16, no. 3.

Madge, J. 1969. "Aging and the Fields of Architecture and Planning." In *Aging and Society, Vol. Two* ed. M.W. Riley, J.W. Riley, and M.E. Johnson. New York: Russell Sage Foundation.

McRae, J.J. 1976. *Elderly in the Environment: Northern Europe*. Gainesville, Fla.: University of Florida.

Neugarten, B.L. 1968. Adult Personality: Toward a Psychology of the Life Cycle. In *Middle Age and Aging*, ed. Neugarten, B.L. Chicago: University of Chicago Press.

Pastalan, L.A. 1973. "Involuntary Environmental Relocation: Death and Survival." In *Environmental Design Research*, ed. W.F.E. Preiser. Stroudsburg, Pa: Dowden, Hutchinson and Ross.

Regnier, V.A. Forthcoming. "Neighborhood images: A case study". In *Community Housing—Choices for Older Americans*, ed. M.P. Lawton. New York: Garland Press.

Shanas, E.; Townsend, P.; Wedderburn, D. 1968. *Older People in Three Industrial Societies*. New York.: Atherton Press.

U.S. Bureau of the Census 1979. "Prospective Trends in the Size and Structure of Elderly Population," *Current Population Reports*, Series P-23; 78. Washington, D.C.: USGPO.

U.S. Congress, Senate Special Committee on Aging 1974. *Nursing Home Care in the U.S.: Failure in Public Policy*. Washington, D.C.: USGPO.

U.S. Department of Health and Human Services. 1980. *Facts about Older Americans: 1979*. Washington, D.C.

Zeisel, J.; Epp, G.; and Demos, S., *Low Rise Housing for Older People*. U.S. HUD 483 (TQ)-76, Washington, D.C.

10 Elements of Geriatric Design: The Personal Environment

Joseph A. Koncelik

For the greater part of two decades, social scientists have been linking concepts such as well-being and independence among the elderly to environment. In most instances, this linkage has meant social environment or the interaction of people with people. However, increasingly there have been attempts (if not successes) in linking these concepts to the design of physical environments. Robert Sommer discussed behavior of elderly women in a mental institution in terms that show his observation of the linkage between physical environment and behavior:

> The ladies sat side-by-side against the newly painted walls in their chrome chairs and exercised their options of gazing down at the newly-tiled floor or looking up at the new fluorescent lights. They were like strangers in a train station waiting for a train that never came. This shoulder-to-shoulder arrangement was unsuitable for sustained conversation even for me. To talk to neighbors, I had to turn in my chair and pivot my head 90 degrees. For an older lady, particularly one with difficulties in hearing and compensation, finding a suitable orientation for conversation was extremely taxing. (Sommer 1970, p. 27)

Sommer's discussion of behavior among elderly women resulted from observations gathered in an institutional setting. Indeed, most of the information generated about behavior and the physical environment of elderly is the result of studies conducted in mental institutions and nursing home environments. Eva Kahana has commented on the environments of nursing homes as being too much a derivative of health-care models and not sufficiently responsive to other psychosocial needs of the elderly:

> Even our best institutions for the aged often operate on a pathology model of aging, viewing the individual as a medical management problem and disregarding his (or her) personal identity. (Kahana 1973, pp. 282–283)

However, whether the question is how to design environments for independent or institutionalized living, there is little doubt that the critical level of interaction between physical environment and the elderly user is at the personal or micro-environmental level as Arthur Schwartz has assessed:

[D]esign of micro-environments for the aged must be aimed not only at the ameliorating of stresses, minimizing the effects of losses, and compensating for deficits but must do so in ways which enhance the individuals' effectiveness, support their competence, and thus help them maintain self esteem. (Schwartz 1975, p. 289)

Distinctions between the micro-environment and the macro are vague. Generally, most researchers and designers would agree that the macro-environment is really an architectural and community level of design and structuring of the physical environment. Micro-environments are characterized by personal scale—the immediate surroundings of an individual. In essence, the micro-environment is that part of the physical environment within reach of a person. The more infirm that person is, the tighter the personal micro-environment becomes. In research conducted at Cornell University (Koncelik, Ostrander, Synder 1973) many elderly persons in institutional settings were interviewed. In response to the question, "Where do you live?" a woman restrained in a geriatric chair responded, "I live in this chair." Other researchers as well as facility administrators have reported similar responses on other occasions.

In the design process usually followed in the creation of special environments for elderly people, the general configuration is top-down. Most design begins from an overall-planning standpoint, without consideration of the environment surrounding each individual in the setting. Frequently, the design process to create personal environments is not even conducted by a designer, but is delegated to an administrator or staff member without design training or experience. Preliminary results from current on-going research bear this out.

In a questionnaire survey of one-hundred architects within the United States (with forty returns), over 50 percent stated that they had been engaged in the specification of architectural building products, while under 20 percent had been engaged in the specifications of furnishings and personal properties for facilities and independent living-units for the elderly. These personal-property elements of the micro-environment include seating, beds, tables, storage units and appliances. In other words, although the importance of the personal micro-environment in relation to the well-being of elderly people has been demonstrated by social scientists, it is the level of environmental relationship receiving the least amount of design attention. The micro-environment is largely a product environment. This means that the spaces relevant to critical levels of functioning are dominated by organized or unorganized collections of furnishings and seating, appliances, tables, lighting and other functional items. The task of the designers of space, whether they are architects or untrained facility personnel, is to coordinate and arrange these items so that they relate and produce a usable and comfortable environment. Since each of the items has been designed without regard to the other, assemblage can be complicated and less than optimally functional.

At present, there is no systematic approach in the design of interrelated products for specific environments. At best, manufacturers will provide performance criteria about the physical characteristics or the output of their products. This is useful information to the degree that it allows matching of one item to another. However, the total effective ambience of the resulting environment cannot be easily measured. Thus, matching of components through output-performance criteria alone does not provide all of the information necessary for effective design. As Lawton (1970) has stated: "Little is known about the factors of design, furnishings and other features of smaller spaces." He was really referring to the lack of information about effective environments or how the micro or product environment influences behavior.

The micro-environment has been described as that part of the physical environment that is within reach. To know that environment in order to reach it, one must be able to sense it—to understand what it is; to determine locations of one component relative to another; to be able to make meaningful adjustments to that environment that place it under personal control. In order for these things to be accomplished, information must be processed through sensory channels. Koncelik's *Designing the Open Nursing Home* (1976) includes discussion of the physiological changes related to aging, among them changes to the sensory modalities. This research has been reviewed in numerous other publications and it is not essential to review the specific findings of the many researchers who have provided useful information. It is important to state that, since there are changes with aging, perceptions are altered, and, in order to cope with the design problem presented by the nature of both physiological change and sensory deprivation, it is necessary to first have a conceptual framework in order to depict and to classify the relationships all people enjoy with the physical setting. This framework enables specific categorization of problems where characteristics of change become an important relationship between the user of the environment and the environment itself. A four-stage framework may be constituted of relationships at increasingly higher levels of sophistication; these relationships are (1) warning, (2) interpretation, (3) negotiation, and (4) responsiveness. The definitions of these terms are

Warning: Stimuli necessary to convey life-threatening situations or harm. They must be clear and free from confusion with other environmental stimuli or background noise. With regard to populations with sensory problems, signals used to convey harmful or life-threatening situations should be backed up with redundant signals or cues that would increase the probability that the signals would be received and acted upon.

Interpretation: The conveyance of information from the environment allowing that user to understand the place. Without appropriate interpretive information, it may be possible to overly confuse the user about a given place. Interpreting environments depends upon two factors: sufficient difference between various parts of a place to insure discrimination from place to place, and information about location and pathways, again redundantly cued, to insure that the user is properly aware of his position in the environment in relation to other places.

Negotiation: This part of the conceptual framework refers to the physical aspect of movement, especially continuous and uninterrupted physical movement through an environment. A user of the environment must be able to move from one place to another within an environment without incurring any obstacles or becoming confused with respect to pathway.

There are two important features any environment must have in order to facilitate negotiation. First, physical barriers that impede the use of a place by the physically handicapped must be removed. Second, signals used throughout the facility must be either repeated or continuous in order to insure that once a person commences movement through a place she will be able to do so continuously and with the assurance of arrival at the anticipated destination. A simple example of design in this regard is the use of a continuous arrow or long band of color to indicate a direction within a corridor.

Responsiveness: The accommodation of both the user and the environment to each other, a subtle and complex communication that can be seen as a dialogue.

The concept of a dialogue takes this notion of communication out of the context of simply marked places. Removal of things which tell the environment user that he is in control can result in a loss of self-esteem and hostility about and toward the environment. If walls protect us, we refer to our surroundings as a shelter. If they constrain us, they become a prison. The dialogue response, when the environment either constrains or confuses—or reduces self-esteem, can be a lashing out against that environment. Sometimes this response is physical and sometimes it is verbal. A visit to a nursing home might very well show an observer certain behaviors that are part of this dialogue. Frequently, people will seem to be talking to the walls, or yelling at them. It is a hasty judgment to call this behavior senile.

The conceptual framework mentioned is essentially a spectrum of communications from the most basic to the most complex. This framework suggests that directed recommendations can be made to permit the accommodation of any given building to either the broadest population or special populations suffering handicaps or sensory losses. Therefore, through implementation of measures to maximize the usability of environments, both physical barriers and then, most important, psychological barriers can either be eliminated or reduced significantly. In many instances, the form of the implementation is a commonsense solution derived from the recognition of the problems of infirmity or sensory loss in the first place. Actually, there are no magical or mysterious devices that need to be employed in the physical setting to counteract confusion, disorientation and barriers to use.

The following categorical listing is an attempt to capsulize some of the ways in which an environment (or specific environment such as an institutional setting) can be improved in regard to the specific elements of the conceptual framework provided earlier. A comprehensive listing of recommendations to facilitate use of environments from the standpoint of all possible handicaps and infirmities would be impossible in this chapter. However, it is possible to project some of the design alternatives derived from a recognition of sensory loss.

Sound Control and Attenuation

Ambient background-sounds in open, reverberating public-spaces can and should be dampened or reduced through the use of such baffling materials as wall hangings of thick woven fabrics, screens, banners, or panels that reduce the reflection of sound from overhead surfaces. In conjunction with this type of baffling, seating arrangements in institutions should have no more than six positions, preferably four positions, to facilitate conversation and eye contact. This measure should also help older people concentrate on the verbal communications of their neighbors at a table and facilitate the reading of lips and facial expressions. General background noises in public thoroughfares or corridors can be reduced through the use of carpeting wherever possible and also through attention to the coating of the ceiling and wall surfaces. Heavily textured surfaces applied by spray techniques can reduce sound reflection; they also provide wall surface allowing greater purchase for the dry hand of the aging person. Ceilings can be flocked with a very dense, sprayed-on, roving material that will do a great deal to cut down high frequency background noises. Elevators can and should be equipped with middle-frequency tones that would sound when safe passage is possible to and from the elevator. In institutional settings, this would also serve to warn others in corridors that the elevator has reached that floor and is available or that there will be traffic coming from that direction. In settings with six or fewer floors, the tones may ring in accordance with the number of the floor itself—serving as a redundant cue with visual signals for the floor—for those people who have visual sensory loss.

Many environments are equipped with prerecorded music. This background is potentially distressing to the sensorily deprived (as well as to many music lovers) because it has a tendency to make the environment more uniform rather than to maximize the differences for ease of place identification. However, the potential of carefully controlled sound sources in specific locations can help to identify the place, especially for the visually impaired person. Dining rooms have sounds and smells that help to identify them, but this might even be enhanced with the lilt of carefully-chosen background music. Evenness of sound throughout an institutional facility would be highly counterproductive. The attempt should be to encourage self-reliance in the negotiation of the environment.

Visual warning devices such as emergency exits should be backed up with auditory middle-frequency sound signals to enhance the identification of the location of the exit. Many visual signals are placed high in the space and cannot be seen in a smoky room.

Visual Signage and Spatial-Recognition Devices

The architecture of many high-rise and institutional settings is made up of repetitious elements that become confusing to the sensorily deprived person. The clients who utilize the services of the designer should be aware of this problem and act as knowledgeable recipients of the designer's services.

It is possible to make changes to existing interiors to alleviate some of the problems caused by the repetitive nature of an environment. Color coding, the use of color in patterns to increase recognition of the spaces they are associated with, can be employed, especially in the institutional setting. Each floor, in a given setting, for example, can be designed with significant color and decor differences so that the specific color becomes recognizable as a distinct place with its own character. Even the partially sighted may be capable of recognizing bold color patterns located in carefully lighted areas. Obviously, for those people who suffer hearing losses, there will be an even greater dependency upon the visual stimuli for the identification of a place.

The figure-ground relationships of signage systems should employ a very high contrast ratio between the symbol and the background upon which it is situated. It is preferable, in the interior of buildings, to use white symbols on dark or black backgrounds rather than the reverse. This treatment is not always possible for a variety of reasons—thus, the concept of maximum difference between the symbol and the background. Signs should be located at wheelchair eye-heights of approximately forty-eight to fifty-two inches because the standing or ambulatory person would still be capable of reading signs at that height.

Glare reduction has become most important, especially in an institutional setting for the aged. The adaptation rates from low-light to high-light conditions coupled with the nonpathological changes in the aging eye make the elderly extremely susceptible to glare. Carpeting floors in corridors wherever possible and greater use of peripheral lighting to increase the subjective total-lighting of a space (as opposed to the direct intermittent-lighting of a space) can reduce glare off surfaces and also provide a better visual sense of the dimension of a space. Window walls must be carefully considered and glazing that reduces total light as well as potential glare should be investigated. Entrance and exit areas of public buildings should be designed so that the slower adaptation rate of the older adult is accommodated. This user of the environment may be momentarily confused or unable to identify places or signage in an interior moments after entry from the outside. One of the most significant problems in this regard is the design of highway underpasses that go from a high-lighted to a low-lighted and then back to a high-lighted condition. In this situation, the elderly eye cannot adapt and the consequences might be very serious and dangerous.

Textural Signage and Markers

Because so many of the occupants of institutional facilities, age- related apartment buildings, domiciliary units, and other environments have more than one sensory deficit (hearing and sight are most frequently effected), there should be markers that identify place through the use of touch. The most obvious form is braille, now in use in public buildings as well as on topographical maps for direction-finding. However, there are other textural markers, such as shape coding of handrails in nursing homes (at intermittent locations, notches or grooves could be cut in the surface of a handrail to identify location), changes in the surfaces of wall textures, and other devices. Care should be taken to give sufficient difference to the textures so that building users do not become confused.

Two visual and tactile problems are presented in figures 10-1 and 10-2, examples of floor and ground surface treatments. Both were found in facilities for older people. In figure 10-1, there is a lack of homogeneity in the surface with portions of the concrete raised up. These changes in the surface would be very hard to discern for many elderly and obviously present hazards in high glare conditions.

In the figure 10-2, the visual pattern of bathroom tile obliterates a critical surface change. Since shallow depth changes in surface cannot be seen clearly by elderly having sustained normal aging losses in vision, this surface also presents a serious hazard, especially in an environment where high glare and wet surfaces are present.

From the standpoint of responsiveness in an environment, institutional settings are almost devoid of richness. For the bedridden in particular, the institutional setting can be a desolate place without stimulus. This is precisely the opposite from the way things should be. An institutionalized older person, for example, should have a multiplicity of textures and personal artifacts around to provide that sense of territoriality and ownership which communicates control.

Product and appliance design as a process has not incorporating information about elderly consumers. (See figures 10-3 and 10-4.) With the aid of "empathic" lenses provided by the University of Michigan's Institute of Gerontology, a comparison of a so-called normal sighted person and one having sustained age-related vision losses can be made. The glare from the controls, reflectivity of the surface, inappropriate graphics and confusing use of symbols make this device difficult to interpret and use by an older adult.

Figure 10–1. Uneven Surfaces in this Geriatric Facility are Especially Hard to Discern in High-Glare Conditions

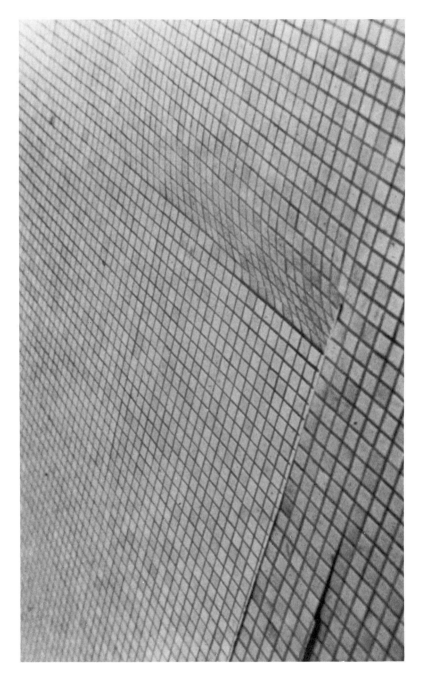

Figure 10–2. Visual Pattern in the Bathroom Floor Masks a Critical Surface Change; Glare and Wet Conditions Add to the Danger

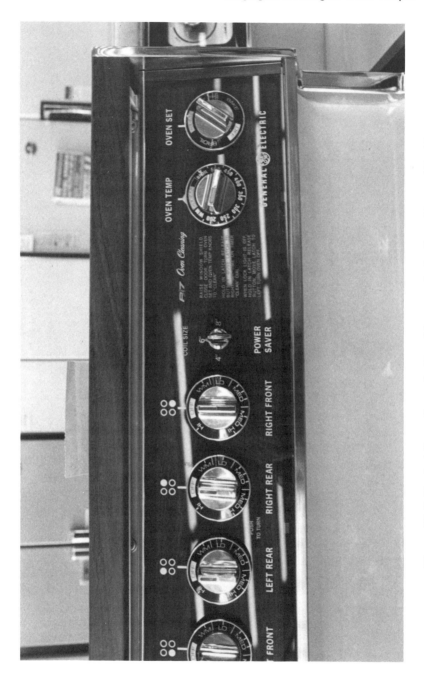

Figure 10-3. Typical Stove Controls: Rear Mounting Is the First Observed Problem

Figure 10–4. Stove Controls as Seen by Vision-Impaired Elderly Reveal Confusing Reflections and Glare, Inappropriate Graphics, and Confusing Symbols

Devices for Control

The architectural hardware used in most buildings has been designed and selected as though all users have no handicaps or no problems with hand/eye coordination. As previously stated, there are over 25 million people in the United States who suffer limitations to activity. A great many of them have sensory problems that interfere with manipulation of controls used to manage, change, open, close and select and actuate environments. This must be regarded as the most serious design oversight facing both the design profession and the American consumer public—perhaps even the Western World—today. If the perspective on this problem is changed to accommodate the real user populations, a massive design program would have to be created to rectify the difficulties brought about by current design standards and the products designed to meet the outdated criteria they stipulate. The standard American doorknob, for example, encourages ulnar deviation contributing to the onset of arthritis (osteo arthritis) through the rotating motion needed to use the device. How many times a day does every American have to turn a doorknob? It can also be argued that the inability to manipulate the architectural hardware presently designed into most buildings communicates a loss of capability to the infirm long before their difficulties really do inhibit environmental use. This same principle can be extended to include such control devices as light switches, window latches, sink or lavatory water-controls, stoves and ranges, television sets—almost an infinite variety of devices found in every environment and taken for granted by most of us. How many people damn themselves or their lack of vision or case of arthritis for their inability to manipulate a control device when even the fully able user may have difficulty due to design defects?

Recommendations Regarding Implementation of Products

Products designed for application to supportive environments such as nursing homes and sheltered housing should be seen as elements in an overall system, not as separate entities without relation to other products. There should be efforts to design products as surroundings (Koncelik 1976) or in combinations for use as integrated subsystems. In other words, if the bed in a nursing-home room is seen as one component of a surrounding, then other products—lighting, room controls, warning systems, work surfaces, tables and other equipment—could be integrated into single-product units.

Insufficient attention has been given to visual and verbal communication utilized on products and packaging and as signage and marker systems in the environment. Inappropriate figure sizes, stroke-width proportions, and figure-ground relationships are all too common. Specifications for appropriate changes can be found in Steinfeld's *Barrier-Free Design for the Elderly and Disabled* (1975) and in Koncelik's *Designing the Open Nursing Home* (1976).

Environments for both independent living and institutional living should receive intensive study and application of current technologies for the reduction of glare. Glare is one of the most significant visual susceptibilities influencing perception (or lack of perception) of the environment by aged people. These studies should not result in research findings, but in product development such as floor, wall and ceiling coverings and coatings, drapery materials and combinations of fibrous materials, and luminaires that are improved as sources of light minimizing unwanted glare.

There is sufficient evidence to show that the elderly prefer warmer interior environments as well as climatic settings. With current technology in place as the aging population increases, energy utilization (fuels of all types) will increase at a time of diminishing resources. New designs for HVAC systems must be developed to provide sensations of warmth while maintaining current or cooler ambient temperature levels.

In the United States, inspection procedures as well as regulatory structures emphasize health and life-safety. These governances and methods of assessment should include the development of procedures for assessment of the psychosocial environment as well. Feldman and Burke (1976) have experimented successfully with designs for such a procedure and it is time for inclusion of these factors as part of the support structure of environments for aging people.

There is confusion in the relationship between designers and manufacturers. Designers are specifying for use in building projects for the elderly products that manufacturers either deny have relevance for aging populations or that they do not market specifically for the elderly. The fallout from this confused state of affairs is possible awareness of criteria for use of products by elderly on the part of designers. Greater efforts must be expended to educate manufacturers about the aging market; to educate architects and designers about criteria derived from the needs of the elderly; and also to educate the aging consumer, who needs to know how to demand effective supportive environments that will allow for their needs and promote personal control.

Regardless of whether the elderly person is independent or institutionalized, the bed, one of the least considered devices in any setting, is occupied by the elderly for almost 40 percent of the total day. Sleeping is obviously the most essential bed activity, but also, during the waking hours, napping, resting, reading, and snacking or eating, plus many other peripheral behaviors, may take place in and around the bed. In double-occupancy rooms beds may be the only space for visitors to sit, so that socialization with friends or relatives, and even conjugal visitations or love making must be considered. Beds should be at a height of twenty inches off the floor to the top of the bedding level to allow for dressing without assistance as well as entrance and egress. The bedding should be carefully considered, especially from the standpoint of the total room decor and aesthetic sensibilities of the resident. If possible, elderly residents should choose their own bed covering.

Chairs can be roughly divided into two categories: lounging and functional. Research reported by Koncelik, Ostrander and Snyder (1973) has shown that the durations of time spent in the seated position range from as much as six hours for the ambulatory to twelve hours for the restrained nonambulatory. In the majority of institutional environments, seating used by nonambulatory patient/residents served as both lounging and functional seating as well as the mode of ambulation through the facility. However, first, it is important to deal with some fundamental notions about seating for the ambulatory elderly.

Once again, this subject is very difficult to cover adequately in a single chapter. However, there are certain fundamental design considerations that can be discussed. First, no chair placed in a facility for the elderly should be without arms. These arms should extend forward slightly beyond the leading edge of the chair to facilitate entrance and egress. Height to the leading edge of both categories of chairs should not exceed seventeen inches, keeping in mind that overall population of elderly people is somewhat shorter than average, and most of the population over sixty-five are women, with the median percentile of their anthropometric range having a standing height of five feet two inches tall. Technologies for improved seating exist and are underutilized. With special regard to lounge seating, springing and damping members of the platform for support to the torso could be greatly improved in most chairs to eliminate bottoming characteristics. With the long durations of seated time, the characteristic of bottoming may promote the incidence of decubitus ulcers incurred from sitting too long. All incidences certainly do not result from long durations in bed.

Nonambulatory elderly should receive special design attention with regard to seating. Very few transfers are made from chair to chair in most nursing homes and, therefore, the ambulatory device must serve as a multifunctional furnishing.

Wheelchairs also should be subject to an intensive design, redesign and evaluation study. There is a host of psychological as well as physiological problems that are exacerbated or in some way contributed to by these poorly designed ambulatory devices. Many elderly people restrained in geriatric chairs, for example, are often ascribed a degree of psychological incompetence by both patients and staff that is not accurate simply because of the impression of illness suggested by the ambulatory device itself. Wheelchair-bound elderly are often capable of moving or fully negotiating their wheelchair, but not by the conventional method of rotating the wheel that requires reaching behind the vertical plane of the shoulders to push the wheels forward. With arthritis and loss of strength, this maneuver is extremely difficult. There is a definite place for the motorized wheelchair and for a design that could be articulated through the seating position to allow increased comfort over longer periods of time. Some of these design ideas are not difficult to employ but do need further development and evaluation.

Chairs necessary for dining and activities can be regarded as functional seating mentioned earlier. Again, these chairs should have arms, and the leading edge should not exceed seventeen inches from the floor. Back supports are an extremely important consideration in functional seating. Younger populations, have a tendency to lean forward and away from the back supports provided in the chair, but not so the elderly. There is loss of strength in the torso and inability to flex the spinal column, greater roll at the shoulders and slumping forward, as well as limited side-to-side head-movement.

Tables should accommodate both the ambulatory and nonambulatory in activity and dining areas to encourage the greatest possible participation and socialization at the meals. Generally, a thirty-one-inch-high table will accommodate both groups of people. The table might be just slightly too high for the smallest person so that a selection of table heights might be necessary. It is possible that a table with a central stem could be made adjustable so that when sittings are arranged for groups of elderly, a height could be selected for each individual group.

The bathroom itself has been the subject of very intensive investigation (Kira 1976, Steinfeld 1975), but the largest concentration of effort with regard to designing for the institutionalized elderly has been from the standpoint of arrangement of components (existing hardware) and the placement of handrails and supports. Little attention has been given to the design of the fixtures and hardware independent of its placement or relationship in the setting. However, there is a great deal of potential in a modular approach to bathroom design wherein the fixtures are really part of the overall wall/floor structure.

The sink, mirror and storage configuration should receive more attention than it has. Mirrors should be placed lower to the surface of the sink and possibly hinged or canted outward so that wheelchair-bound residents are able to see themselves with little of the difficulty they presently have. The sink should be shallow draft and the wastepipes as well as the hot water feed-pipe should be shrouded to prevent burns to the legs of wheelchair users. Control devices should be easy to grasp and easy to use by people with very little strength in their hands.

Toilets are another concern. One of the chief problems is mounting and egress for both the ambulatory and nonambulatory users. There should be two different designs for each group or modifications that could be made to an existing flexible unit. One system to permit mounting and egress for both groups will not work.

Bathtub design is another important area not given sufficient attention. Quasi-seated or semisupine bathtubs should be available, however, with so little available except for very inappropriate and old-fashioned equipment, there is no question of the necessity for support of development in this area. Again, ease in entrance and egress of both bathtubs and shower-stall units is an important problem. Showers are generally considered safer because there is no change of body position from standing to sitting and no stress in awkward positions transferred through arms and legs. Showers should incorporate a bench or other seating, as well as grab bars.

Activities of the Elderly and Evaluation of Their Surroundings

In order to evaluate environments that support the activities of the elderly—and especially those elderly who are infirm and institutionalized—it is necessary to realize just what is meant by the term *activities of daily living* (ADL) and to provide some definition of activities the elderly are truly engaged in. To the health-care professionals (physical therapists, occupational therapists and also recreational therapists), ADL has significance in terms of accomplishing therapies that allow people to resume those functions associated with normal everyday-life. For the most part, these functions are commonplace and unnoticed; rarely are they "active" activities in the sense that a game of tennis is an activity requiring athletic ability, concentration, reflexes, and stamina. However, reduction of certain basic functional-activities would mean that some people might be in serious trouble physiologically as well as psychologically. Leon Pastalan, professor with the Institute of Gerontology of the University of Michigan, has shown that if activities are reduced to too-low a level, institutionalized elderly may die. Also, activities may be limited by sensory changes and changes in perception of the environment.

A relatively old publication is still a good source of information about the daily living activities of older people. In Beyer and Wood, *Living and Activity Patterns of the Aged* (1963), the results of extensive interviews with 5200 elderly persons provide a good basis for understanding how ADL should be supported as well as with what kinds of devices. Beyer and Woods show that out of the twenty-four-hour day the median time spent in wakefulness was fifteen hours. Among these independent elderly, four to five hours were spent doing housework. It is interesting to note that the housework deemed most difficult was the care of furnishings, equipment and facilities; nine out of every ten independent elderly do their own laundry. Personal care and hygiene occupied one to two hours of wakefulness. Dining, both in and out of the residence, was especially important and those people fortunate enough to have a spouse, companion or family ate very regular meals. Those without companionship tended to eat less regularly.

When this large number of elderly people was interviewed about activities beyond obligated time, where they exert choice over what they do, the results were very interesting. Seventy percent of the elderly interviewed stated that they watched television three to four hours per day with the median being three hours. Over half interviewed spend one to two hours either napping or in idleness. Twenty-eight percent of the elderly stated that they were engaged intermittently in shopping and related activities, but the largest proportion of this population does not engage in these activities. Reading occupied most of the elderly for about an hour per day. Only one of five elderly did any gardening; one of ten took regular walks and, only 1 percent of those interviewed stated that they had a hobby or personal interest. Only 4 percent of those interviewed stated that they were ever engaged in some form of social or church activity. Sixty percent of the aged did not belong to any organization. When asked what they preferred to do most, visiting relatives and friends was the activity highest on the list. Watching television and reading were very close in second place with other activities composing a very scattered hierarchy of interests.

The overall picture of activity seems rather sedentary and passive in profile, with the largest portion of the day being consumed by maintenance of self and residence. However, there is a good deal of evidence that younger generations of elderly people are much more active and involved—perhaps to some degree in reaction to the image of the elderly being quite sedentary. However, these older data are not easily discounted even now and even if dramatic changes ensue in the coming years, a far clearer conception of the framework for environmental supports has been established.

A significant goal of congregate or sheltered housing is the encouragement of continued feelings of independence with a supportive, yet stimulating, environment. The importance of activities including gardening, pets, crafts, and others resides in the fact that there are limited opportunities in sheltered housing for activities beyond those relating to maintenance of self and the personal environment. The possibilities for activity programs are infinite and largely unexplored, but a well implemented program should prolong the active lives of residents, both socially and physically.

To summarize this discussion of activities, it has been shown that independent elderly people have very limited activities to begin with and that there is a great deal of passivity inherent in their major activities during the day. Most residents of any institution have even more severely curtailed activities with even greater passivity.

The surroundings of greatest and most immediate concern are those elements of the environment with which the elderly must contend during the greater part of their day. The elements of these surroundings are the bed, the various forms of seating, tables and work surfaces and bathroom fixtures. Only after these devices are truly supportive of the use given them by elderly people and after they are no longer an obstruction or impediment in the way of general maintenance activities can there be a real improvement in the supportive quality of the physical environment.

More important, the design fields currently failing to collaborate must realize that they represent a continuum of design effort that must be synthesized for effective results. Purely self-interested focus and a lack of balance between aesthetic concerns, business enterprise and human-needs assessment will be counterproductive. If the needs of elderly populations are not approached satis-factorily in building and product design, then the inevitable future for the design professions will be reduced participation and more limited professional practice. To some degree, signs of this negative prognosis already exist. Designers have the capacity to change, but if designers move into the twenty-first century without addressing the problems stated, many face an uncertain future. Those that survive will have defined a new approach to practice and to designing. They will be the architects, product designers and interior-design specialists who set the pace, and by collaborating give new definition to the practice of design.

References and Additional Resources

Beyer, G.H., and Wood, M. 1963. *Living and Activity Patterns of the Aged*, Research Report No. 6. Center for Housing and Environmental Studies. Cornell University, Ithaca, N.Y.

Birren, J.E. 1964. *The Psychology of Aging*, Englewood Cliffs, N.J.: Prentice-Hall, Inc., Chapter 4.

Bloomer, H.H. 1971. "Speech and Language Disorders as a Function of Aging," *Hearing and Speech News*. November/December, p. 14–15.

Comfort, A. 1956. *The Biology of Senescence*. London: Routledge and Paul.

Corso, J.F. 1971. "Sensory Process and Age Effects in Normal Adults," *Journal of Gerontology* 26: no. 1, 90–105.

Corson, S.A., et al. 1976. "The Socializing Role of Pet Animals in Nursing Homes: An Experiment in Non-verbal Communication Therapy," a paper presented at the Symposium of Society, Stress and Disease: Aging and Old Age, Stockholm, Sweden, June 14–19.

Feldman, J., and Burke, R. 1976. "Quality Evaluation System: An Effective Multidisciplinary Team Evaluation for Long Term Care," a paper presented at the Annual Meeting of the Gerontological Society, New York, October 14.

Gerard, R.W. 1964. "Aging and Organization." In *The Psychology of Aging*, ed. J.E. Birren. Englewood Cliffs, N.J.: Prentice-Hall, Inc., pp. 264–278.

Gilbert, J.G. 1957. "Age Changes in Color Matching," *Journal of Gerontology* 12:210–15.

Gottesman, L.E. 1957. "Nursing Home Research Project: The Study of Aged Patients and Nursing Home Services," *Institute of Gerontology* 12:210–215.

Kahana, E. 1973. "The Humane Treatment of Old People in Institutions," *The Gerontologist* 13, no. 3:282–289.

Kira, A. 1966. *The Bathroom*. New York: The Viking Press, revised in 1976.

Koncelik, J.A. 1976. *Designing the Open Nursing Home*. Stroudsburg, Pa: Dowden, Hutchinson and Ross.

Koncelik, J.A., Ostrander, E. and Snyder, L. 1973. *The New Nursing Home: Conference Proceedings*. Ithaca, N.Y.: College of Human Ecology, Cornell University.

Kuhlen, R.G. 1964. "Aging and Life Adjustment." In *The Psychology of Aging*, ed. J.E. Birren. Englewood Cliffs, N.J.: Prentice-Hall, Inc., pp. 852-900.

Lawton, M.P. 1970. "Ecology and Aging." In *Spatial Behavior of Older People*, ed. L.A. Pastalan and D.H. Carson. Ann Arbor, Mich.: University of Michigan Press, 40-67.

Lawton, M.P., and Nahemow, L. 1971. "Ecology and the Aging Process." In *Psychology of Adult Development and Aging*, ed. M.P. Lawton and K. Eisdorfer. Washington, D.C.: American Psychological Association, 619-666.

NSPB Factbook, 1966. National Society for the Prevention of Blindness, New York.

Pastalan, L.A. 1975. "Age Related Sensory Deficits." In *Environments and Aging, Concepts and Issues*, ed. T. Byerts, et al. Washington, D.C.: Gerontological Society, A-1-13.

———. 1973. "Age Related Sensory Deficits." In *Environments and Aging, Concepts and Issues*, ed. T. Byerts, et al. Washington, D.C.: Gerontology Society, pp. 21-3.

———. 1970. "Privacy as an Expression of Human Territoriality." In *Spatial Behavior of Older People*, ed. L.A. Pastalan and D.H. Carson. Ann Arbor, Mich.: University of Michigan Press, pp. 89-101.

Reinchenback, M., and Mathers, R.A. 1964. "The Place of Time and Aging in the Natural Sciences and Scientific Philosophy." In *The Psychology of Aging*, ed. J.E. Birren. Englewood Cliffs, N.J.: Prentice-Hall, Inc., pp. 43-80.

Rupp, R.R.; McLauchlin, R.M.; Harless, E.; and Mikulas, M. 1977. "The Spector of Aging—Golden Years Tarnished," *Hearing and Speech News* November/December, pp. 10-13.

Sanoff, H. 1969. "Visual Attributes of the Physical Environment." In *Response to Environment*, ed. G. Coates and K. Moffet. Raleigh, N.C.: North Carolina State University, 18:37-62.

Schwartz, A.N. 1975. "Planning and Micro-Environments for the Aged." In *Aging*, ed. D.S. Woodruff and J.E. Birren. New York: Van Nostrand Company, 277-312.

Shock, N.W. 1953. "Aging of Homeostatic Mechanism." In *Cowdrey's Problems of Aging*, ed. A. Lansing. Baltimore: Williams and Wilkins, pp. 415-556.

Sommer, R. 1969. *Personal Space*. Englewood Cliffs, N.J.: Prentice-Hall, Inc.

Sommer, R. 1970. "Small Group Ecology in Institutions for the Elderly." In *Spatial Behavior of Older People*, ed. L.A. Pastalan and D.H. Carson. Ann Arbor, Mich.: The University of Michigan Press, pp. 25-39.

Spivak, M. 1973. "Archetypical Place." In *Housing and Environment for the Elderly*, ed. T. Byerts. Washington, D.C.: Gerontological Society.

Stea, D. 1969. "Environmental Perception and Cognition, Toward a Model of Mental Maps." In *Response to Environment*, ed. G. Coates and A. Moffet. Raleigh, N.C.: North Carolina State University.

Steinfeld, E. 1975. *Barrier-free Design for the Elderly and the Disabled*, (Learning Modules in four parts). Syracuse, N.Y.: Syracuse University Gerontology Center and Center for Instructional Development.

Studer, R. 1970. "The Organization of Spatial Stimuli." In *Spatial Behavior of Older People*. ed. L.A. Pastalan and D.H. Carson. Ann Arbor, Mich.: The University of Michigan Press, 102–123.

Sunturia, B.H., and Price, L.L. 1971. "Otolaryngological Problems in the Geriatric Patient." In *Working with Older People*, ed. A.D. Chinn. Vol. 4 pub. no. 1459. Rockville, MD: U.S. Public Health Service, pp. 113–23.

U.S. Department of Commerce, Bureau of the Census 1975. *Statistical Abstracts of the United States*, 96th Annual Edition. Washington, D.C.

Walle, E.L. 1971. "Communication Problems of Chronically Ill and Aged in the Institutional Setting," *Hearing and Speech News*, November/December, 16–17.

Part IV:
Services and
Management

Managing sheltered or congregate housing and delivering services requires a facility for strategic intervention. Need in many cases does not equate with use or desire. Beyond the baseline of standard housing-management practices there is responsibility for providing a flexible package of services. There is also a limit to that flexibility that must be clearly understood by resident and management.

11 Service Options in Congregate Housing

Elaine M. Brody

Congregate-housing arrangements with service options should be seen in the context of their role and position in what has come to be called the continuum of long-term care. Not too many years ago, long-term care referred solely to care in various types of institutions. Since support services were virtually nonexistent, the two options for older people were living in one's own home or that of a relative on the one hand, or in an institution such as a nursing home or home for the aged on the other. Both of these approaches originated with the English poor laws, emerging during the nineteenth century as indoor relief (that is, in almshouses) and outdoor relief (usually in-kind grants). The almshouse, as indoor relief, was the ancestor of the nursing home; public assistance programs, as this century's outdoor relief, eventually culminated in Supplemental Security Income (SSI). During the past two decades, the notion has gradually gained acceptance that a variety of housing situations could be combined with services to offer another option—congregate-living arrangements. This represents yet another attempt to respond to the long-term care/support requirements of an increasing population of chronically-disabled older adults.

Though there is no generally accepted definition of long-term care, a tentative definition recently formulated by the Division of Long-Term Care of the Health Resources Administration states:

> Long-term care consists of those services designed to provide diagnostic, preventive, therapeutic, rehabilitative, supportive and maintenance services for individuals . . . who have chronic mental and/or physical impairments in a variety of institutional and non-institutional health care settings, including the home, with the goal of promoting the optimum level of physical, social and psychological functioning. (HRA 1977)

The definition calls attention to the chronicity that characterizes the ailments of older people and which dictates sustained services, rather than diagnosis alone to function as the determinant of which services are necessary, and to the social and psychological as well as physical aspects of functioning.

To realize that definition and its goals an adequate long-term care system should be coherent and comprehensive. It should include thorough multidisciplinary assessment, a spectrum of facilities providing options for an extremely diverse population, criteria for matching the individual to the most appropriate service(s) and setting, monitoring over time, and reformulation of treatment goals, linkages among facilities, and services to facilitate orderly movement along the continuum of care as changing needs dictate, on either a temporary or sustained basis. It also implies that care is available and accessible to those who need it.

The continuum is being filled much more rapidly on a theoretical level than in practical development. What does exist at present is an incomplete network of facilities and services that does not constitute a system fulfilling those conditions. Components of a model continuum can be categorized as: (1) a variety of living arrangements with different home-service patterns to which people move; (2) services delivered into one's own home (for example, homemaker, home-health, delivered meals); (3) programs that combine institutional and community care (for example, day care for the impaired, or respite care); (4) linkages to connect individuals with needed services (for instance, counselling, transportation, information and referral); and (5) acute hospital care for the intermittent acute problems often experienced by those needing long-term care.

Two pivotal services deserve special mention. The central importance of accurate multidisciplinary diagnosis and functional assessment as the point of entry to the long-term support system is indicated by its position on (figure 11-1), developed by S. Brody (1979) at the University of Pennsylvania. The chart illustrates the array of services/facilities needed for a complete system of long-term care. There is also universal agreement about the need for a service to mobilize and orchestrate the other services. Such a service has been called variously casework, advocacy, case-management, coordination, and other names, depending on the moment in time when it is discovered afresh.

No matter where older people may be along the continuum, including congregate housing, they share common needs to be addressed in service planning. Many taxonomies of human needs and of services to meet them when individuals cannot do without assistance have been developed. One group of services includes personal services, maintenance services, extended medical services, counselling, and linkages (Brody, S., 1973). To that listing should be added psychosocial and enrichment services that speak to the quality of life, that is, to enjoyment, dignity, work, creativity, and the continuity of values (Brody, E., 1976).

Some of the reasons for the growing importance of congregate housing as part of the continuum of long-term support are relatively straightforward. First, the enormous heterogeneity of the aging population dictates that there be a wide spectrum of options to meet diverse needs and preferences. Secondly, demographic developments have resulted in a massive increase in the number and proportion of older people requiring services. In 1900 there were 3 million

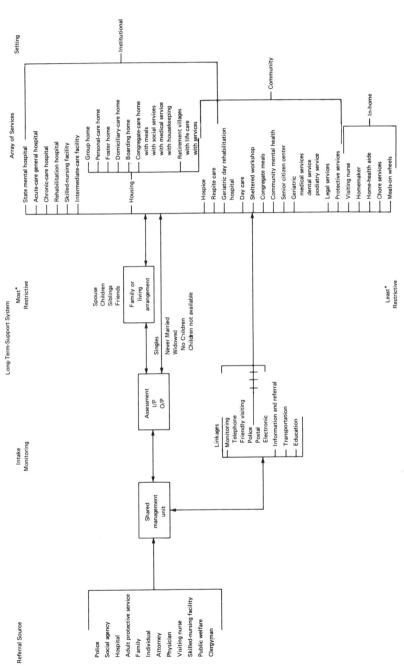

Source: S. Brody, "Data for Long-Term Care Planning by HSA's," *American Journal of Public Health* 70, no. 11 (November 1980): 1197. Reprinted with permission.

Figure 11-1. Inventory of Recommended Available Services, Appropriate to a Long-Term-Care/Support System

people sixty-five and over (4 percent of the total population) compared to 24 million at present (11 percent of the total population or one in every nine Americans). By 2020 there will be 45 million older people and by 2050 there will be 55 million who will represent one in six Americans. More significant than the absolute and proportionate increase of older people is the fact that the aging population is growing older. That is one of the keys to the long-term care issue. In the decade between 1960 and 1970, the over-seventy-five population grew at three times the rate of those sixty-five to seventy-four. During the rest of this century, those sixty-five to seventy-four will increase by 20 percent, those between seventy-five and eighty-four by 56 percent, and the over-eighty-five group by 84 percent. As a result, needs for long-term care will increase steadily, since the disabilities of the old requiring service supports are age-linked.

A third factor contributing to the need for housing options with services flows from the preference of older people to live independently and thus to preserve maximum control over their lives. Advances in income supports, primarily SSI and the Employees Retirement Insurance Security Act (ERISA), have reduced poverty as the primary barrier to community living. In recognizing the doctrine of the "least-restrictive alternative," however, one should not assume that congregate housing and other services are alternatives that would eliminate the need for institutional care. There will always be a need for such facilities for an irreducible proportion of the aged (Brody, E. 1979a). In contrast with the grandiose estimates sometimes made of the proportion of older people who are inappropriately institutionalized, the recent report of the General Accounting Office (GAO) states that 11 percent of older people in institutions could use congregate housing (1977).

A fourth rationale for service-supported congregate housing is that as many as one-third of the aged (about 8 million) either have no adult children or have children who are not close enough to provide help. For them, congregate housing can act as a surrogate family as their functional capacities decline. Among those who do have what Cantor (1977) calls "functional family," there are many who prefer congregate housing to living with an adult child. As research has indicated, most older people prefer to live near, but not in the same household with, children.

Since the mix of formal and informal supports is of direct concern to planners of congregate housing, the family relationships of older people are relevant to both site selection and service options. Service-supported living arrangements, as community-provided services in general, can supplement and complement family services, but not replace them. Beyond any doubt, families provide the vast majority of services to older people in need. They provide 80 percent of the medically-related services and personal care (HEW 1972). Ninety percent of home-help services (personal care, checking, homemaker, meal preparation, continuous supervision) and transportation are provided by family and friends (GAO 1977). The help given by friends does not, of course, approach in level or duration the help given by families (Cantor 1977; Brody, S. 1979). Apart from a spouse, adult daughters are main providers of care to the noninstitutionalized elderly (Shanas 1961; Sussman 1965; Stehouwer 1968; Litman 1971; Gurland et al. 1978). In short, the services provided by the informal-support system (primarily family) dwarf those provided by the formal system (voluntary and government agencies) in providing health and social services (Brody, E. 1979b).

Another relevant aspect of the long-term-care continuum issue is the appropriate mix of formal and informal supports. The myth of family abandonment of the aged continues to be strong, while at the same time the family is being told that it has played an important role in support of older people and is being cheered on to greater efforts. The other major myth is that provision of community services will weaken family loyalties despite evidence that such services complement and supplement, but do not substitute for family help.

Major demographic and social phenomena argue that the community inevitably must increase its share of service provision for the old. The radically changing demography has resulted not only in fewer caregivers (adult children) proportionate to those in need of care, but also those who are depended on are more often in middle age and early old-age with their caregiving capacities diminished accordingly.

In addition, the broad social trend of women's changing roles has potential for further straining family resources. Middle-aged women, who are the traditional primary caregivers to the old, are entering the labor force more rapidly than any other group. Between 1940 and 1978 the proportion of married working-women between the ages of forty-five and fifty-four rose from 11 percent to 56 percent. Women's multiple and often competing roles suggest that they may be less available to provide supportive services to the old, or, if they continue as in the past, they may be at risk of severe stress. Either way, it is apparent that the family must have help if it is to continue to care for its elderly members in the form of expanded community services and service-supported living-arrangements.

The family of the tenant in congregate housing, then, is both client and service-provider. The housing is supportive not only of the older person, but also of the family. The family is partner to the formal provider, so much so that many in-home service agencies require that family be present as a criterion for the offering of on-going services.

In turning to practical considerations of designing service options in congregate housing for older people, the basic decision is who (which segment of the population in need) will be served. That determination dictates the answer to the issue of what services should be offered.

Though the factors described above portend an increase in the service-needy population of older people, research indicates that at present a minimum of 30 percent of all noninstitutionalized older people need one or more services

(Brody, S. 1973; Pfeiffer 1973; GAO 1977; Gurland et al. 1978). Of those, about one-third require nursing care and surveillance and, hence, are not appropriate candidates for congregate housing. The remaining 20 percent constitute a potential universe from which tenants could be drawn. That estimate is supported by the GAO's Cleveland study, which states that 18 percent of noninstitutionalized older people "could use" congregate housing (GAO 1977).

It cannot be assumed, however, that those who could use such facilities would, in fact, use them if they were available. There are many filtering processes between could and would. The issue of how to translate need to services is a difficult one. Among the complexities of such translation are (1) in identical situations several different service/facility options may meet the need; (2) need as defined by professionals is not invariably paralleled by a feeling of need on the part of the potential service recipient; (3) need and wish are not identical; and (4) older people are more likely to recognize their need for concrete services (such as home help) than to recognize benefits as social recreational services (GAO 1977) or counseling.

Further, experience with many programs, again confirmed by the GAO study, tells us that the existence of a service by no means ensures its use. In Cleveland, of those eligible for federal programs, 89 percent were not using public housing, 77 percent were not using food stamps, 52 percent were not using SSI, and 29 percent were not using Medicaid (GAO 1977). Among the reasons for this phenomenon are lack of availability of the services or facilities; unawareness of their existence on the part of those eligible; determination by those eligible that the service is unacceptable because of its eligibility criteria, or terms, or the environment in which it is offered; and failure to package the service so as to be consonant with the life-style and ethnicity of the potential recipients. In addition, the strength of individual personalities and preferences should not be underestimated. Many individuals who need and even want a service, or need and want to move to a different environment, do not do so because of deep-rooted psychological barriers.

Thus, the 18-20 percent figure of *could* users does not provide an estimate of the yield of *would* users for congregate housing. Nevertheless, as others have pointed out, long waiting lists for existing congregate-facilities attest to the need for their greatly increased development.

The mutual interdependence of population characteristics and service options is illustrated clearly by the findings that emerged from Lawton's (1975) broad study of thousands of older people in high-rise buildings across the nation. He found that the amount and nature of the services actually provided in various housing environments are major determinants of the characteristics of people who move in. Service-rich housing attracted older, less healthy, less socially active people and those with lower morale than did housing without supportive services. Parenthetically, data on the effects of moves to specialized housing are unanimously positive. Simply stated, older people self-select to go where their level of service-needs can be met, a proposition that might be characterized as "Lawton's Law."

To underline, then, the task remains to determine which segment of the population the congregate housing is to serve and to design the service pattern as well as the physical structure accordingly.

The effects of services on tenant well-being require a good deal more research. Again drawing on Lawton's studies, when tenants who moved to a service-rich high-rise were compared to those who moved to a building with fewer services, the service-rich building was found to produce higher morale and housing satisfaction, and reduction in the solitary status of its tenants (though the effect was small); the low-service group improved (or had less decrement) in participation in activities and social interaction (Lawton 1976). That investigator, therefore, suggested that maximum choice be provided for potential housing applicants along the continuum between no-service housing and service-rich housing; that sensitized management of congregate housing attempt to compensate for tenants' reduction in interaction with the community by stimuli such as proximity to resources, access to transportation, and programming for outside involvement; and that both inner satisfaction and behavior maintenance be used as criteria in evaluating the impact of environments.

While over-service may have potential for increasing dependency, at this time the proponderance of evidence makes it safe to conclude that there is no imminent danger of saturating old people with services or of creating an over-abundance of supportive environments (Brody, E. 1977). It is self-evident that services that enable older people to improve their functioning are not over-service. On the other hand, dependency can be fostered by overprovision of services in the interest of the provider. The outstanding illustration is the routine feeding and dressing of institutionalized older people because it is less demanding of staff than individualization and encouragement of self-care. When total care facilities such as hospitals and institutions are over-used because lesser levels of care are not available, that, too, is over-service. In the main, when options are real, older people do not seek over-nurturing environments. The vast majority, for example, do not apply to institutions until they cannot function in their community environments and unless suitable options are unavailable.

Within that framework of incomplete knowledge, definitions of congregate housing developed by the Comptroller General of the United States, by M. Powell Lawton, and by the National Conference on Congregate Housing for Older People have some common points and therefore offer some guidelines as to the nature of services to be provided.

Congregate housing is defined as housing where eight main services are provided, namely: meals, social-recreational, education, transportation, medical care, homemaker, counseling, and security. It differs from institutions in that it does not provide such services as full-time nursing care and continuous supervision. (U.S. Comptroller General October 15, 1979).

Planned housing that contains both the physical plant and the staffing capability for delivering a variety of supportive services, including as a bare minimum a common dining facitity and the on-site serving of at least one meal per day. Other services, while optional, will frequently include homemaking, home health, delivered meals, counseling, medical dispensary service, and others. (Lawton 1979).

An assisted independent group living environment that offers the elderly who are functionally impaired or socially deprived, but otherwise in good health, the residential accommodations and supporting services they need to maintain or return to a semi-independent life style and prevent premature or unnecessary institutionalization as they grow older. (Housing Resource List, *Generations* 1979).

The central fact is that by definition congregate housing includes services. Lawton states clearly that such housing includes as a "bare minimum, a common dining facility and the on-site serving of at least one meal per day." Both he and the Comptroller General list other services such as delivered meals, counseling, medical service, homemaking, home-health, social, recreational, education, transportation, and security. Nursing care and continuous supervision are excluded either explicitly or by implication.

Apart from Lawton's emphasis on the inclusion of one meal a day as part of service provided with the housing arrangement, the various definitions of congregate housing leave open the issue of whether the services should be provided by staff of the housing itself or through arrangements with other agencies in the community. Such decisions depend on many factors such as the proximity of the housing to essential and enrichment services, (for example, grocery stores, movies) the availability to transportation, the size of the facility, and its staffing capability.

Parenthetically, though the most familiar congregate arrangements are high-rise buildings for older people with varying service patterns, attention should also be called to the small facilities that have been developing, many stimulated by the Philadelphia Geriatric Center's (PGC) Community Housing Project which began (Brody, E. 1978). In contrast to federally-assisted housing in which about 800,000 older people reside (Lawton 1979), the total number of people served in these small-scale facilities is not majestic. Almost all utilize houses or apartments originally intended as ordinary housing rather than buildings planned as institutions (Liebowitz 1978). They occupy varying positions on the continuum of living arrangements. The PGC is the most independent. Its essential components of bed-sitting room, kitchen, and bath are not shared and services are either optional (frozen main-meals and housekeeping) or not provided directly by the sponsor. At the other extreme are those with live-in or part-time staff and a rich-service pattern, which, in some, includes nursing supervision. In addition to service provision, the characteristics most of these arrangements have in common are nonprofit sponsorship and fiscal management, often buttressed by financial supplementation (Liebowitz 1978).

Whatever the size or service pattern, it is essential that the physical design of congregate housing permit the delivery of the services. Basic examples of such congruence between environment and service requirements are a dining area for group meals, an office and equipment for medical services and spaces for social/recreational services. The environment/services fit measures a successful environment according to the extent to which it (1) obviates or minimizes the need for services; (2) facilitates the development and delivery of those that are required; and (3) can be flexible in accommodating to the changing services needs of changing elderly individuals and population (Brody, E. 1979c).

The essential congruence between services and environment extends to the community or neighborhood as well, since no congregate arrangement can be totally self-contained and since, to serve its tenants well, it must relate to community service resources. Thus, the GAO study found that impaired people living dispersed in resource-poor neighborhoods were not receiving appropriate services. By contrast, those concentrated in public housing received more attention from social service agencies. It is ironic that the most impaired people were less likely than the unimpaired to receive social/recreational services. That is, those with least capacity to meet such needs themselves were also least likely to receive help in doing so.

Research provides some indications as to what older people see as their service priorities in housing. Safety from crime is an overriding concern (Sundeen and Mathieu 1976; Toseland and Rasch 1978; Davis and Brody 1979). Lawton's review of the literature (1979) indicates that the expressed wish of 60–75 percent of older people is first for on-site medical services (dispensary with nurse and physician); next in popularity is meal service (28–35 percent).

The *what* of service options relates also to the *mix*—the combination of basic services provided on an ongoing basis and those that are optional and/or intermittent. Some tenants will want some services even if they do not need them. For many of those whose capacities fit with the service pattern, there will be occasions when a richer service pattern will be needed temporarily. The high rates of hospitalization of older people speak to their intermittent needs for convalescent care (personal care, meals, and so forth) and rehabilitative services.

The services mentioned thus far are visible and concrete. Special attention should be drawn, therefore, to services of a somewhat different order. At least as important as the services offered to tenants during their residency in any congregate-housing environment are those offered to the older people (and their families) when they first consider moving in and when consideration is first given to their moving out. During the past two decades, a major stream of research on relocation has definitively established that the process by which environmental change is effected is as crucial as the move per se to the well-being of the elderly mover.

The original concept of the relocation effect, (that is, the negative impact of moving institutionalized older people from one environment to another, including excess morbidity and mortality) has been modified by subsequent research. The effects of moving were found to be qualified by the characteristics of the movers, the qualities of the receiving environment, the reasons for the move and its significance to the mover, and the ways in which the moves were managed. The physically ill, depressed, confused, and involuntary movers were the most vulnerable to negative effects. On the other hand, improvements occurred in movers who were physically well and those who moved voluntarily into senior-citizens' housing. Negative effects were reduced or avoided when older people participated in the decision-making process, were offered options, and were carefully prepared for moving through individual counseling and pre-move orientation. The well-being of the movers is positively related to a favorable or upgraded psychosocial environment in the new residence, that is, to a natural life-style; personalization; encouragement of autonomy and social interaction; and warmth and positive staff attitudes. There is also evidence that the adjustment period and therefore the need for services extends several months beyond the actual move (Relocation Symposium 1974; Community Housing Symposium 1978).

Such information has strong implications for the service patterns of congregate housing. Since those in need of such living arrangements are not completely intact, their moves are not likely to be prompted solely by a desire to leave the old environment, but may be in response to the need for varying levels of help. To that extent there is the element of lack of choice which makes them vulnerable and which therefore requires skilled counseling help.

What of those older people who need to move and express a wish to do so but not actually follow through? Research has identified many whose environments are not congruent with their capacities to function, some of whom live under extreme stress in high-crime neighborhoods (Brody, E. 1977). Many older people may be psychologically unable to leave their homes and the familiar neighborhoods in which they have been rooted for many years. Others may be experiencing declines, often subtle, that prevent them from mobilizing the necessary psychic and/or physical energy, and that lead them to give up. What is the nature of the responsibility of congregate housing to extend helping services to such individuals? Does it reach out actively to facilitate the moving process for those who are immobilized in that manner?

The related issue, of course, is the nature of the services offered to those who must move out of congregate housing. Inevitably, as they age, many tenants will experience the normal declines of aging as well as the disabilities of catastrophic illness or the progress of chronic ailments. Service needs will increase and some will be at risk of institutionalization. When service needs are beyond what the housing can provide, the same service supports indicated during the in-move and adjustment phases are necessary in order to manage the move constructively. The elderly tenants, and their families as well, are again often immobilized at this point. Their congregate housing has achieved the status of home; an additional move connotes decline, may have psychological over-tones of death, and is resisted.

The aging and decline of the tenant population and the resultant change in service needs over time pose a dilemma common to all congregate housing. The dilemma arises when the limits of person-environment-congruence begin to be stretched (Lawton 1979). Lawton's research explores precisely how they change and how the housing itself and the community change to maintain (or not maintain) need satisfaction for tenants and benefits or costs for the community (1979). Though such data are not yet available to guide decisions, it is evident that sponsors have two options: They may elect to hold firmly to the original service-pattern and admission criteria for tenant capacities, offering to the declining tenant only those services initially planned; or they may plan to add services as need arises so that the facility itself changes to accommodate such changing capacities.

If the auspice opts for change, how far can the sponsor go without changing the nature of the facility itself? At some point, an enriched service-pattern demands a different physical environment: a nurse cannot monitor an individual who is behind a locked apartment door. Apart from the inability to meet the life-safety-code requirements for nursing homes, the result of the change option may include a metamorphosis in the character of the facility. New applicants meeting the original criteria will not apply; for that group the appropriate facility will have disappeared. In any event, if planners choose the change model, the ultimate limits of the service package must be determined and the structure planned so as to have the capability of incorporating the additional services. If the other option is chosen—that is, if tenants must retain their original functional capacities to a significant extent in order to be permitted continued residence and the service package remains largely inflexible—there is likely to be a high rate of turnover with a need for elaborate referral services. Either way, the sponsor must think ahead, relating criteria for eligibility to the service options provided and to the ultimate parameters of those services.

Congregate housing with service options for older people undoubtedly is a clear, positive direction. As the target population for congregate housing grows older and increases numerically, we must be aware that value judgments and misconceptions concerning services to older people often influence the planning of services, whether in congregate housing or in other settings. The word service itself is value-laden since it implies dependency. In our culture a positive value is ascribed to independence, with the notion that dependency per se is bad. Although there is general belief in the desirability of maintaining maximum functioning levels throughout the life span, the general direction in old age is decline. In contrast with the transitional dependencies of child-hood, those of old age are most often chronic and may augur further depen-dency. Though older people are not children, many of their dependencies, are no less normal. Whatever the criteria for applicants to congregate housing, it is inevitable that the tenants will change over time and that this will result in increases in their service needs. Their dependencies must therefore be expected, accepted, made legitimate and planned for (Brody, E. 1977), rather than be regarded with negative judgmental attitudes.

Another common notion is that services to meet dependency needs actually foster continuing dependence. On the contrary, services can increase independence much in the way that a crutch enables a disabled person to ambulate. As has been pointed out, the delicate decisions have as their object a correct balance between service provision on the one hand and encouragement of the judicious exercise of skills on the other (Lawton and Nahemow, 1973). Implicit in that concept is the goal: services should maximize independent functioning when possible and meet needs that the older people cannot meet themselves.

Further, dependency is a complex concept that requires sorting out. Individuals vary in the extent to which they accept dependency and in what they regard as dependency. Thus, older people often view services in their own homes (such as homemaker) or service-supported congregate housing as enabling them to live independently rather than be dependent by living with or unduly burdening their children (Brody, E., 1979d). There is also variation among elderly individuals on which types of dependencies are easier to accept psychologically. Financial, physical, and emotional dependencies may have quite different inner meanings.

There are differences, too, regarding the acceptability of depending on different kinds of service providers. For example, at the Philadelphia Geriatric Center, we are studying three generations of women in terms of their preferences for receiving certain types of help from different sources. The women in all three generations are united in preferring adult children as confidantes and financial managers, an expression of family bonds and responsibility, but they saw those services as quite different from the actual giving of money (which they did not want from children) and concrete services. With regard to the latter—personal care, household tasks and maintenance—there were generational differences and ethnic differences expressed as the women chose preferred service providers from among family members, friends and neighbors, paid workers, and community agencies (Brody et al. 1979). These findings confirm the need to be aware of ethnic, religious, and other characteristics when planning services. They also signal the need for flexibility over time as new cohorts are graduated into the aging phase of life (there is a one-third turnover in the over-sixty-five population every five years), rather than cementing services into rigid patterns unresponsive to changing needs. These new groups will have differing perceptions of service needs and of acceptable packaging of those services.

In short, there are different meanings placed on differing dependencies on different people, and therefore preferences and degrees of acceptability vary. Service options, then, must take note of such changing individual and cultural preferences as well as of differing levels of functioning.

Following World War II a massive increase occurred in that form of long-term care called the nursing-home industry. The number of beds rose from about 25,000 in 1939 to 450,000 in 1954 to more than 1.4 million in 1981. The developmental direction of those facilities was guided primarily by the hospital model. Discussions elsewhere (Brody, E., 1973) have documented the imposition of the hospital atmosphere and routines on living arrangements in which one-third of the older residents live for one to three years, another third for more than three years (U.S. Bureau of the Census 1978; U.S. National Center for Health Statistics 1978) and in which they become patients rather than people.

So that there is no misunderstanding—medical services are sine qua non in service options in congregate housing, whether they are provided by the housing itself or through linkages with community agencies. However, to the extent that the population of congregate housing is impaired functionally, the risk of its becoming a medical facility increases. As nursing-home history has taught us, medical/nursing services tend to rise in prominence relative to the human services that speak to the quality of life. That direction is reinforced by funding keyed to the life-safety code and medical services and grossly neglects social/recreational needs and a natural life-style. I believe, therefore, that congregate housing should develop under social-agency auspices or be free-standing rather than have health-facility sponsorship.

Recognition that congregate housing is part of the long-term support system has not been paralleled by social-policy implementation of that concept. Reimbursement, in the main, has been for medically related services, with medical rather than social need triggering the availability of public and other third-party funding for services. We must be vigilant, then, that dependency is not equated solely with medical needs by the public-policy decision makers.

In 1960, Arthur Waldman developed the Philadelphia Geriatric Center's York Houses, the first congregate housing to include a significant package of services. Noting the trend toward the development of high-rise apartment buildings and smaller congregate arrangements with services, he wrote that they have many elements of the institution "restructured and made palatable with a new acceptable facade" (Waldman 1965). His message is clear. In the interest of well-being of congregate-housing residents, let us make their living arrangements palatable by creating environments that reflect the value of home—that keep them people rather than turning them into patients or inmates.

References and Additional Resources

Brody, E.M. 1979a. "Long-Term Care of the Aged: Promises and Prospects," *Health and Social Work* 4:29–59.

Brody, E.M. 1979b "Women's Changing Roles, the Aging Family and Long-Term Care of Older People," *National Journal*, pp. 1828–1833.

Brody, E.M. 1979c. "Service-Supported Independent Living in an Urban setting: The Philadelphia Geriatric Center's Community Housing for the Elderly." In *Environmental Context of Aging.* ed. T.O. Byerts, S.C. Howell and L.A. Pastalan. New York: Garland Publishing, Inc., 191–216.

Brody, E.M. 1979d. "Aged Parents and Aging Children." In *Aging Parents,* ed. P.K. Ragan. Los Angeles: University of Southern California Press, 267–287.

Brody, E.M. 1978. "Community Housing for the Elderly: The Program, the People, the Decision-Making Process, and the Research," *Gerontologist* 18: 121–128.

Brody, E.M. 1977. "Environmental Factors in Dependency." In *Care of the Elderly: Meeting the Challenge of Dependency.* ed. A.N. Exton-Smith and J.G. Evans. London: Academic Press; New York: Grune and Stratton.

Brody, E.M. 1976. "Basic Data Requirements: Individual Care and Internal Management of Geriatric Institutions and Services," *Medical Care* 14, Supplement: 72–82.

Brody, E.M.; Davis, L.J.; Fulcomer, M.; and Johnsen, P. 1979. "Three Generations of Women: Comparisons of Attitudes and Preferences for Service Providers," paper presented at the 32nd Annual Meeting of the Gerontological Society, Washington, D.C.

Brody, E.M.; Kleban, M.H.; and Moss, M. 1974. "Measuring the Impact of Change," *Gerontologist* 14: 299–305.

Brody, E.M., 1973. "A Million Procrustean Beds," *Gerontologist* 13: 430–435.

Brody, S.J., 1979. *Planning for the Long-term Support/Care System: The Array of Services to be Considered.* Philadelphia, Penn.: Health Services Council, Inc., Region III, Center for Health Planning.

Brody, S.J. 1973. "Comprehensive Health Care of the Elderly: An Analysis," *Gerontologist* 13: 412–418.

Cantor, M.H. 1977. "Neighbors and Friends: An Overlooked Resource in the Informal Support System," paper presented at 30th Annual Meeting of the Gerontological Society, San Francisco.

Davis, L., and Brody, E.M. 1979. *Rape and Older Women, A Guide to Prevention and Protection.* Washington, D.C.: U.S. DHEW, NIMH, National Center for the Prevention and Control of Rape, Government Printing Office.

Gurland, B.; Dean, L.; Gurland, R.; and Cook, D. 1978. "Personal Time Dependency in the Elderly of New York City: Findings from the U.S.-U.K. Cross-National Geriatric Community Study," *Dependency in the Elderly of New York City*, Community Council of Greater New York.

Health Resources Administration, Division of Long-term Care 1977. *The Future of Long-term Care in the United States–The Report of the Task Force.* Washington, D.C.: Government Printing Office.

Kleban, M.H., and Turner-Massey, P. 1978. "Short-Range Effects of Community Housing," *Gerontologist* 18: 129–132.

Lawton, M.P. 1979. "Changing Service Needs of Older Tenants, Proposal to Administration on Aging." Philadelphia Geriatric Center, mimeograph.

Lawton, M.P., ed. 1979. "Housing Resource List," *Generations* (Winter):3.

_____. 1976. "The Relative Impact of Congregate and Traditional Housing on Elderly Tenants," *Gerontologist* 16: 237-242.

_____. 1975. "Final Report: Social and Medical Services in Housing for the Aged." Philadelphia Geriatric Center, mimeograph.

Lawton, M.P.; Brody, E.M.; and Turner-Massey, P. 1978. "The Relationships of Environmental Factors to Changes in Well-Being," *Gerontologist* 18: 133-137.

Lawton, M.P., and Nahemow, L. 1973. "Ecology and the Aging Process." In *The Psychology of Adult Development and Aging*. ed. C. Eisdorfer and M.P. Lawton. Washington, D.C.: American Psychological Association, 619-674.

Liebowitz, B. 1978. "Implications of Community Housing for Planning and Policy," *Gerontologist* 18: 138-141.

Liebowitz, B. 1974. "Impact of Intra-Institutional Relocation: Background and the Planning Process," *Gerontologist* 14: 293-295.

Litman, T.J. 1971. "Health Care and the Family: A Three-Generational Analysis," *Medical Care* 9:67-81.

Locker, R., and Rublin, A. 1974. "Clinical Aspects of Facilitating Relocation," *Gerontologist* 14: 295-299.

National Conference on Congregate Housing for Older People. 1975. Washington, D.C.

Patnaik, B.; Lawton, M.P.; Kleban, M.H.; and Maxwell, R. 1974. "Behavioral Adaptation to the Change in Institutional Residence," *Gerontologist* 14: 305-307.

Pfeiffer, E. 1973. "Multidimensional Quantitative Assessment of Three Populations of Elderly," paper presented at Annual Meeting of the Gerontological Society, Miami Beach, Fla.

Shanas, E. 1961. *Family Relationships of Older People*, Health Information Foundation, Research Series 20 Chicago: University of Chicago Press.

Stehouwer, J. 1968. "The Household and Family Relations of Old People." In *Old People in Three Industrial Societies*, ed. E. Shanas. New York: Atherton Press, 177-226.

Sundeen, R., and Mathieu, J. 1976. "The Fear of Crime and Its Consequences among Elderly in Their Urban Communities," *Gerontologist* 16: 211-219.

Sussman, M.B. 1965. "Relationships of Adult Children with Their Parents in the United States." In *Social Structure and the Family*, ed. E. Shanas and G.F. Streib. Englewood Cliffs, N.J.: Prentice-Hall, Inc., 62-92.

Toseland, R., and Rasch, J. 1978. "Factors Contributing to Older Person's Satisfaction with Their Communities," *Gerontologist* 18: 395-402.

U.S. Bureau of the Census. 1978. *1976 Survey of Institutionalized Persons: A Study of Persons Receiving Long-term Care.*

U.S. Department of Health, Education and Welfare, Public Health Service. 1972. *Home Care for Persons 55 and Over, United States: July 1966– June 1968*, Vital and Health Statistics, Series 10: No. 73.

U.S. General Accounting Office. 1977. *The Well-Being of Older People in Cleveland, Ohio: Report to the Congress by the Comptroller General of the United States*, Washington, D.C.

U.S. National Center for Health Statistics. 1978. *Advance Data, A Comparison of Nursing Home Residents and Discharges from the 1977 National Nursing Home Survey: United States*. U.S. Department of Health, Education, and Welfare, PHS, No. 29.

Waldman, A. 1965. "Non-Institutional Living Arrangements for the Aged: Fact or Fiction." In *Selected Papers, Fifth Annual Conference of State Executives on Aging*, U.S. Department of Health, Education and Welfare. Washington, D.C.: USGPO.

12 A Management Overview

Diana L. McIver

Critical to the success of a congregate-housing development is quality management. Although design, construction, and location contribute substantially to the viability of a development, no aspect controls the future of the facility as significantly as does management, which has the capability to enhance or destroy even the best-laid foundation.

The Role of Management

For the reason stated above, management must be a prime consideration long before the doors open. A professional management agent should assist the development team throughout the planning, design and development stages. Although it is often tempting to spend less on the management component in an effort to allocate more money to construction, a continued allegiance to quality management can result in substantial cost savings over the life of the facility.

In a speech before the First National Conference on Congregate Housing for Older People in 1975, Frances M. Carp asked the question: "What is to be congregated—living units? old people? services?" The management of congregate housing must address these same questions—are we managing people, housing or services? The effective housing manager recognizes the interaction between these three components and strives to manage all three. The management goal should be to provide an efficient, effective housing program with a high degree of resident satisfaction.

Types of Management

The management role is obviously a necessary one; the accomplishment of this role, however, may be performed in numerous ways.

The first choice to be made by the housing sponsor is whether to self-manage the development or whether to hire a professional management firm. That choice will be affected by the following factors: size of the development, location of the development, sponsor's related experience in housing for the elderly, particularly congregate housing, financial resources available for project operations. The management of congregate housing should not be attempted by a novice. If the owner does not have sufficient experience and capability in the area of management, professional management should be sought. In selecting a professional management firm, the owner should look for a firm with: successful track record in housing management; experience in the management of housing for the elderly, preferably congregate housing or housing with extensive services; management philosophy sensitive to both social and fiscal issues; responsive management plan, and day-to-day operating systems procedures, preferably in manual form.

An alternative for the sponsor who wishes to be involved in management but does not have sufficient experience is turn-key management. Under this system, a professional management firm provides on-the-job training to the sponsor's staff for a two-to-three-year period during which the reins of operation are gradually turned over to the sponsor. The management firm serves as the management firm of record during this training period.

Once the sponsor has selected the type of management, there are several organizational structures which may be employed in the management of congregate housing. Examples of possible structures are shown in figures 12-1 through 12-2.

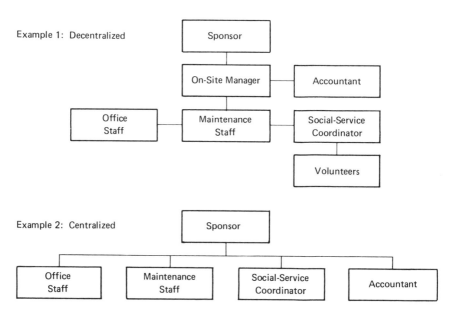

Source: National Center for Housing Management, *Housing for the Elderly* (November 1978). Reprinted with permission.

Figure 12-1. Self-Management

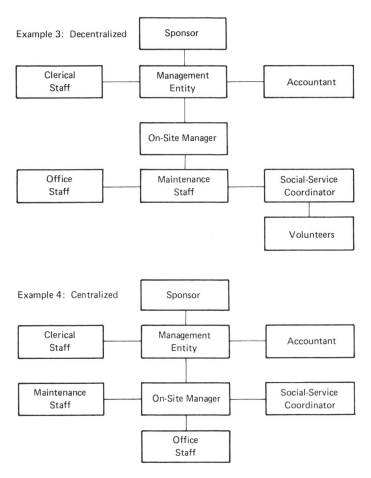

Source: National Center for Housing Management, *Housing for the Elderly* (November 1978). Reprinted with permission.

Figure 12-2. Management Agent

Figure 12-1 portrays decentralized and centralized organizational structures for self-management housing-developments. In figure 12-1, example 1, the housing sponsor employs an on-site manager who has day-to-day responsibility for housing operations. All project staff report to the on-site manager who in turn will be directly responsible to the sponsor. In figure 12-1, example 2 the housing sponsor assumes direct responsibility for all day-to-day project operations. Unless the sponsor has both the time and experience to assume this responsibility, this format is not suggested.

Figure 12–2, examples 3 and 4, depicts decentralized and centralized organizational structures for developments utilizing a professional management firm. In example 3, the sponsor employs a management entity to handle accounting and certain clerical functions in its central office. The management entity in turn employs an on-site manager who directly supervises the project staff. Under this arrangement, the project staff reports directly to the on-site manager, an employee of the management entity. While the principal duties are performed at the on-site staff level, the responsibility for performance still rests with the management firm. In example 4, the sponsor contracts with a management entity which hires the on-site manager. In this model, however, the management entity performs most major functions from its central office, with day-to-day supervision performed by the on-site manager. This model is sometimes employed when the pooling of staff among several developments can result in the provision of more specialized or cost-effective service programs. Smaller congregate projects may tend to benefit from participation in such a system.

There are, of course, many variations to these themes and congregate-housing sponsors must determine which model or variation best suits the needs of their residents.

Management Components

Regardless of your management structure, your management system will include the following components: Occupancy, maintenance, nonshelter services, safety-security, personnel, budgeting. The first four of these components—occupancy, maintenance, nonshelter services, and safety-security—constitute subsystems of the management system, while the latter two—personnel and budgeting—affect the entire system.

Occupancy

Occupancy is regarded as that part of a manager's work. It is centered around moving people into and out of a housing development. The occupancy cycle includes marketing, resident selection, preoccupancy procedures, move-ins, recertification and reexamination, and move-outs. While this cycle is typical of all apartment management, special concerns arise in the management of congregate housing for the elderly and handicapped. Resident selection is one area that should be of particular concern to the managers of congregate housing. Resident selection criteria should address age, income, health, physical limitations or disabilities, family composition, and credit rating. It is vitally important that resident-selection criteria complement the nonshelter service program offered. No one wants to admit residents with needs that cannot be served. Further, it is best to keep a balanced mix of residents (that is, age, physical abilities, marital status, race, and so on) to enhance future marketing. Further, the initial mix of residents tends to create a lasting image and tends also to be hard to alter, except as it becomes increasingly old and frail.

In addition to establishing entrance criteria, congregate-housing managers should also establish exit criteria that should be clearly explained to the resident at the time of entry into the development. These criteria should address the type of health and support needs that can and cannot be met by the management and the point at which other more appropriate accommodations must be sought for the resident.

The ability to maintain full occupancy along with resident satisfaction directly effects the economic viability of the development. A firm but understanding approach to occupancy issues is usually successful.

Maintenance

Maintenance includes all activities that improve the appearance of buildings and grounds; optimize the performance of working parts and insure dependability of performance; correct physical, mechanical, and other defects; reduce accidents; and extend the productive life of the property in general.

In congregate housing, special attention must be given to any failures or deficiencies that would endanger the well-being of a frail population. Further, special instruction should be provided to residents on the maintenance and utilization procedures for any equipment or appliances located in their apartment units. Maintenance employees should be instructed to alert management to possible resident problems, such as housekeeping neglect, which may indicate poor health on the part of the resident. Management should also be alert to residents with numerous requests, since these requests may indicate a need for companionship and conversation rather than a true maintenance need.

Well maintained buildings and grounds are a major factor in the decision to move in, and in continuing resident satisfaction.

Nonshelter Services

Nonshelter services constitute a major management component in congregate housing. This area encompasses those services not related to the physical plant or shelter aspects of housing but necessary to the well-being of the residents. These services include: nutrition programs (always); health and medical services; housekeeping/home-chore services (always); transportation; social, educational; and recreational programs; personal services; counseling, information and referral services; and commercial services. Since the coordination, development and delivery of these services tend to be the most difficult management-issue in congregate housing, this will be discussed more fully later in this chapter.

Safety/ Security

Safety/security is that area of housing management that insures that residents are provided with a safe living-environment. It includes (1) protection against crime, (2) psychological well-being, and (3) personal safety. From a managerial standpoint, safety and security measures fall into two categories: hardware and software. Hardware incorporates site hardening and the physical side of security; software is an umbrella label for a variety of management techniques such as resident-education programs. In congregate housing for the elderly, security and safety take on a special meaning because of the physical vulnerability of most residents. Further, anticipated patterns of income (for example, Social Security checks arriving the first of the month) make elderly persons particularly susceptible to criminal intrusions.

Personnel

Personnel as a component of management involves hiring, training, supervising, and evaluating project employees. To adequately implement the concept of congregate housing, a variety of staff professionals must be employed. The number and types of staff positions will vary depending on project location, size of development, type and extent of services, and financial resources. In determining staffing patterns, careful consideration should be given to management functions that might best be handled by outside contractors. This is especially important in the social-service area, where licensure and insurance requirements may be in effect for employees involved in food service or medical procedures.

Typically, the one-hundred-unit apartment complex with minimal or no services would need the following full-time staff: resident manager, clerk/secretary, maintenance superintendent, maintenance assistant, and groundskeeper. To include a service package at least one full-time social-service coordinator will be necessary. Additional service personnel will be required, depending on the volume of services. It is also possible to contract with outside agencies to provide these services, particularly nutrition, in full or part. Under these circumstances, the staff will be employees of the agency and not of the development.

In the selection of personnel, it is important to find people who are not only qualified and competent, but also sensitive to the needs of elderly persons. It is important to provide training for employees on a continuing basis and to have regular staff meetings at which employees can discuss problems and ideas.

Budgeting

Budgeting is critical to the fiscal success of a congregate-housing development. The annual budget of a housing development serves four vital functions:

The budget is a planning tool for the management of the development. In order to prepare a budget properly, the manager must pre-plan the full operation for the coming year.

The budget serves as a day-to-day control for the manager's administration of the development.

The budget is a monthly evaluation tool for project operations.

Budget data combined with other operating data become a major input into the annual management review of the development.

In congregate housing for the elderly, budgeting must include services in addition to ordinary operating costs. Since service costs are often not covered by rental income, the manager must consider what financial resources (resident or nonresident) will be used to support these services. Generally, a manager must utilize a combination of resident fees and government and private funding-programs to provide an affordable service-package. Both the U.S. Department of Housing and Urban Development and the U.S. Farmers Home Administration have underway demonstration programs that combine federal-service dollars with federal-construction dollars to provide congregate housing for low-and-moderate-income elderly people.

It becomes obvious that all of the management components described above are interrelated; no single component can operate in a vacuum.

The Management Cycle

The functions of management fall within the following categories: needs assessment, planning, program design and development, implementation, monitoring, evaluation. These functions constitute a management cycle, a cycle which should encourage constant updating and improvement of management operations. Depending on staffing arrangements, these functions may be performed by various personnel. It is important, however, that the manager integrate these six functions into the overall management-system being utilized.

Managing the Nonshelter Services: Special Concerns

Perhaps the most challenging aspect of managing congregate housing is that of coordinating and operating the nonshelter services. The extent to which these services are provided will vary from development to development. To determine the level of services to be provided in a particular congregate development, or any housing-for-the-elderly complex, the following service-level checklist (figure 12–3) developed by the National Center for Housing Management may be used.

Service levels should be in direct proportion to an individual's level of independence. Although they will not directly correspond to chronological age, the levels will bear relation to physiological age as indicated in the continuum of service needs.

The continuum also illustrates the relationships between essential and nonessential services. As people age, they become increasingly frail. Services that were earlier considered nonessential or luxury services become essential to the support of that individual in an independent or semi-independent living-situation. For instance, housekeeping assistance may be a nonessential service for an able-bodied person, yet essential to the physical well-being of an elderly person with arthritis.

Typically, the manager of congregate housing for the elderly is serving a constitutency with varying levels of service needs. From a management stand-point, it is generally advisable to restrict the number of persons with heavy service needs to 15–20 percent of the population. With this, the manager can achieve a balance of resident population between the young-old, middle-old, and old-old, making it possible to continue to attract a more independent population and avoid an old-folks-home identity. Although a population mix is clearly desirable to maintain full occupancy, the manager must avoid overservicing or underservicing residents. This can be accomplished through proper planning.

In planning a nonshelter service package, managers must consider: needs of the residents, financial capacity of the sponsor and residents, staff capability and availability, location of the development, design of the development, service availability. These service considerations are interrelated; that is, a sit-down-meals program cannot be initiated if the space (design element), staff, and financial resources are not available. Moreover, since circumstances change, nonshelter service programs must be continually monitored, evaluated and updated in accordance with these elements.

The key ingredient insuring the success of a nonshelter service program is flexibility; it is necessary to build and maintain a nonshelter service package that can adapt to the ever-changing needs of elderly residents. Further, it is critical that, within this flexibility, the program demonstrates reliability and credibility. Creating false expectations by making unrealistic promises must be avoided. Elderly residents need the security of knowing that the services they depend upon will be there when needed, and the manager must be prepared to back up commitments.

In addition to being both flexible and reliable, the service package should be versatile, that is, it should maximize the options available to elderly persons.

Place a mark in the box under the specific services for each service offered by your development opposite the service level which MOST CLOSELY DESCRIBES the level of service your development offers.

	Nutrition/ Meals	Health and Medical	Housekeeping	Transportation	Commercial	Social, Recreation, Education	Personal and Counseling
• Residents obtain or arrange for services privately.							
• Management inventories and informs residents of off-site community resources.							
• Management identifies and informs residents of special services and facilities for the elderly (discounts, programs, and so on) off-site and how to obtain them.							
• Management solicits improvement of off-site services and delivery to the elderly.							
• Management provides space for on-site services arranged for by residents (community rooms, and so on).							
• Management assists in scheduling and obtaining equipment and assigns space for on-site service delivery arranged for by residents.							
• Management solicits on-site delivery of volunteer or other free services to residents.							
• Manangement arranges for on-site service delivery of services by concessionaires, community resources, contractors, and so on,							
• with payment to be arranged between provider and individual users.							
• and collects a per-use charge from individual users.							
• with a monthly service fee paid by all residents.							
• with costs included in rent.							
• Management provides on-site service delivery by staff							
• on a fee-for-service basis to individual residents.							
• with a monthly service fee paid by all residents.							
• with costs included in rents.							

Independent ←——————→ Dependent

Source: National Center for Housing Management, *Housing For the Elderly* (November 1978). Reprinted with permission.

Figure 12-3. Service-Level Checklist

Independence is treasured by all people regardless of age, and availability of choices gives a greater degree of independence in determining life patterns. It is important that managers remember that the presence of choice implies more control on the part of the residents; the absence of choice implies more control on the part of the management.

Developing a Service Package

The following steps must be undertaken in the development of a congregate service package:

1. *Assessment.* (a) Prepare a resident profile including such information as age, number of residents, physical limitations, income, sex, marital status, and so forth. (b) Determine resident needs and demands through questionnaires and through examination of physical and financial status. (c) Inventory existing nonshelter service-programs. (d) Determine needs and demands of residents versus availability of existing services.

2. *Planning.* Outline goals and objectives to include both short-term and long-term objectives.

3. *Designing a Service Package.* When a service package is designed, technological (space and equipment), organizational (labor), and financial (resident or nonresident) factors must be considered. Remember that services can be provided off-site as well as on-site. After the service package has been designed, check it for appropriateness to resident needs, cost feasibility, staff utilization and space utilization.

4. Once the preceding steps have been completed and the congregate-services program is ready for implementation, staffing, supervision, scheduling, purchasing and record keeping may proceed. If you plan to contract for services, this will be done in lieu of or in addition to staffing.

5. *Monitoring.* It is vitally important to monitor the operation of the service package. It is important to insure that programs are appropriate to resident needs, well-run and cost-effective.

6. *Evaluation.* Evaluation of programs should be done on a periodic basis, preferably semi-annually. The information thus retrieved should give a factual assessment of program viability.

Conclusion

Management is an important but often overlooked ingredient in the housing-development process. In the area of congregate housing, its importance is even greater, since this type of housing requires more sophisticated management operations. Professional management advice must be sought in the early developmental stages to insure that the physical structure is designed and constructed to endure years of wear and tear and consequently to provide a decent, safe, and sanitary home for its occupants. Moreover, throughout the life of the facility, it is management that will directly effect the quality of living for the population served.

Suggested Resources

The Housing Manager's Resource Book, National Center for Housing Management, 1976.
Managing Housing and Services for the Elderly, National Center for Housing Management, 1977.
Housing for the Elderly: A Model Management System for Nonprofit Sponsors, National Center for Housing Management, 1978.
Congregate Housing for Older People, International Center for Social Gerontology, 1977.

13 Health-Care Needs of Elderly in Congregate Housing

Richard W. Besdine and
Sylvia Sherwood

The demographic imperative has emerged as a powerful argument for more and better services for the elderly American population. Although it is well known that vigorous middle age can persist beyond age sixty-five and even into the seventies in the absence of disease, sixty-five years of age will mark old age for statistical convenience. Seventy-five years ago, 4 percent of the American population (approximately 3 million people) was over sixty-five-years old. Currently, the more than 24 million Americans over age sixty-five constitute 11 percent of our population (U.S. Bureau of the Census 1977). Maximum human life-span has changed little in 100 or even 1000 years, in America or anywhere else, remaining approximately 100 years. The dramatic change accounting for the shift toward oldness of the American and many European populations is an increase in mean life-expectancy. In 1900, the average citizen lived less than fifty years. Now that American is living more than seventy years, with about an eight-year survival advantage for women over men. One obvious effect of this increased average longevity of the population is prolonged old age. According to current projections, a sixty-five-year old man has a life expectancy of thirteen more years, and at seventy-five he will live nine more years. A sixty-five year old woman has an eighteen-year life expectancy, and at age seventy-five she will live twelve more years (Kovar 1977). The most startling presentation of the demographic imperative indicates that of all the people who have ever survived on earth to age sixty-five, a majority are alive today, and this statistic will continue to be correct to the year 2000 (Dans and Kerr 1979).

The sharp increase in the elderly population in most Western cultures has resulted in a proportional demand for appropriate housing. Because the prevalence of disease and disability increases sharply with age, particularly in the older segment of the elder population (the old-old, as opposed to the young-old), the housing needs of this group must be specially addressed. If housing is not adapted to their needs, long institutional stays can be predicted for the frail elderly. Bernard Isaacs, a prominent Scottish geriatrician, has vividly identified the impact on health and welfare services of the growing infirm British elderly population, a phenomenon he calls *Survival of the Unfittest* (1972). Society's aging has produced a need for new and more services for the impaired elderly. Previously unimagined numbers of people are surviving into extremes of old age with burdens of medical disease, emotional vulnerability, social disadvantage, and the inevitable poverty these burdens create.

Medical-care needs are beginning to be addressed by the provider community as well as by health planners, but the provision of basic services, with housing in the forefront, seems to have lagged behind the more dramatic health-care issues. Though the over-sixty-five population in America is growing rapidly, the group over seventy-five is growing most rapidly of all. This is precisely the group with the highest prevalence of dependency needs and disease, and the group most vulnerable to institutionalization. Though only 5 percent of Americans over sixty-five-years of age live in nursing homes, nearly half those over eighty years will die in a nursing home (Butler 1978). Citizens seventy-five-to-eighty-four years old have a threefold increased prevalence of service need compared with those sixty-five-to-seventy-four (Institute of Medicine 1978). Housing for our old-old population should anticipate increasing frailty and the need for community-based services in order to avoid future institutionalization. In Great Britain, a housing experiment has been underway for at least ten years in which sheltered housing for the elderly has been provided on a large scale. Sheltered-housing descriptions are available elsewhere (Anderson 1976), but a brief summary of the services which have, in Britain, allowed elderly individuals to remain in the community and out of institutions is needed. Sheltered housing in Great Britain describes congregate housing for the elderly in which certain services are provided. There is a manager on the premises who is responsible for keeping in touch with and being aware of any difficulties encountered by the elderly residents. Various forms of checking, communications, and emergency warning-systems have been tried, but an intercommunication system between the manager and the elderly resident has been essential. The security, protection, and sense of comfort provided the residents of such housing is an important factor in maintaining frail elderly in their community setting. Sheltered housing additionally provides one hot meal a day, both for nutritive and socializing values. Housing designed to maintain frail elderly in the community needs to be specially adapted for disability, including such arrangements as wide doorways, no steps, grip rails at toilet and bathtub, and appropriately low counters and storage space. In Great Britain, specially adapted sheltered housing has allowed very frail, disabled elderly to stay at home for very long periods, avoiding even terminal institutional care (Anderson 1976).

In the British experience, health services for the elderly in sheltered housing have been provided by the comprehensive National Health Service with its special apparatus exclusively for elderly individuals. In America, where no special geriatric health services exist, a medical-care component must be developed as part of the design of congregate housing for frail elderly.

Medical services for elderly in congregate housing should have as their goals avoidance of institutionalization, maintenance of resident health, and early intervention in the disease process. The reimbursement and organizational structure of the multiple relevant services is complex. Navigating the maze of services and service organizations is often an impossible task, especially for an ill old person. Therefore, much has been written recently about the channeling of services—an easy pathway of access to services for old people. The channeling can be organizational or individual; that is, there can exist a definite pathway which, once entered upon, has a set sequence of experiences for the old person, or there can be a navigator-advocate who assists the old person in obtaining the appropriate intervention. In either case, health services connected to sheltered housing for the elderly are intrinsically channeled for the resident. Another reason for providing health services in elderly congregate housing is that old people appropriately have increasing anxiety about their health. The prevalence of disease rises with age, as do doctor visits and utilization of all health services (Institute of Medicine 1977). Old people are justified in expecting that they will have more illness and more need for health services. Allaying anxiety concerning the availability of services by providing them within the residence of elderly people makes a substantial contribution to a better life quality. Available health services ensure that old people will have earlier intervention when they are ill and thus a greater likelihood of recovery (Anderson 1976).

If older people behaved as younger ones when they are ill, health-care services for the old would not need any special components. The structure could be identical to the current American system which functions quite well in general for young and middle-aged patients. Unfortunately, the elderly patient does not have the same health or illness behavior as the younger individual. It is precisely these differences that account for the generally poor record of the American health-care system in dealing with the problems of the elderly. Accordingly, we must understand what these behavioral differences are before we can constructively plan health services for elderly individuals in congregate housing.

A classic fact of geriatric medicine is that, when they are ill with legitimate symptoms, old people conceal, or at least do not report, those symptoms until very late in the course of the disease. Nonreporting of illness by the elderly virtually guarantees that, in a health care system that does not actively intervene to assess the health status of elderly individuals, disease will be discovered late, be treated late, and likely have a disappointing outcome. Many studies have examined the health status of the noncomplaining, community-dwelling elderly. The earliest investigations were performed in Scotland after implementation of the National Health Service, which provided everyone with free medical care supervised in the community by general practitioners who were retained by the health service to provide out-patient care. The care was free and the doctors' offices were conveniently located. In spite of what appeared to be an adequate network of care, the iceberg phenomenon in geriatrics was first described in these early studies. A burden of undiscovered, uninvestigated, untreated disease was found in a majority of the community-dwelling elderly subjects (Anderson and Cowan 1955). The disease burden of this population was not esoteric, but rather a collection of common treatable conditions with substantial functional consequences. The common conditions brought to light included malnutrition, vitamin B-12 or iron-deficiency anemia, congestive heart failure, poor oral hygiene interfering with nutrition, foot disease interfering with walking, deafness from ear wax, diabetes, tuberculosis, gastrointestinal bleeding, and, most dramatic of all, a 25–40 percent incidence of serious depression (Williamson et al. 1964).

How could this happen? Why did these elderly patients not seek medical care for their symptomatic illnesses? In analyzing these early and subsequent data, three explanations accounted for this peculiar habit of the elderly. Ageism, with all of its negative implications, emerged as a major factor explaining non-reporting of symptoms by the elderly. A nearly universal assumption in our ageist society is that old age is a time of sickness and disability—to be old is to be sick. Sick-old is in danger of becoming a single word in our culture. This myth about aging is shared equally among young and old, lay and professional. An abundance of good gerontologic research data informs us that this ageist myth is incorrect. In fact, old age is healthy with good feelings and function for most individuals. Although there are biological and functional declines gradually developing with age, abrupt functional decline is the elderly—in those who are already old—is almost always due to disease, not aging. Whether the disease producing the functional impairment is curable, treatable, or incurable must await diagnostic evaluation; but to assume that no treatable condition exists and that the disability is due to old age, is to deny the elderly patient his or her just health services. Sick old people are sick because they are sick, not because they are old.

A second explanation for the lack of reporting of disease and symptoms by the elderly themselves is inherent in their disease burden. Prevalence of the dementia syndrome (intellectual impairment) increases sharply with age, rising to 30 percent over the age of eighty. Depression has already been identified as a common disorder of the elderly. The presence of either a dementia syndrome or of depression retards the diagnostic enthusiasm and thoroughness of the physician in evaluating the afflicted patient (Miller et al. 1976).

A third explanation for lack of reporting of disease by the elderly resides in the medical memories of the current elderly population. Three generations ago, doctors and hospitals were people and places concerned primarily with death in the elderly; and their current avoidance of health care is natural, at least in historical perspective.

With the discovery that self-reporting of disease by elderly persons was not an adequate first-line of health defense, there emerged another surprise concerning disease in old age. The phenomenon of multiple pathology in geriatric medicine was identified in some of the same studies of community-dwelling elderly people (Williamson et al. 1964). Multiple pathology describes the finding of several or even numerous disorders in an elderly person being treated for a single obvious problem. In one early study, the average number of serious pathologic conditions in a randomly surveyed elderly population was nearly five, and more than half of those disorders had never been reported to or treated by the responsible physician (Williamson et al. 1964). As subsequent studies accumulated, it was found that the older the patient population the more numerous the associated pathologic conditions. In addition to providing unexpected complications during the diagnosis and treatment of a single disorder, unattended multiple pathology has a further hazard. There is a potential vicious circle of decline in the elderly, multiply-diseased, untreated patient in which the advance of one disease stresses another already-damaged system which then begins to further fail; and so on, creating what ultimately becomes an irreversible chain of events leading to infirmity, dependency, and eventually, if uninterrupted, death (Korenchevsky 1961).

Another phenomenon unique in ill elderly individuals was described in a study of elderly persons dying in the city of Glasgow, Scotland (Isaacs et al. 1971). A high proportion of deaths in old age, nearly 75 percent, was preceded by a period of increased dependency; usually due to immobility, incontinence, or dementia, frequently in combination. Duration of community dependency increased only modestly with increasing age; but the hospital stay preceding death, termed predeath, increased sharply with increasing age (figure 13-1). For hospitalized patients over age eighty-five who were destined to die, the hospital stay prior to death exceeded nine months. It seemed that prompt evaluation and treatment during the early period of dependency might have avoided the long and discouraging hospitalizations that were documented. The cost in misery and in health resources of these preterminal hospitalizations is substantial. Thus, loss of function in elderly individuals, generated by immobility, incontinence, or dementia, usually heralds serious underlying pathology demanding prompt assessment.

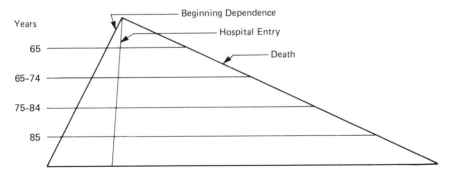

Figure 13-1. Dependence, Hospitalization, and Death

Gerontology, the study of normal human aging, collects data from biological and behavioral sciences contributing to our understanding of age-related change. Objective data confirm in scientific detail what is grossly obvious—old people are different from younger individuals. Gerontological research contributes to our ability to distinguish normal human aging from the effects of disease in old age. As humans age, disease becomes more and more prevalent, and locating healthy subjects for study becomes increasingly difficult. Gerontological research suggests that individual variability increases with age and generalizations are dangerous. However, many age-related biological changes demonstrate development and positive growth for about three decades with subsequent linear decline until death, into the ninth and tenth decades. The assumption that human functions peak at eighteen, remain static until the sixties, and then abruptly decline, is a common ageist myth (Rowe 1977). Biological functions that decline with age include renal function, cardiac output, muscle mass, ability to clear glucose from the blood, and skin thickness and elasticity, but certain functions remain the same and a few even increase (Finch and Hayflick 1977). Though more and better gerontological research should be encouraged, a substantial body of knowledge about normal human aging already exists. These often obscure data are the intellectual frontier of care of the elderly, and they must be included in the mainstream of medical education received by these elderly patients' physicians. Equally dangerous to the elderly patient, and likely in the absence of geriatric-educational programs, is the confusion of normal human aging with disease and vice versa. Assuming that a change in an elderly person is due to normal aging when, in fact, it is due to disease, and therefore neglecting it, has a predictably adverse outcome for the patient. Likewise, assuming that a phenomenon of normal human aging is due to a disease and trying to treat it with drugs or surgery, is at least equally hazardous to the patient. When illness is superimposed on normal changes of aging, distinguishing one from the other can be exceedingly difficult, even for the physician acquainted with the body of gerontological data. The physician deprived of this body of knowledge faces confusion and frustration when caring for the elderly.

In order to adequately understand the health services and their organization necessary for ambulatory elderly, it is necessary to understand how disease differs in old age. Disease in the elderly can be classified under two broad headings (Besdine 1980). Diseases in the first group are those which usually occur in elderly patients. These diseases, although not necessarily common, usually are found in elderly individuals:

Stroke

Decubitus ulcers

Normal pressure hydrocephalus

Urinary incontinence

Accidental hypothermia

Diabetic hyperosmolar nonketotic coma

Parkinsonism

Basal cell carcinomas

Herpes zoster

Chronic lymphatic leukemia

Tuberculosis, especially miliary

Gammopathies, including multiple myeloma

Prostatic carcinoma

Causes of falls

Causes of the dementia syndrome

Metabolic bone disease, including osteoporosis

Osteoarthritis

Hip fracture and its rehabilitation

Polymyalgia rheumatica

Angioimmunoblastic lymphadenopathy with dysproteinemia

The second group of diseases requiring special knowledge relevant to the elderly patient is less circumscribed. These are disorders which, though common in both young and old individuals, behave differently in elderly patients. These are diseases influenced by the normal age-related changes found in elderly humans. The altered anatomy, physiology, biochemistry and psychology of elderly persons influence the presentation, clinical course, complications and outcome of a wide variety of diseases. A principle of geriatric medicine is that any condition with a characteristic presentation and course frequently occurs in elderly persons with few or none of the usual findings (Hodkinson 1973). The standard manifestations of disease in the young are replaced in the elderly patient by one or more nonspecific but functionally devastating problems. These include loss of appetite, acute confusion, new or worsening dementia, incontinence, falls, dizziness, and failure to thrive. The appearance of any of these symptoms or signs in an elderly patient is never due to normal human aging. To attribute any to aging is to adopt an ignorant attitude and deny the patient the benefit of professional care. Although any disease theoretically can be present atypically in old age, certain disorders do so repeatedly, including depression, drug intoxication, hypothyroidism, alcoholism, acute myocardial infarction, pulmonary embolism, bacterial pneumonia, carcinoma, particularly breast, lung or colon, acute abdomen, and hyperthyroidism.

In the medical care of elderly persons, the aforementioned multiple pathology must be sought and identified. If a single disease is treated while other associated illnesses are ignored, the outcome is likely to be decline of the patient and worsening of disease. The elderly patient is especially vulnerable to drug-drug and disease-disease interactions, producing intellectual and physical decline. Some of the most common coexisting conditions in elderly patients are congestive heart failure, chronic renal failure, angina pectoris, osteoporosis, osteoarthritis, frail gait, chronic constipation, urinary precipitancy, venous and arterial insufficiency in the legs, diabetes mellitus, chronic pain, sleep disturbance, depression, dementia syndrome, and multiple drug regimens with poor compliance. When numbers of these problems coexist in one elderly individual, pursuit of diagnosis and treatment of one without careful consideration and evaluation of others may cause further functional impairment for the patient.

Drug therapy, as well as disease, presents special problems in the elderly patient. Old people are more susceptible to side and toxic effects of most drugs (Vestal 1978). Older Americans purchase 25 percent of the prescription drugs sold annually, filling more than thirteen prescriptions and spending twenty percent of their personal available money on drugs (Basen 1977). Symptom-directed reflexively prescribed psycho-active agents are especially dangerous for the elderly and must be avoided. Old people are more vulnerable to adverse drug effects for many reasons. First, the increased prevalence of disease usually means that older individuals take more therapeutic drugs and thus increase the risk of reaction. Second, lean body mass declines with age, and, therefore, when standard doses are used, older individuals get more drug per pound-body-weight of metabolically active tissue than do younger persons. Third, intellectual and visual impairment, both increasingly prevalent with age, make drug errors likely. Fourth, normal aging brings a predictable and steady decline in renal function, resulting in a 50 percent decline in creatinine clearance by age eighty (Rowe et al. 1976). This diminished ability to clear drugs from the blood increases the risk of drug accumulation and toxicity whether the drug is cleared unchanged by the kidney or metabolized to substances which are then renally excreted. The increased prevalence of adverse drug reactions in the elderly argues for extreme caution when initiating new drugs or continuing multiple-drug regimens.

Nonreporting of illness, multiple pathology, and predeath predispose to late diagnosis and treatment of disease and disability in elderly individuals. Late intervention, coupled with diminished physiological reserve, puts old people at particular risk of institutionalization following acute illness. This palpable vulnerability to loss of home makes old people and their advocates fear medicine and hospitals. Unusual aspects of disease in old age, coupled with multiple pathology and its negative interactions, and pitfalls of drug use in elderly patients, also make it likely that treatment of disease in old age will be hazardous. Community-dwelling, functional elderly need active surveillance of health status allowing early intervention when disability, usually provoked by underlying occult disease, appears. This surveillance need, coupled with medical services, can be met in a congregate-housing setting providing a mechanism for the early detection of disease in the residents.

As has been emphasized in the foregoing discussion of the medical needs of elderly persons, medical surveillance is essential. Large proportions of elderly persons who have severe health problems report that they are healthy (Maddox and Douglas 1974). It has been presumed that the elderly do not recognize health problems, but it is also possible that they are unwilling to admit illness. A study of 2,000 elderly (Ostfeld 1968) revealed that conditions considered by the elderly themselves to be age-related were diagnosed by their physicians as treatable disease. Absent medical surveillance allows the possibility that potentially reversible conditions will go untreated, resulting in permanent disability and dependency.

Nevertheless, the majority of the elderly, including those with serious medical conditions, are able to function with minimal supports in the community. An important recent development is public housing for the well elderly providing architectural modification to facilitate functioning (no sills, emergency alarm buttons, and common spaces for social activities). Barrier-free housing is recognized as important in maintaining independent functioning. The less energy required to negotiate the environment, the easier it is to function despite physical impairment.

Designed for the independent aged, however, housing for the elderly was not imagined as a supportive environment appropriate for persons requiring long-term care. Recognized as a public-housing option only in the 1970s, congregate housing overtly recognized the role of living arrangement and supportive services in maintaining community independence of elderly persons with special needs. Congregate housing represents a combination of living arrangements, shared services and common areas. Although some accommodations had been in existence through imaginative developments in one form or another in both the private and public sectors prior to that time, the 1970 Housing Act finally gave legislative support specifically for building service spaces within public housing. Congregate housing was given further support by the Housing and Community Development Act of 1974, when responsibility for meeting the special needs of occupants through congregate housing was specified (although no funds for operating programs per se have yet been made available through HUD). Federally sponsored housing that specifically embraced a public health or maintenance perspective was finally constructed. Congregate housing, including architectural features, site location, and supportive services, was considered an aid to physical functioning and health.

When the concept of housing specifically for the elderly was originally introduced, it was highly criticized, but within a year after its opening, it received high acclaim and its architecture copied. Indeed, even architectural features subsequently found to be disadvantageous to the elderly were copied; for example, placing the refrigerator on a block to prevent bending was found to be extremely inconvenient because it also prevented many of the elderly from reaching the top shelves.

Currently most forms of congregate housing share the availability of some meal service (Urban Systems 1976). Meal service is important from a social as well as from a nutritional and physical-function perspective, but meal service may be less important to the elderly than the availability of medical services. Support for this position comes from a large study of elderly persons in various housing situations (Lawton, 1969), including community people not living in age-integrated public housing, as well as residents in traditional public and congregate housing for the elderly. Regardless of current residential living arrangements or income status (lower and middle income), elderly persons valued medical services above all others. Medical service was also found important in a restudy of an early United States example of what is now considered traditional retirement housing for the elderly, Victoria Plaza in Texas (Carp 1976). Eight years after the study of its first operational year, in response to questions about features which would enhance living in Victoria Plaza, 64 percent indicated that Victoria Plaza would be better if it had a hospital unit. Nursing care in clinic facilities (62 percent) and a medical clinic (52 percent) were also specified as desirable services. In addition, a sizeable proportion in each case replied "it depends," the proviso most often being the necessity for maintaining such facilities away from the living units and social areas but otherwise easily accessible. When asked about new construction, none of the men living in the building and only 6 percent of the women opposed building medical facilities; but again, residents wanted a clinic separate from the living areas.

Some have been concerned that medical facilities in the housing setting would necessarily change the character from community living to an institutional milieu. This fear has been allayed. A study of twenty-seven congregate-housing facilities in different states, twenty-three of which provide either in-patient or out-patient medical services to residents, concluded that "Congregate housing is not an institutional environment" (Urban Systems Research 1976). Highland Heights, the medically oriented congregate housing to be discussed in more detail, has had similar experience. Creation of an institutional environment in congregate housing is, then, a function of poor management. Despite multiple additional services, an institutional environment is not inevitable.

A recent, long-term, longitudinal study of a congregate-housing facility, Highland Heights, shows that medically oriented congregate housing can have a positive impact on the elderly and be a viable alternative to long-term care.

Highland Heights, located in Fall River, Massachusetts, is a low-income, federally supported, medically oriented congregate-housing project for the physically impaired and elderly. The search for options in long-term care, providing viable alternatives to institutionalization, was a prime motivation to develop this type of specialized housing.

Through the joint efforts of the Fall River Housing Authority and the municipal hospital for the chronically ill (Hussey Hospital), HUD approved the building of a low-income fourteen-story apartment house providing 110 studio and 98 two-room apartments designed specifically for the physically impaired (usually elderly) adult living alone or with one other person. In addition to the building design and hardware features, specialized features include health and other community services. It was constructed on the grounds of Hussey Hospital. The out-patient clinic is located in the basement of the apartment house, and includes physical therapy, occupational therapy, and out-patient treatment rooms. Since the closing of the in-patient wards of Hussey Hospital in December 1974, the medical services initially provided by hospital personnel have been maintained by the municipal government.

When applications were taken for this building, congregate housing was not a reality; thus, problems arose concerning architectural design of space for services. For instance, in addition to problems in providing space for medical facilities, there was also no way of approving space for congregate dining if kitchens or kitchenettes were to be included within apartments. Before the building was approved, an agreement between the Fall River Housing Authority and the municipality specified that the land would be given to the Fall River Housing Authority by the municipal hospital; in exchange, the basement floor, to be used as an out-patient clinic (as well as providing space for congregate dining, if necessary), was to be rented for $1.00 a year by the municipal hospital for the next forty years, and the provision of clinic services within the building for forty years was also guaranteed.

Before the opening of this sheltered housing facility, it was recognized that a valuable opportunity existed to gain knowledge concerning this new approach in long-term care. In June 1970, a HUD-HEW-funded contract (H-1275) for demonstration study was signed with the Fall River Housing Authority with a subcontract to the Department of Social Gerontological Research, Hebrew Rehabilitation Center for Aged (HRCA) in Boston. Subsequent research efforts have been supported by HEW/NCHSR Grant HS00903 and HUD Contract H-2180R (Sherwood et al. 1978). Beginning some months before the building was opened for occupancy in the fall of 1970 through January 1977, the Highland Heights experience was intensively studied, including the impact of medically oriented housing on the health and well-being of its residents.

The initial HUD contract had two associated demonstration aims: (1) the development and implementation of appropriate screening techniques to select the occupants of the housing project (including social-medical eligibility as well as the standard housing-authority criteria); and (2) the development and stimulation of a program to help meet resident medical and social-service needs as identified in the screening process. Since then, both the screening process and social-planning consultation have been continued.

In addition to standard criteria of housing authority tenant selectors, medical status and social criteria were used. Applicants were rated (by demonstration interdisciplinary team clinicians, primarily social workers and nurses) by degree of need for residency (from 1, very little or almost not at all, to 4, extreme need, residence a viable alternative to institutionalization). Persons assessed as functioning too poorly for this type of residential environment (for example, needing twenty-four hour surveillance) were considered ineligible for residency by medical-social health criteria. Persons applying alone who were assessed as having borderline functioning were referred to the demonstration-project physician (Dr. David S. Greer, coinvestigator of this demonstration project) for a final determination of eligibility.

Pressure was on the Housing Authority to rent all the apartments as soon as possible after the facility opened, and apartments were offered to all eligible applicants. Since then, those with a rating of a 3 or 4 by social-medical criteria have been given a higher priority. The highest priority is given to applicants from institutional settings for whom Highland Heights is seen as an alternative to institutionalization.

The Impact Study Design and Experimental-
Control-Group Samples

The ideal research design to study the effects of medically oriented housing would have included basic randomization. A randomized controlled study was the goal of the Highland Heights study, with random allocation of the applicant population into experimental and control groups; residency in Highland Heights constituting the experimental status. Although applications were officially taken only shortly before opening, it had been assumed that there would be a large pool of available applicants. The Fall River Housing Authority had agreed that, if such were the case, the apartments would be offered on a lottery basis to eligible applicants. This would have both constituted a democratically equitable system for allocating apartments and provided a sound method for studying impact. However, considerably fewer applicants at opening accepted admission than were originally anticipated. Thus, the financial pressure on the Housing Authority to fill the facility and the only slightly greater number of eligible applicants than available apartments excluded randomized design.

Rather than randomized allocation of applicants to control and experimental groups, individual-to-individual matching was employed. An unusual methodology was used in an attempt to avoid the pitfalls (Campbell and Erlebacher 1970) of matching to select a control group. Multivariate-statistical handling of theoretically important variables was used, along with detailed case-by-case selection of appropriate matches by interdisciplinary (social worker-nurse) team members in which residents (the experimentals) were matched with elderly and physically-impaired persons who applied for residency in Highland Heights, but who had not yet become residents (the controls).

Although the population had extensive diagnosis and impairments, both experimental and control populations fell into four major diagnostic categories:

1. Cardiovascular: Heart disease of any etiology, hypertension with or without cardiovascular disease, and peripheral arterial disease. Stroke was not included in this group (42.5 percent of the experimentals and 46.5 percent controls fell into this group).

2. Arthritis: Symptomatic joint disease of any etiology (29.4 percent of the experimentals and 27.2 percent of the controls).

3. Metabolic: Metabolic diseases of various etiologies, principally diabetes mellitus; but also including thyroid abnormalities and chemical imbalances such as calcium-related bone disease (17.1 percent of the experimentals and 21.9 percent of the controls).

4. Neuromuscular: Central nervous system or primary muscular diseases, either congenital or acquired (15.4 percent of the experimentals and 12.3 percent of the controls).

Additionally, over 9 percent of the experimentals and 15 percent of the controls had had strokes. Only about 9 percent of the experimentals and controls were considered to be normal, that is, individuals with no health problems identified.

In five years, 228 residents (the experimentals) were matched with 228 applicants (the controls), and the efficacy of the pairs obtained through these multivariate-clinical-matching procedures was tested in a variety of ways (Sherwood et al. 1975). The primary justification for using the matched samples resides in the similarity (comparability) at the application date of controls and experimentals with respect to the study variables, including background factors (used in the matching procedures) and outcome variables (which, for methodological reasons, were not used as operationalized variables in the matching procedure).

Impact for up to five years was studied for the total sample with respect to acute hospitalization, institutionalization and death. Data collection included yearly interviews with willing and available experimentals and controls. Using those pairs for whom comparable data existed, impact up to five years was studied with respect to housing, health, social isolation, and cognitive and emotional variables.

Findings

This study of medically oriented housing indicates benefit to its residents (Sherwood, et al. 1978). One surprising finding was that the experimentals were less likely to die during the first four years of the impact period, when thirty-four experimentals died compared with fifty-five controls (P ≤ .01). By the end of the fifth year, however, forty-seven experimentals had died as compared to sixty-one controls (P ≥ .10); but the average number of days alive was significantly greater for experimentals compared with the controls by the end of the fifth year (P ≤ .002). Much of the reduced mortality was in the cardiac group. Medical evidence suggests that psycho-social stress plays a role in the genesis of various cardiovascular diseases. Reducing health anxiety by providing medical services may have been important in reducing psycho-social stress and mortality among the Highland Heights residents.

The impact findings also validate the major goal of the Highland Heights intervention, to serve as a viable alternative to institutionalization. Throughout the five-year-impact-study period, "Highland Heights residents were significantly less likely to become institutionalized and spent less time in a long-term care facility as compared with their matched controls. Of the pool of over 200 matched pairs, thirty-nine experimentals as compared with fifty-six controls were in a long-term care facility for at least some time during the impact period (P ≤ .05). The average stay for persons who were in long-term care facilities during this period was 261.08 days for the experimentals and 586.28 days for the controls.

During the five-year-impact-study period, experimentals were more likely than controls to have been in an acute hospital. Of the total pool of matched pairs, 127 of the experimentals and 98 of the controls were hospitalized for one or more days during the study period (significant at the ≤ .01 probability level). The total number of hospital days for the first two impact-study years was approximately the same for both groups, although significantly more experimentals than controls were hospitalized. By the fifth year, the experimentals spent significantly more total acute hospital days during the five-year period than the controls (P ≤ .015). Controls may have spent fewer days in hospitals because many more controls were in long-term care facilities which could manage some acute illnesses without hospitalization.

Data concerning persons who moved to Highland Heights directly from long-term-care facilities were also very encouraging. Between 1970 and 1976, fifty-one persons from long-term care facilities moved to Highland Heights and were followed from their time of occupancy through December 1976. Ages ranged from nineteen to ninety-five, with 76 percent forty-five years of age or older. The residents sixty-five years or older who moved to Highland Heights from an institutional setting had been institutionalized for less than two years, contrasted with the younger group who had been institutionalized much longer.

Most individuals moving to Highland Heights were clinically assessed as meeting the Medicaid medical standards concerning appropriate institutional placement. The experiences of this deinstitutionalized group demonstrate that very disabled persons can be deinstitutionalized and maintained in a supportive environment which also allows maximum freedom and individual discretion. All but one of the persons moving to Highland Heights from what was apparently a permanent institutional placement lived in Highland Heights for more than one year, and some individuals who had been institutionalized for many years lived almost totally independently in Highland Heights for over six years.

Finally, while a cost benefit analysis was not part of the original research design, the generally positive findings urged such an analysis. Based on estimates derived from data on 214 experimental-control matched-pairs, institutional dollar charges not incurred as a consequence of Highland Heights residency were estimated for an impact period of three years at $525,295.19 for the first twelve months; $789,914.44 for the first twenty-four months; and $831,984.71 for the total three-year period. Charges not incurred by the controls during the same period were estimated to be $185,583 for twelve months, $308,520 for twenty-four months, and $376,562 for thirty-six months. The cumulative benefit-cost ratio for the three year period was calculated to be 2.21. For each of the 214 Highland Heights residents in the sample, there was an average savings of $2,986 over the three-year period; or about $995 per year (a total of $639,004 for the three year period).

These findings, then, demonstrate that not only is medically-oriented congregate housing a viable option which can have positive effects on the health and well-being of its residents, but also, despite increased acute hospitalization, that it is a financially sound option.

Conclusions

Old people are at high risk for late diagnosis and treatment of disease because of (1) ageism, (2) nonreporting of illness, and (3) the unusual presentation of disease. Late intervention for acutely ill elderly produces high risk for institutionalization because of multiple pathology and its negative interactions, and the phenomenon of predeath. Special aspects of disease in old age require special physician skills and knowledge. Sheltered or congregate housing for elderly providing medical services for residents has a positive effect on health, reduces institutionalization risk, and thereby can save money. Easy access to acute-care services in a professional setting familiar with the supportive capabilities of the congregate housing is essential for optimum utilization.

Providing the health services outlined above can make a substantial contribution to the health, well-being, and security of elderly people in congregate housing. Data presented above strongly suggest that such services would, additionally, save money.

References

Anderson, W.F. 1976. *The Practical Management of the Elderly*, 3rd ed. Oxford: Blackwell Scientific Publications.

Anderson, W.F., and Cowan, N.R. 1955. "A Consultative Health Center for Older People," *Lancet* 2:239.

Basen, M.M. 1977. "The Elderly and Drugs–Problem Overview and Program Strategy," *Public Health Reports* 92:43.

Besdine, R.W. 1980. "Geriatric medicine: An Overview," *Annual Review of Gerontology and Geriatrics* 1:135-153.

Bureau of the Census, 1977. Current Population Reports, Series P25, no. 311, July 1965 and Series P25, no. 704, July.

Butler, R.N., "Overview on Aging". 1973. In *Aging: The Process and the People*. ed. G. Usdin and C.J. Hofling. New York: Brunner/Mazel Inc.

Campbell, D.T., and Erlebacher, A., 1970. "How Regression Artifacts in Quasi-Experimental Evaluations Can Mistakenly Make Compensatory Education Look Harmful." In *Compensatory Education: A National Debate* ed. J. Hellmuth, 3. New York: Branner/Mazel Inc.

Carp. F.M. 1976. "User Evaluation of Housing for the Elderly," *Gerontologist* 16:102.

Dans, P.E., and Kerr, M.R. 1979. "Gerontology and Geriatrics in Medical Education," *New England Journal of Medicine* 300:228.

Finch, C.E., ²and Hayflick, L., *Handbook of the Biology of Aging*. New York: Van Nostrand-Reinhold.

Hodkinson, H.M. 1973. "Non-Specific Presentation of Illness," *British Medical Journal* 4:94.

Institute of Medicine. 1977. *The Elderly and Functional Dependency*. Washington, D.C.: National Academy of Sciences.

Institute of Medicine. 1978. *Aging and Medical Education*. Washington, D.C.: National Academy of Sciences.

Isaacs, B., et al. 1972. *Survival of the Unfittest*. London: Routledge and Kegan Paul.

Isaacs, B., et al. 1971. "The Concept of Pre-Death," *Lancet* 3:1115.

Korenchevsky, V. 1961. *Physiological and Pathological Aging*. New York: Basel/Karger.

Kovar, M.G. 1977. "Elderly People: The Population 65 Years and Over. In Health United States 1976-1977." National Center for Health Statistics, DHEW, Pub. No. (HRA) 77-1232.

Lawton, M.P. 1969. "Supportive Services in the Context of the Housing Environment," *The Gerontologist* 9:15.

Maddox, G.L., and Douglass, E.B. 1974. "Self-Assessment of Health." In *Normal Aging II* ed. E. Palmore. Durham, N.C.: Duke University Press.

Miller, D., et al. 1976. "Physicians' Attitudes Towards the Ill Aged and Nursing Homes," *Journal of the American Geriatric Society* 24:498.

Ostfeld, A.M. 1968. "Frequency and Nature of Health Problems of Retired Persons." In *The Retirement Process*, ed. F.M. Carp. USPHS Pub. No. 1788, Washington, D.C.

Rowe, J.W. 1977. "Clinical Research on Aging: Strategies and Directions," *New England Journal of Medicine* 297:133a.

Rowe, J.W., et al. 1976. "The Effect of Age on Creatinine Clearance in Man: A Cross-Sectional and Longitudinal Study," *Journal of Gerontology* 31:155.

Sherwood, C.D.; Morris, J.N.; and Sherwood, S. 1975. "A Multivariate, Nonrandomized Matching Technique for Studying the Impact of Social Interventions." In *Handbook of Evaluation Research,* ed. E.L. Struen, and M. Guttentag. 1:183, Beverly Hills: Sage Publications.

Sherwood, S.; Greer, D.; Morris, J.N.; Mor, V. 1978. *The Study of the Effects of Medically Oriented Housing, Dept. of Social Gerontological Research.* Boston: Hebrew Rehabilitation Center for Aged.

Urban Systems Research and Engineering, Inc. 1976. *Evaluation of the Effectiveness of Congregate Housing for the Elderly.* Washington, D.C.: USGPO.

Vestal, R.E. 1978. "Drug Use in the Elderly: A Review of Problems and Special Considerations," *Drugs* 16:358.

Williamson, J., et al. 1964. "Old People at Home: Their Unreported Needs," *Lancet* 1:1117.

Part V:
The Future

Creating attractive but supportive, functional but residential environments for sheltered living poses one set of relatively fixed, though still not totally explored, problems. Balancing services rendered between oversupport and undersupport, while adjusting to constantly shifting demands, presents even more difficult problems. To achieve better solutions, researchers, architects, sponsors and managers must work together to plan, implement, and evaluate new models for congregate living.

The complex problem of creating sheltered housing for elder people is exacerbated by government underspending and over regulating. A new alliance must be forged between the public and private sectors if the burgeoning need is to be met. Creative solutions will provide an accommodating environment, one in which individuals with a wide range of functional ability may live. Husbanding of resources will require careful assessment of recipients, going far beyond rudimentary qualifiers of age and income.

14 Daring to Explore and Apply: A Research Agenda for Congregate Housing

Sandra C. Howell

Our knowledge of alternative forms of supportive housing is primarily descriptive rather than analytic. Since this is so, there is now little valid research on which to base the multitude of decisions required in the planning, design, tenant selection, and service programming of these types of settings.

The information currently used to develop congregate housing is based on good evidence of an existing and growing need among aging people for residential and service packages that vary widely in characteristics and intensity to meet variation in need.

In order for future research to be useful in planning congregate housing, most of the questions for which answers are sought must be systematically built into the actual development process. This is particularly true in relation to alternative-design solutions as they relate to (1) the changing space needs of frail elderly, (2) tenant compositions, and (3) in-house service variations.

If, as Marie McGuire Thompson (chapter one) has indicated, we would choose to test Lawton's recent models (Lawton 1980), particularly the accommodating one on which I will elaborate, then presumed accommodating variables in physical design, management policies or practices, and service inputs must be systematically varied across settings and tenant compositions. This kind of effort requires collaboration both among researchers and between them and planner-practitioner groups. This is so partly because, as it now stands, each of us tends to move into our own selected field-research setting(s) with our own variables and instruments, a few of which only occasionally match. Since everyone knows you cannot compare apples and oranges, even though both are fruit, our problems of aggregating diverse data are considerable and the validity and generalizability of our efforts is often rightly questioned.

I owe to my colleague, Lucille Nahemow, a new method for organizing my several years of thought on research needs in housing and aging. Out of her work on cases in Geriatrics (Nahemow, in press) while Director of Gerontology Training at New York University Medical School, a clear theme repeatedly emerged. Living environments for the aging, she says, must be extending capabilities where both the physical attributes of the setting and the service/ delivery packages are flexible to meet a wide segment of needs not always predictable on an individual basis. Nahemow is finding increasing numbers of people who cannot meet the current criteria for fitness to either community-based service delivery or various housing types, and whose support network would only continue to function if programs could be integrated to their needs. The policy-related research that this information implies has never been directly addressed. At this time, we do not know how to organize and administer either facilities and services to deal with temporary stays in varied settings or back-up crisis services to respond to a family under duress in their caretaking of a frail older member. What mechanisms can be developed that would allow a congregate setting to take in, for a week-end or a month, a guest resident and, for that matter, to allow a permanent resident's unit to be held while he/she proceeded through a rehabilitation process outside the facility with the assurance of coming home? Our current rigid programming, including the accounting designations of levels of care, disallows settings and often services for those in duress on housing waiting lists. What do they do in the meantime? We do not know. In a project I am leading, we may begin to discover how some of these stressed elders and their families deal with limited environmental options.

Research in program flexibility also extends to management in rental housing and condominiums, where exchange of living units within and between projects is required to continue the independence of a single tenant or couple. I have consistently been puzzled by the notion that the units for well elderly could not house people whose potential disability might make the setting inappropriate. In fact, several such cases have come to my attention in public housing.

Policy research relative to flexibility also extends to the arena of the housing and housing-fixtures industry. What incentives would be required to break the lock on the one-size-fits-all mentality generated by anthropometric standards of average reach, grasp, spatial movement, etc? Most of these standards are still based on young samples. How do we convince HUD and other housing producers that variability, rather then central tendency, is the rule of survival and support of independence in aging?

What, really, are the reasons for the unavailability of necessary or flexible hardware for elderly housing units? Is it the lag in recognition of a market? A resistance on the part of construction trades and subcontractors to deal with procedural change? An unwillingness to retool for production of different fixtures? Thoughtless time pressures on the developer/architect?

Figure 14–1 shows a woman transferring herself from wheelchair to shower stool. Were she a left hemiparetic, the grab-bar system would not have worked and the towel rod on the glass door would certainly not have sustained her weight and may have posed a safety hazard. Policy/program research includes exploring methods of assuring accountability for design and program decisions. Where, in the planning-production and management processes of housing facilities and services, do the breakdowns occur? Where is information lost or unused, and why?

Our knowledge of older people who have moved to some form of supportive housing (and this includes subsidized age-segregated settings with minimal services) is quite good. What we know about those who do not seek or choose options, or who will not even consider options is slim in terms of policy/program

Source: U.S. Department of Health, Education and Welfare.

Figure 14-1. Patient Transferring from Wheelchair to Shower

enlightenment. We need to be able to identify key collative situations and events to which aging people and their families (networks) are not now responding with sufficient alertness, in order to review short and long-term alternatives. As Brody and many others have pointed out, the majority of aging people do not apply prematurely for alternative residential service. In fact, for many of us there appears to be a strange reticence to plan for older life the way we did for child-rearing and education, vacations, and previous housing along with other investments. In order to be able to reach out and to assist in planning and providing truly alternative and flexible housing-service-packages we need to know what the gaps in both perception of need and knowledge of options are and why they exist. For example, are the kinds of buildings being erected (and their locations) inappropriate to the perceptions of habitability of many older people? Extremely few housing demonstrations now exist relative to the vast growing aging populations in America's working and middle-income suburban communities. Here, to an extreme, are the underserviced and isolated of the near future (problems not incidentally due to monolithic transportation planning and bizarrely inappropriate land-use planning, that is, single-use zoning). We know that elderly prefer to remain in familiar neighborhoods and benefit from geographic proximity to family; yet planning distribution of settings and services based on this knowledge has been exceedingly poor relative to this largest elderly segment and their suburban middle-aged children. Multidisciplinary research that would bring threads together from gerontology, planning-design, sociology, housing economics, and medicine is clearly needed. Categorical research-policies are as detrimental to problem solving as categorical programming has been to long-term-care-service development. The problem of developing settings and services for the aging is often stated as one of correcting a housing disequilibrium (Struyk and Soldo 1980). This implies that the solutions are simply a matter of increasing supply of proper-size units and of changing the evident need into effective demand by presenting financial-incentive programs accessible to the consumer. This position focuses on external and seemingly rational issues. The consistent absence of any trend in the mobility of older home-owning-Americans in over five decades belies the purely economic explanation, and points, rather, to a perception-affect explanation: home as part of identity. (Howell 1980).

Research needs to disentangle this relationship between self and place, separate out the types of attachments and the ways in which attachments can either he reinforced or substituted through housing or service programs.

The term social integration implies both a modification of social-interaction patterns and an adaptation to a new social environment. To measure integration requires a series of steps: first, to know the past levels and character of social interaction and, second, to know the nature of both the adapted-to and the adapted-from situation. In psychology, we would probably call these issues social learning, and we are beginning to address, both theoretically and experimentally, the features of social learning across the life span (Baltes and Schaie 1973).

For the aging person moving into a new environment, there are new social interactions and adaptations that must occur. If the new environment has already established rules and a formal social structure reinforced by a building-type, such as is often the case in a nursing institution, the issues of integration and adaptation might seem rather clear. When a newly completed facility such as high-density, high-rise, age-segregated housing, is occupied simultaneously by the initial tenant population, for all of whom it is an untried social-residential form, there are virtually no rules to guide initial social interaction. This is especially true with regard to the use of unfamiliar semi-public spaces in such settings.

To my knowledge, with the exception of studies conducted by Tobin and Lieberman (1976) relative to the psychological processes accompanying moves to nursing homes; Lawton, Brody, and Turner-Massey (1978) relative to moves to supportive housing; and Carp (1968) relative to a move to a single age-segregated-housing project, there are no United States studies of social integration that have adequately elaborated upon Rosow's (1967) description of patterns of social interaction among elderly in residential settings. None of these explicitly address the issue of what is learned in an environmental change, but rather, deal with one of the following issues: (1) the impact of a move relative to cognitive-affective decline; (2) adjustment and activity levels of movers compared with nonmovers; (3) satisfaction, morale, and social activity levels of the movers (Lawton and Cohen; 1974), though Lawton and Simon (1968) has touched upon used and unused spaces in elderly housing. In western gerontology, we have nothing analogous to Michelson's (1977) recent four-year study of changes in behaviors of families concomitant with moves to new housing (see Schulz and Brenner 1977).

My research has dealt with social interaction and environmental use of older United States populations whose health and activity level is, in general, quite high. If the character of their physical environments influences social interaction and adaptation, how must the physical environment impinge on those elderly who are becoming frail?

In congregate housing the main objective is to reduce the incidence of institutionalization of the frailer elderly. For the most part, the settings being built or adapted under this program are design reproductions of large scale, high-density apartment-buildings with fifteen-to-thirty units per floor and with all sharable spaces concentrated in a single building-location. The apartment units are typically smaller than those allowed under family-unit standards, and some do not include a kitchen.

In my work I have addressed the issue of private space and its meaning for the aging person in the United States, arguing that neither vast increases in numbers of available age-peers nor provision of spaces for services and social interaction (where the definition of the spaces is left to chance) compensate for limitations in the private unit.

Congregate housing, or any setting for frail elderly, requires reduction in scale and compensatory social spaces proximate to clusters of living units, no matter how many units are involved. The activity level of frail elderly is, by definition reduced, as is their capacity to handle complex environmental-social stimuli. To expect them to traverse long corridors (150–200 feet), to manipulate elevators (6–30 floors), and to risk encounters with 100–300 strangers in unaccustomed spaces and particularly at meals (previously a family activity) is creating stress, not enhancing the quality of their life. The opportunity for choice in selecting the number of encounters, the places of to-be-expected encounters and the situations personally appropriate for encounter can be designed into buildings.

In the case of the frail elderly, the to-be-learned social behavior ought to be that of adapting to decreasing physical, perceptual, and cognitive competency. To enforce, by design, a set of values that require high levels of social activity and interaction is not to provide a supportive learning-environment.

Change over time is the major applied-research focus required to understand and plan for supportive housing settings for aging. Lawton's (1980) discussion of congregate planning models addresses the issues, but the varied paths, uneven and often circuitous, that people and events follow in their quest for supportive environment are often not clearly understood.

The roles of families, the private market, health and social services, weave both effectively and ineffectively throughout these individual histories.

Study of these complex linkages is essential to the development of the support continuum we all talk about. Understanding the varied characteristics of people, events, and settings in a systematic and replicable way is the only foundation for policy and program development of congregate housing. Who are we planning for? a question often asked at workshops, cannot be answered because we do not have the kind of taxonomic research focusing on dynamics and change, that is required.

Finally, the most informative type of research is based on intervention. Every congregate setting should be viewed as an hypothesis and its characteristics (variables) and their presumed effects specified. We need to develop and monitor a range of models and study them, in action, over time.

References

Baltes, P.B., Schaie, K.W. 1973. *Life Span Developmental Psychology*. New York: Academic Press.

Collier, I.G., Oliver, D.B. 1979. *Relocation and Mobility Patterns of 421 Residents: A Longitudinal Study Covering a 16 Year Period*. Paper presented at the Gerontological Society Annual Meetings, Washington, D.C., November.

Figure 14–2. Social Area in Congregate Housing

Carp, F. 1968. "Effects of Improved Housing on the Lives of Older People." In *Middle Age and Aging: A Reader in Social Psychology*, ed. B.L. Neugarten. Chicago, ILL.: University of Chicago Press, 409-416.

Howell, S.C. 1980a. "Environments as Hypotheses in Human Aging Research." In *Aging in the 1980s*, ed. L.W. Poon. Washington, D.C.: American Psychological Association, 424-432.

Howell, S.C. 1980b. *Designing for Aging: Patterns of Use*. Cambridge, Mass.: M.I.T. Press.

Lawton, M.P. 1980. *Environment and Aging*. Monterey, Cal.: Brooks-Cole,

Lawton, M.P.; Brody, E.M.; Turner-Massey, P. 1978. "The Relationship of Environmental Factors to Change in Well-Being," *The Gerontologist* 18: 133-137.

Lawton, M.P., and Cohen, J. 1974. "Generality of Housing Impact on the Well-Being of Older People," *Journal of Gerontology* 29:194-204.

Lawton, M.P., and Simon, B. 1968. "The Ecology of Social Relationships in Housing for the Elderly," *The Gerontologist* 8:108-115.

Michelson, W. 1977. *Environmental Choice, Human Behavior, and Residential Satisfaction*. New York: Oxford University Press.

Nahemow, L., and Pousada, L. Forthcoming. *Geriatric Diagnostics*. New York: Springer, Inc.

Rosow, I. 1967. *Social Integration of the Aged*. New York: The Free Press.

Schultz, R., and Brenner, G. 1977. "Relocation of the Aged: A Review and Theoretical Analysis," *Journal of Gerontology* 32:323-333.

Struyk, R.J., and Soldo, B. 1980. *Improving the Elderly's Housing: A Key to Preserving the Nation's Housing Stock and Neighborhoods*. Cambridge, Mass.: Ballinger Publishing Company.

Tobin, S.S., and Lieberman, M.A. 1976. *Last Home for the Aged*. San Francisco: Jossey/Bass.

Index

Rehabilitation, 95, 103, 105
  Act of 1973, 134
  cost, 104
  economics of, 105
  services, 169
  versus new construction, 105, 106, 107,
    108, 110
Reimbursement, 21, 23, 24
Relationships, primary group, 54
Relocation, effects of, 39–41, 53, 60–62,
    74, 131, 169
Rent, supplement programs, 103
  "rent-up," 90, 100
  Section 8 program, 118
  subsidies, 93, 118
Residents
  guest, 23, 210
  handicapped, 22
  mix of, 181
  nursing-home, 18. *See also* Tenant
    selection
Respite care, 23, 210
Retirement hotels, 127. *See also* Housing
Retirement village, 131. *See also* Campus
    environment, Housing
Richter, C.P., 15
Risk factors, 123
Rodin, J., 16, 18
Role models and social learning, 37–38
Rosenthal, R., 18
Rosow, I., 213
Rural development, 9
  European, 10

Safety. *See* Security
Schwartz, Arthur, 139
Seating. *See* Chairs
Security, 107, 168, 169, 182, 190
  lighting, 130
  personal safety, 182
  protection against crime, 182
  psychological well-being, 182
Seed-money, 123
  schedule, 97
  source of, 97
Seligman, M.E.F., 17
Sensory decrements, 130
Services, 115, 159, 161
  channeling of, 191
  counseling, 168, 181
  crisis, 210
  developing package, 186
  educational, 168, 181
  enrichment, 168
  essential versus nonessential, 184
  flexibility, 210, 212
  home-chore, 181
  home-health, 164, 168
  housekeeping, 181

inventory of (figure 11–1), 163
  meals, 108, 169
  medical, 168, 169, 173, 190
  needs, 170, 172
  nonshelter, 181, 183
  nutrition, 181
  overservice, 167
  oversupport versus undersupport, 207
  providers, 172
  rehabilitative patterns, 170
  referral, 171, 181
  scattered, 3
  security, 32, 83
  service-level checklist, 185
  service-rich environment, 166, 167
  social, recreational, 169
  subsidy, 5
  supportive, 4, 8, 59, 72
  transportation, 168, 181
  variations, 209
Shanas, E., 129
Sheltered housing (Maryland program),
    9, 10
Sherwood, Sylia, 199
Shopping, 155
Shower stalls, 153, 154, 210, 211
  See also Bathrooms; Tub/showers
Signage, 144, 145, 150
Site, 75
  control, 89, 93, 94, 120
  information, 96
  selection, 89, 93, 94
Sleep patterns, napping, 154
Snyder, M., 18
Social integration, 212
Social Security, 1
Social services, 99, 100, 127
Sommer, R., 12, 139
Sound, control, 143
  attenuation, 143
  background noise, 143
  music, 143
Sponsor, 121, 168
  management role, 178, 179
Sprinkler systems, 104, 106
SSI. *See* Supplemental Security Income
Staff, 43
  congregate housing, 60
  health-care professionals, 23
  training, 118
Steinfeld, E. 150
Storage, 190
Stress, 15, 39, 51, 53, 54, 85, 202
  psychological, 16
Stroke, 194, 201
Structural system, 4
Supplemental Security Income (SSI),
    161, 164
"Survival of the unfittest," 189

About the Contributors

Jerry Avorn, M.D., is assistant professor of social medicine and health policy at Harvard Medical School and staff internist in the gerontology division of Beth Israel Hospital, Boston.

Richard W. Besdine, M.D., is with the Division on Aging, Harvard Medical School, and the Hebrew Rehabilitation Center for Aged, Roslindale, Massachusetts.

James N. Broder, Esquire, is a partner in the firm of Thaxter, Lipez, Broder and Micoleau, Washington, D.C. He served on the congressional staff involved with drafting the original 202/8 program and authored studies on housing and tax relief for the elderly.

Elaine M. Brody, M.S.W., is director of the Department of Human Services and senior researcher of the Philadelphia Geriatric Center. She is past president of the Gerontological Society of America and author of *Long Term Care of Older People*.

Thomas O. Byerts, A.I.A., is director of the Gerontology Center and associate professor of architecture at the University of Illinois in Chicago.

Maria B. Dwight, M.S.G., is vice-president of Gerontological Planning Associates in Santa Monica.

Louis E. Gelwicks, A.I.A., is president of the Gerontological Planning Associates, Santa Monica, and author of *Planning Housing Environments for the Elderly*.

Lorraine G. Hiatt, M.A., an environmental biologist and gerontologist, is director of the Unit on Aging of the American Foundation for the Blind.

Sandra C. Howell, Ph.D., M.P.H., is associate professor of behavioral science, Department of Architecture, at the Massachusetts Institute of Technology.

Joseph A. Koncelik, M.A., is a professor in the Department of Industrial Design of The Ohio State University. He is president of Design and Research Services, Inc., in Columbus, Ohio.

Ellen J. Langer, Ph.D., is professor of psychology at Harvard University.

Diana L. McIver is a partner in the real-estate-development firm of Conroy and McIver. She has developed a model management system for the National Center for Housing Management.

Edward H. Marchant, M.B.A., vice-president of John M. Corcoran Company, East Milton, Massachusetts, is lecturer in the Department of City and Regional Planning, Harvard University Graduate School of Design.

Elizabeth W. Markson, Ph.D., is research coordinator of the Gerontology Center of Boston University, where she is an associate research professor in the Department of Sociology. She is coeditor of *Public Policies for an Aging Population* (Lexington Books, 1980).

Sylvia Sherwood, Ph.D., is director of social gerontological research at the Hebrew Rehabilitation Center for Aged, Roslindale, Massachusetts.

Chia-Ming Sze, A.I.A., is an architect specializing in elderly housing developments and is the lead consultant on the Farnsworth congregate-housing model project, Boston.

Marie McGuire Thompson serves as housing specialist for the International Center for Social Gerontology, Washington, D.C.

About the Editors

Robert D. Chellis, M.P.H., is a certified housing manager and licensed nursing-home administrator. A graduate of Princeton University and Harvard University, he has spent the last eight years doing original research and fieldwork for a large multilevel retirement and nursing center. He is president of the New England Gerontological Association and vice-president of the Association of Massachusetts Homes for the Aging. His consulting work and service on the volunteer boards of elderly-housing providers in the Boston area has impressed him with the many potentials of congregate housing.

James F. Seagle, Jr., is the executive director of Rogerson House, a multilevel long-term-care facility in Boston. He is a graduate in sociology from Denison University and a licensed nursing-home administrator. Currently, he is actively developing congregate-housing programs for both Rogerson House and for the Farnsworth Housing Corporation. Mr. Seagle is the immediate past president of the Massachusetts Association of Homes for the Aging.

Barbara Mackey Seagle is a free-lance writer and editor with a central interest in family health. She received the B.A. in English from Denison University in 1970 and is currently a premedical student at Boston University.